I0124457

Aging, Work, and Retirement

ELIZABETH F. FIDELER

ROWMAN & LITTLEFIELD
Lanham • *Boulder* • *New York* • *London*

Executive Editor: Mark Kerr
Editorial Assistant: Courtney Packard
Higher Education Channel Manager: Jonathan Raeder
Executive Channel Manager: Karin Cholak
Interior Designer: Rowman & Littlefield

Credits and acknowledgments for material borrowed from other sources, and
reproduced with permission, appear on the appropriate pages within the text.

Published by Rowman & Littlefield
An imprint of The Rowman & Littlefield Publishing Group, Inc.
4501 Forbes Boulevard, Suite 200, Lanham, Maryland 20706
www.rowman.com

6 Tinworth Street, London SE11 5AL, United Kingdom

Copyright © 2021 by The Rowman & Littlefield Publishing Group, Inc.

All rights reserved. No part of this book may be reproduced in any form or by any
electronic or mechanical means, including information storage and retrieval systems,
without written permission from the publisher, except by a reviewer who may quote
passages in a review.

British Library Cataloguing in Publication Information Available

Library of Congress Cataloging-in-Publication Data
Names: Fideler, Elizabeth F., author.
Title: Aging, work, and retirement / Elizabeth F. Fideler.
Description: Lanham : Rowman & Littlefield Publishers, 2020. | Includes bibliographical
  references and index. | Summary: "The text reflects a growing interest in and concern
  regarding aspects of aging, ageism, labor market challenges, workplace issues, plus
  gender and racial/ethnic similarities and differences in employment history and
  extended worklife opportunities, as they affect older workers in this country and
  abroad"— Provided by publisher.
Identifiers: LCCN 2020005392 (print) | LCCN 2020005393 (ebook) | ISBN
  9781538139608 (cloth) | ISBN 9781538139615 (paperback) | ISBN 9781538139622
  (ebook)
Subjects: LCSH: Older people—Employment. | Age and employment. | Older people—
  Health risk assessment. | Discrimination in employment. | Retirement.
Classification: LCC HD6279 .F513 2020 (print) | LCC HD6279 (ebook) | DDC
  331.3/98—dc23
LC record available at https://lccn.loc.gov/2020005392
LC ebook record available at https://lccn.loc.gov/2020005393

Contents

Preface

This volume updates the findings I reported in *Women Still at Work* and *Men Still at Work*, which were published in 2012 and 2014, respectively.[1] Coincidentally, those discussions about older workers' reasons for staying on the job appeared when *The Oxford Handbook of Work and Aging* was commenting on the dearth of research on factors influencing late-career workers' participation in the labor force, such as their objectives and motivation for working, for staying with, or for joining an organization.[2] And now, at the ten-year mark following the Great Recession, it is important to take a new and deeper look at why older workers are still staying on the job in record numbers, as well as to compare today's discoveries with earlier findings and explore salient differences about the factors influencing their decision making. Thus the book looks closely at current and projected demographic and workforce changes and the socio-economic context within which the employment picture for older workers has changed since the 2008 recession.

Aging, Work, and Retirement is primarily intended for use in graduate and undergraduate courses across a wide spectrum of fields—sociology, gerontology, industrial/organizational psychology, social work, and business management—all of which are affected directly or indirectly by trends in labor force participation. The information will be of immediate value as well to corporate leaders, human resources managers, professional organizations, policymakers, journalists, older workers themselves, and the generations coming behind them. The text reflects a growing interest in and concern regarding aspects of aging, ageism, labor market challenges, and workplace issues, plus gender and racial/ethnic similarities and differences in employment history and extended work-life opportunities, as they affect older workers in this country and abroad.

The following is a brief outline of the chapters in *Aging, Work, and Retirement*—an aid to readers who are accustomed to proceeding from start to finish as well as to those who like to skip around among topics. The introduction presents an overview of expanding interest in and knowledge about older workers, providing useful context for subsequent chapters that discuss the reasons so many well-educated professionals are bypassing retirement or coming out of retirement in order to work. Chapter 2 presents a demographic composite of the older working professionals who responded to the survey for this study. Chapter 3 examines their reasons for choosing work over retirement, including who and what influenced such an important decision. Retirement itself is the subject of the next chapter, which looks at the ways retirement is being reconfigured as a process and why organizations are becoming more willing to extend their mature employees' work lives. Chapter 5 discusses the career fields populated by well-educated professionals and specifies where they are working, their employment status, and how well they are compensated in terms of income and benefits. The next chapter focuses on the significance of good health and well-being vis-à-vis the aging workforce. Chapter 7 uncovers an array of challenges and concerns often but not always associated with working in the retirement years, including the pernicious effects of ageism. Chapter 8 treats working as a volunteer or in an "encore" career with the respect it deserves and reviews the spectrum of activities older workers enjoy in their free time. The final chapter summarizes persuasive arguments for encouraging older men and women to stay in the workforce as long as they are willing and able to do so.

Of special appeal to students and faculty are the highly engaging stories— twenty-four in-depth profiles of remarkable women and men who are working well past conventional retirement age—that put a face to the statistics and focus on the drivers behind that decision. In addition to the text's robust array of topics and examples, readers will find extensive notes, a full bibliography, and resources to enhance the course experience.

The research methodology is basically unchanged from my earlier studies: the current survey asks the same questions as the earlier ones in order to ensure comparability of data. New, in-depth interviews of twenty-four women and men selected from the pool of survey respondents follow essentially the same protocol that was used before. Profiles based on the interviews provide a more complete picture of the respondents' lives, their overall work experience, and their attitudes toward working past traditional retirement age and about retirement itself.

Initial data collection for this study began in September 2017 when I sent the survey via email and regular mail to women who had responded in 2010 and to men who had responded in 2013, asking them to complete the survey if they were still working and to refer or recruit other older working women and men who might be interested in participating in the project. As before, eligible respondents had to be at least sixty years of age and in the *paid* workforce either full time or part time. Again, the survey snowballed and 168 responses came from all around the country: seventy-three responses from men and ninety-five from women. (Three-quarters of the survey responses from women [seventy-one] came from women who were new to the project, and just under two-thirds of the survey responses from men [forty-five] were from men who were new to the project.)

Indeed, this research method is what sociologists call "snowball sampling." Passing from colleague to colleague, friend to friend, or between relatives, the survey draws responses from people who tend to share a number of characteristics pertaining to socio-economic status, educational attainment, types of occupation, race and ethnicity, and so on. Although female respondents to the survey divide fairly evenly among low-, medium-, and higher-income brackets and male respondents tend toward higher income levels (see chapter 5), with at least moderate financial security, they are all fortunate in being able to choose whether to retire or to continue working.

In contrast, for poorly educated older workers employed in low-wage, low-skill, high-turnover jobs, necessity is frequently the driver. Barbara Ehrenreich's 2001 book *Nickel and Dimed: On (Not) Getting By in America* was a masterful portrait of their plight. In a similar vein, Alisa Quart's aptly titled 2018 book *Squeezed—Why Our Families Can't Afford America* makes the case for members of the "Middle Precariat." They are young and struggling parents who are pressed economically, burdened by heavy if not impossible debt loads, and finding themselves downwardly mobile despite training or background that should have ensured a comfortable middle-class existence. They are also unemployed older workers, many still carrying student debt, who are anxiously trying for another shot at the labor market. (Downward mobility is not confined to families in the United States. Since 2008, middle-class households in European Union countries have been experiencing "unprecedented levels of vulnerability" and "reduced economic mobility" that are comparable to the income instability and inequality now besetting many middle-class American households.)[3]

When a survey does not extend throughout all social and economic groups, the findings to be discussed do not represent and cannot be generalized to the entire population of older workers, many of whom are working simply to make ends meet, as stressed previously. This is a drawback of snowball sampling.

Before proceeding, another caveat is in order. Retirement is the goal for many mature adults; in fact, it is clearly the norm in this country. Retirees have many valid reasons to exit the workforce, be they financial, physical, job-related, or personal. Forced retirement can be due to poor health, layoff or termination, or family caregiving responsibilities. Desired or anticipated retirement is often associated with the allure of leisure-time activities and the freedom to pursue them in the so-called bonus years. A severance package or other incentive to retire falls into a category of its own in which retirement is not entirely forced or desired; instead, "tempting" might be the way to describe it. In effect, the wave of older men and women electing to delay retirement and keep working, as described herein, goes against the tide surging in the opposite direction . . . at least for now.

I would like to thank all of the people who supported my efforts in writing this book. First and foremost are the women and men who participated in my survey and those who agreed to be interviewed and then profiled in the book. I am also grateful to colleagues, friends, and family who encouraged my efforts all along the way and recommended often valuable print and online resources. Very special recognition is due to editor Rolf Janke, who initially shepherded the book along at Rowman & Littlefield with the help of editorial assistant Courtney Packard, and to Rowman & Littlefield editor Nancy Roberts who adopted the project and brought it to successful completion.

NOTES

1. Fideler, Elizabeth F. *Women Still at Work: Professionals Over Sixty and On the Job*. Lanham, MD: Rowman & Littlefield, 2012, 2017; *Men Still at Work: Professionals Over Sixty and On the Job*. Lanham, MD: Rowman & Littlefield, 2014.

2. Hedge, Jerry W., and Walter C. Borman, eds. "Advancing Research and Application in Work and Aging." In *The Oxford Handbook of Work and Aging*. New York: Oxford University Press, 2012, 697–98.

3. Alderman, Liz. "The Middle Class Shrinks in Europe." *New York Times*, Business, February 16, 2019, B1, B4.

1

Introduction

CHAPTER OBJECTIVES

---

1. Reviews macro-economic trends, U.S. labor market trends, the changing workforce landscape, current and projected labor force participation rates by gender
2. Examines changing retirement patterns, working longer by choice or necessity
3. Portrays human resource managers' perceptions and practices with respect to older workers, organizational rhetoric versus reality
4. Highlights age-friendly, age-diverse companies worldwide
5. Explains the author's research methodology and outlines the chapters that follow
   Note: Throughout all chapters, the author's research findings are compared with pertinent national and international studies and reports.
   Note: After the introduction, older worker profiles in all chapters illustrate major themes, thus putting a face to the statistics.

Working in the retirement years appeals to many people for a host of different reasons. Foremost among them, it is often assumed, is income generation. The money is certainly appreciated, but it is not the real reason a growing number of older men and women give when they are working by choice rather than by necessity. This book uses profiles of older workers to tell their stories, and in so doing, reveals their reasons for bypassing retirement. Equally important, it explores salient gender and socio-economic differences among older workers and lays out the arguments for encouraging older men and women to stay in the workforce as long as they are willing and able to do so.

Although economic well-being is by no means enjoyed by all Americans—growing inequality seems unstoppable and the middle and working classes are feeling squeezed—compared with massive job cuts during the Great Recession that was in full swing ten years ago, the picture has improved for many. The U.S. economy is said to be humming; the prospect of continued economic expansion appears to have momentum for at least another year. The Dow Jones industrial average and the Standard and Poor's 500-stock index have reached all-time highs, followed by inevitable (and scary) drops and rebounds. The unemployment rate held at under 4 percent through the first months of 2020, with new applications for unemployment assistance at a level last seen in 1969. The economy has added jobs for nearly one hundred straight months, average hourly wages have risen, and consumer spending is up.

Meanwhile, a trend that was already under way but little remarked upon in 2008—older workers, especially women, bypassing conventional retirement age and staying on the job—has continued to accelerate. The U.S. Bureau of Labor Statistics (BLS) says women sixty-five and older will comprise 25.3 percent of the female labor force and older men will comprise 21 percent of the male labor force by 2024. The overall labor force participation rate for the total civilian non-institutional population, counting those who have a job and those who are unemployed and actively looking for one, was 63 percent in July 2019. The rate for people *seventy-five and older* is growing faster than the rate for any other age group. To be sure, plenty of older adults are working out of necessity, often in low-skill, low-wage jobs. And a small but growing number of older Americans (age sixty-five and over) are in financial trouble and filing for bankruptcy. But for those who are well-educated and accomplished, the rising labor force participation rate is for the most part only loosely related to weak or strong economic conditions, allowing them to choose work over leisure for reasons other than financial.

The trend also represents a noticeable turnaround for employers who freely shed older, experienced workers previously and are now beginning to realize how much they need them and their valuable store of institutional knowledge. This volume presents stories of many fortunate individuals who are choosing to work past conventional retirement age, focuses on what that decision means to them, and depicts the socio-economic context within which the employment picture for older workers has changed since the 2008 recession.

First, several anecdotal examples. More and more often, I encounter older women and men who are still in the labor force, engage them in conversation, and take note of their reasons for working. The friendly seventy-eight-year-old seated beside me on a plane to Phoenix, Arizona, is one example. Diane Conrey tutors traditional- and non-traditional-age students, including international students and veterans, who come to Arizona Western College's Student Success Writing Center for help with reading and writing. A former high school English and English-as-a-Second-Language teacher, she had retired ten years earlier, was bored after six months, and started working part-time at the community college in Yuma. The pay is not great, but she is not doing it for the money. "I grew up with a very strong work ethic," she told me. "Between tutoring and going to Silver Sneakers at the YMCA, I have a satisfying framework to my day. I have no plans to retire again."

On the same trip to western states I went hiking with a friend in Colorado's Heil Valley Ranch in Boulder County, a recreational gem covering 6,231 acres at the intersection of the Great Plains and the Southern Rocky Mountains. Stopping to talk with an older gentleman we met on the Lichen Loop trail (a pedestrian-only trail where we would not run into mountain bikes and horses), my friend and I shared our admiration for the dramatic vistas. He told us a bit about the geology and history of the ranch and how grateful he is to be employed as an environmental educator there for the nine months of the year when the trails are open. It hardly seems like work to him.

I encountered ninety-two-year-old Sir David Attenborough only in the sense that I heard him interviewed by the *New Yorker* magazine's David Remnick on the radio. They were speaking about the English broadcaster and naturalist's latest project, "Blue Planet II," which was about to début. When Remnick asked, "How do you view the end of things?" Sir David replied that he thinks about mortality every time he gets up in the morning. He has contemporaries who cannot walk or cannot remember things and considers it entirely a matter of luck that he *can* do those things. "Not to do them if you can do them seems to be an act of extraordinary ingratitude," he asserts.

Sir David's contemporary, Tony Bennett, is still touring, releasing new albums, and collaborating with talents less than half his age. Lady Gaga and Tony Bennett are sympatico—together they have "a conversation with jazz," she told a *Telegraph* reporter in 2014 when their album "Cheek to Cheek" was released. In 2018, Diana Krall and Tony Bennett released their take on Gershwin classics, an album called "Love is Here to Stay." "It's too late to retire," quipped the ninety-two-year-old phenomenon. Likewise, another outstanding recording artist, Barbara Cook, was known to insist that she had "absolutely no desire and no thought of quitting ever." The cabaret and concert singer and voice teacher was still wowing audiences until she died in 2017 at age eighty-nine. And then there is Plácido Domingo, who at age seventy-seven still has leading roles in the opera as both singer and director. Quoted as saying, "When I rest, I rust," he has performed nearly four thousand times in a career spanning six decades and has recorded more than one hundred albums. Folk singers Joan Baez, seventy-seven, and Paul Simon, seventy-six, say they are retiring from touring but assuredly not from performing. Elaine May, half of the one-time Nichols and May comedic duo, is starring in "The Waverly Gallery" at Broadway's John Golden Theater at age eighty-six.

Associate Justice of the Supreme Court Ruth Bader Ginsburg, eighty-six years of age as of this writing, was adamant about not leaving the bench . . . until she had to deal with cancer surgery. She has hired law clerks to work with her through June of 2020, and she wants to serve as long as she can go "full steam." In the 2018 documentary film *R.B.G.*, we learn that her role model is Justice John Paul Stevens, who stepped down as a justice in 2010 at the age of ninety. Among the many adjectives used to describe her are *formidable, inspirational,* and, in a play on the name of a rap star, *notorious.*

RBG's contemporary Dianne Feinstein is the oldest member of the U.S. Senate. Whereas Supreme Court justices enjoy lifetime appointments, senators can be voted out of office. Announcing her intention to seek a sixth term, the senator from California ran into criticism from younger Democrats who said she should pass the torch and make way for new blood. Her reply? She has the experience, energy, and strong support needed for the job, and her mind is fine. Senator Chuck Grassley of Iowa is fewer than three months younger than Feinstein and Senator Orrin Hatch of Utah is nine months younger than Feinstein, but younger Republicans do not call (at least not publicly) for them to step aside. (In January 2019, Hatch left office as the longest-serving Republican U.S. Senator in history.) Two other powerful politicians from California are Nancy Pelosi, age seventy-nine, who became the fifty-second Speaker of the U.S. House of Representatives in 2019, and

Representative Maxine Waters, age eighty-one, who chairs the House Financial Services Committee.

Traditional ideas about aging, career paths, and retirement are out the window. Media coverage of older workers, those who are well known and those who are unknown, has been gradually increasing in accord with greater recognition of the never retire, later retirement, working in retirement, and *un*retirement trends. Clearly, what "working during the retirement years" looks like depends on individual preference and circumstances, as well as incentives and job conditions. Moreover, retirement itself no longer means total withdrawal from the labor force for many people. "The 'once-and-done' model of aging—one degree, one career, one direction—is no longer relevant."[1]

Newspaper and magazine columns on aging occasionally deviate from health topics, including adults' physical, cognitive, emotional, and financial health, to make the connection between aging and work. They feature men and women in various professions explaining why their work is more than a mere job or livelihood. Veteran National Public Radio correspondent Ina Jaffe is alert to the phenomenon, as are journalists writing for the fifty and up population in the "Work and Purpose" segment of PBS's digital platform Next Avenue, whose motto is "Where grown-ups keep growing." A *Washington Post* blog says, "America's aging workforce has defined the post-Great Recession labor market." Pointing to the sharp rise in workers age *eighty-five or older* (an increase of 2.6 percent since 2006), the *Post* defines it as "the era of the very old worker," characterized by "U.S. residents over the age of fifty-five working or looking for work at the highest rates on record," and workers age thirty and younger "staying on the sidelines at rates not seen since the 1960s and '70s, when women weren't yet entering the workforce at the level they are today."[2] *Quartz at Work* comments on the skyrocketing number of Americans working in their seventies, their labor force participation levels rising over the past twenty years from less than 10 percent to nearly 15 percent today, according to the U.S. Census Bureau's Current Population Survey.[3] The *Star Tribune* also employs explosive language in reporting a gain in the labor force participation rate by people sixty-five and older: older workers "blasted through another milestone" (from 10.8 percent in 1985 to 20 percent today, according to BLS data).[4] Looking at these shifts from the organizational viewpoint, a *New York Times* Special Section on Retirement features several award-winning employers who are hiring, retaining, training, and supporting older workers because it makes good business sense and is a win-win for management and labor. Each year, the Mailman School of Public Health at Columbia University designates a dozen or so "Age-Smart" businesses and non-profits in New York City that put a premium on talent, expertise, experience, mentorship, maturity, and reliability.[5]

Then, too, the media occasionally paint a less rosy picture of the employment marketplace, such as stories about the pain of age discrimination in the workplace (see chapter 7). A *Wall Street Journal* article finds the jobs environment for seniors to be "surprisingly bleak" and at odds with the official unemployment rate of 3 percent for older workers. In "the worst retirement [income] shortfall in decades," eight million older Americans are out of work, discouraged and no longer looking for work, or stuck in low-quality part-time jobs for various reasons, including age bias. Consequently, they are unable to improve their situation and have little chance for a comfortable retirement. A comfortable retirement is also out of reach for another 5.8 million older workers (ages fifty-five and up) with full-time, year-round jobs that pay poorly and offer no health benefits. The jobs market can be tough for seniors, even when age bias is not a factor.[6]

Major insurance companies and financial services institutions have a vested interest in changing retirement patterns. Writing for the TIAA-CREF Institute, economists Quinn, Cahill, and Giandrea remark on our entry into "a new era of retirement in the United States" in which the relative appeal of work and leisure in later life has shifted in favor of work. They also point out how well the rising labor force participation rate trends for older men and women "survived the worst job market recession since the 1930s."[7] Exploring what it calls the "New Retirement Landscape," Merrill Lynch, in partnership with Age Wave, identifies four types of working retirees: "driven achievers" at the top of their game and not slowing down, "caring contributors" giving back and making a difference through volunteering or paid work, "life balancers" enjoying flexible work schedules and maintaining social connections, and "earnest earners" still needing to work and not happy about it.[8]

The Society for Human Resource Management has also taken note of the Great Recession's "outsized impact on labor patterns," which made prolonged work life one answer to the problem of recouping lost wealth. At the organizational level, recession-fueled layoffs and retirements posed companies with "a huge risk of a brain drain and a massive loss of intellectual capital." Yet many employers have been slow to explore ways "to capture and transfer older workers' knowledge and sophisticated understanding of workforce tasks."[9] Consequently, the SHRM Foundation convened leading researchers, thinkers, and practitioners at an Executive Roundtable on the Aging Workforce. They were asked to help SHRM to examine the workforce landscape in recent decades and what is projected in years to come, the implications of an aging workforce in both the short and long term, and areas where further research is needed to measure the impact of an aging workforce and to identify best practices for retaining, hiring, and managing older workers.

AARP is paying closer attention to its members for whom retirement is not the goal or for whom it has proved less than satisfying. Professional organizations like the Gerontological Society of America and the American Society on Aging are beginning to expand their focus beyond the "downers," that is, the dismal "d"s of aging—decline, dysfunction, disability, dementia, disengagement, and dependency. And a host of life planning coaches and networks are encouraging the "p"s—positive aging, productive aging, and pro-active aging—plus *non*-"p"s— conscious aging, successful aging, vital aging—whereby elders try to find purposeful engagement, although the later-life journey need not involve paid employment.

In addition to anecdotal examples and popular sources, scholarly work provides evidence of the trends. University researchers studying aging, work, and retirement include economists, demographers, sociologists, gerontologists, social workers, psychologists, neuroscientists, and experts from other fields such as public policy and business management. Some are asking whether working in the senior years, for pay or as a volunteer, is associated with better health and longer life. Building on research showing that adults who work have higher levels of cognitive functioning compared to those of the same age who are retired, the Stanford Center on Longevity is studying the relationship between cognitive performance and working versus retiring in later life, focusing on personal characteristics, engagement behaviors, and occupational characteristics and activities.[10]

The Pew Research Center is tracking the increase in American workers ages sixty-five and older, about nine million people, and notes that they are spending more time on the job (nearly two-thirds are employed full-time).[11] The oldest Baby Boomers (those born in the mid- to late 1940s) are staying in the labor force at the highest annual rate for people their age in more than half a century, Pew researchers observe. According to their analysis of official labor force data, 29 percent of Boomers ages sixty-five to seventy-two were working or looking for work in 2018, exceeding the labor market engagement of the Silent Generation (born 1928 to 1945) at 21 percent and the Greatest Generation (born 1901 to 1927) at 19 percent when they were the same age.[12] The Brookings Institution refines this point, saying older men and women with more schooling and better-paying and more enjoyable jobs are propelling the "clear rise" in full-time employment.[13] Harvard economists Goldin and Katz zero in on the strong attachment of women over fifty years of age to full-time and year-round employment rather than to part-time work. They say the increased participation of older women in the workforce "is a change of real consequence." This development is populated primarily by college graduates in good health who have advanced in and enjoy the rewards of their chosen professions. Most have a partner who is also working in their later years or are not currently married.[14]

The Transamerica Center for Retirement Studies Eighteenth Annual Survey of workers across all age groups (working full-time or part-time in a for-profit company employing five or more people) has identified reasons for working in retirement ranging from need to enjoyment. Of 6,372 workers, more than half (56 percent) said they had not fully recovered financially from the Great Recession. The majority of Transamerica respondents (53 percent) plan to work past age sixty-five and 56 percent plan to work in retirement; among those, most are planning to do so on a part-time basis. Many would like to transition into retirement (47 percent) by shifting to reduced hours or a less demanding and more satisfying role. Just over two-thirds of the Baby Boomers in the Transamerica survey plan to work at least past age sixty-five or do not plan to retire at all. In contrast, 58 percent of the youngest respondents (Millennials) expect to retire at age sixty-five or sooner.[15]

Boomers and Millennials are two of the oft-cited and oft-compared generational cohorts that include "Traditionalists" (the aforementioned Silent Generation) born between 1928 and 1945, "Baby Boomers" born between 1946 and 1964, "Gen-Xers" born between 1965 and 1980, and "Millennials" (or Gen-Yers) born between 1981 and 2000. Members of a generational cohort are said to experience significant social, economic, and cultural life events at similar critical stages in their development.[16] The Great Depression, World War II, and the Vietnam War are oft-cited examples. By extension, there are cohort effects: people who come of age in the same time period share attributes, such as work-related attitudes, values, and perspectives.[17] U.S. Census Bureau projections are sure to astonish Gen-Xers and Millennials: by 2060 nearly all of them will be sixty-five or older and will constitute close to 25 percent of U.S. residents; of that number, 19.7 million will be eighty-five or older. (To this author's surprise, one of her Millennial grandsons has already been thinking about how long he will have to work. While opening Christmas presents with the family this year, Winsloe, age twenty-four, pointed to his grandfather and announced to his younger siblings and cousins, "Poppi got the gift none of us will ever see—retirement!")

Researchers in the U.S. Department of Labor's BLS and the Department of Commerce's Bureau of the Census track demographic shifts, a variety of retirement patterns, and labor market participation rates, among many other topics. Retirement, whether forced or welcomed, was the norm for several generations and is still the norm for older Americans—some ten thousand of the seventy-six million Baby Boomers retire every day. The average retirement age at present is sixty-five years for men and sixty-three years for women, says the BLS. Although the lower average age for women suggests a preference for earlier retirement, the average retirement age for women has been unidirectional, climbing steadily between 1962 (when it was fifty-three years) and 2016, whereas the pattern for men has been erratic: from sixty-six years in the 1960s it dropped throughout the 1980s and 1990s before climbing back up in the 2000s.

As for labor market participation, the BLS also reports that the labor force participation rate (63 percent in July 2019, as previously mentioned) for the total civilian non-institutional population, counting those who have a job and those who are unemployed and actively looking for one, was well below the peak in 2000 when it was 67.3 percent. Strikingly, more than one-fifth (currently 22.8 percent) of the total is aged fifty-five or older, the only fast-growing segment of the labor force. As the Baby Boomer cohort has aged, so too has the labor force. Labor force participation rates for two age groups—*sixty-five to seventy-four* and *seventy-five and older*—are expected to increase the fastest through 2024, whereas participation rates for age groups younger than fifty-five will be stagnant or declining. The BLS estimates that some thirteen million Americans aged sixty-five or older will be in the labor force then. (By the year 2024, all the Baby Boomers will be between the ages of sixty and seventy-eight.)[18]

The share of women (all ages) in the labor force has progressively increased over recent decades, narrowing the gender gap. By 2024, the female share of the labor force is projected to reach 47.2 percent (77.2 million). Since 2000, the median age of women in the labor force has been higher than that of men. Along with that trend, the BLS notes significant increases in the labor force participation rates of older women, and that growth pattern is expected to continue for ten years and to become more racially and ethnically diverse. Of particular interest: the participation rate for women ages sixty-five and older is projected to rise from 15.3 percent in 2015 to 18.4 percent in 2024, the rate projected for men sixty-five and older will rise but more slowly (from 23.4 percent to 25.7 percent), whereas the rates for younger women and men in the cohorts following the Baby Boomers are expected to decrease, owing to the smaller size of the age groups and their declining labor force participation.[19]

Another way of looking at the vigor of the labor force is seeing who is unemployed. Unemployed people aged sixteen or older are counted as participating in the labor force provided that they have been available for work and actively looking for a job within the four-week period prior to each month's Current Population Survey.[20] "Underemployed" (involuntary part-timers) are counted as participants in the labor force. People who are "marginally attached" (meaning they have looked for work in the past year but not in the past month) or "discouraged" (marginally attached and long-term unemployed who have given up trying to find work) are not counted as participating in the labor force. (Once unemployed either voluntarily or involuntarily, older workers seeking to return to the labor force have often faced long-term unemployment owing to hiring managers' negative stereotypes about their skills and productivity. That dynamic may change now that companies with labor shortages are beginning to see the wisdom of recruiting and retaining experienced older workers.) The low unemployment rate smooths out telling differences among unemployed groups. Asians and whites have the lowest unemployment rates (3.4 percent and 3.8 percent, respectively). American Indians and blacks have the highest (7.8 percent and 7.5 percent, respectively), whereas the unemployment rate for Hispanics is 5.1 percent.[21]

The Center for Retirement Research (CRR) at Boston College uses such data to explore financial and non-financial factors that affect the decision to retire or keep working. A particular focus is the relationship between socioeconomic status, as measured by educational attainment, and the retirement decision. CRR researchers have found that "higher-paid workers, those most capable of saving on their own, will likely be the ones to stay in the labor force."[22] Moreover, regardless of gender, the average retirement age is higher in New England and in other states with a similarly high cost of living. One CRR study uses data from the Census Bureau's Current Population Survey to show that adults past age sixty-five who are in the workforce are typically those with the most advanced levels of education and the most financial security. Conversely, individuals with the least education are not only poorer but also apt to be in poorer health and anticipating a shorter lifespan; being less able to delay taking Social Security benefits, they are more likely to retire early. Based on a similar comparison, other retirement research has shown that "a sense of personal control over the decision to work or retire is of primary importance to the well-being of older adults." And "job satisfaction for employed older workers may be partly a function of the *voluntariness* of their employment situation" (italics added).[23]

Another Boston College research group, the Center on Aging & Work, has investigated how older workers perceive their own strengths and weaknesses, for example in terms of their productivity, and how they are perceived by human resource personnel and by younger co-workers. A different Center on Aging & Work study focused on engagement of highly educated older adults in paid or unpaid work, caregiving, education, and training. The authors define *engagement* as deep investment of the self in a role benefitting the individual as well as the organization. Purposeful and meaningful engagement is more than mere involvement or staying busy; it is "a major dimension of healthy aging" offering challenge, creating excitement, and strengthening a feeling of dedication.[24] These authors and other Center on Aging & Work researchers have also looked at time- and place-management tools, policies, and practices, such as options for workers seeking flexible work arrangements. In addition, they examined obstacles to employment of older workers, including employer attitudes toward hiring, training ("upskilling"), and retention of this demographic. The recently formed Sloan Research Network on Aging & Work at Boston College tracks and disseminates studies led by a multi-disciplinary, international group of affiliated investigators addressing the phenomenon of working in later life in this country and abroad.

What was foreseen in 2008 by gerontologist Robert N. Butler, M.D., as the "longevity revolution" is a now a global phenomenon. Butler's work called attention to the benefits and challenges associated with living a long life, as well as their implications for society. Birth rates are falling and life spans lengthening throughout the developed and developing world. Consequently, report Burke, Cooper, and Field, "the aging workforce has emerged as a major issue for individuals, organizations, and countries."[25] Furthermore, Paul Irving, chairman of the Milken Institute's Center for the Future of Aging, adds: "For the first time ever, a growing resource populates the world—millions of mature people. They are better educated and healthier than prior generations of older people, motivated to make a difference and knowledgeable and emotionally stable enough to do so."[26]

Information from the UN Department of Economic and Social Affairs, Population Division, confirms those trends. The number of people eighty or older worldwide is growing faster than the number of older persons overall and faster than any other age group: between 2015 and 2050 the number of "oldest olds" will have tripled. "Population ageing," says the United Nations, "is poised to become one of the most significant social transformations of the twenty-first century, with implications for nearly all sectors of society." Correspondingly, social welfare costs, including pensions, are escalating. In response, government policymakers in many countries are raising the pension age to discourage early retirement. Some governments are urging companies to become "age-friendly" not only to benefit society (e.g., by permitting flexible work arrangements that enhance work-life balance for both older and younger employees), but also because it has been shown to be good for business. Of further concern, the decline in birth rates, coupled with a smaller age cohort on the heels of the Baby Boomers and continual increase in world populations aged sixty and older, as predicted between now and 2050, means a raft of labor shortages, particularly a shrinking supply of skilled knowledge workers, will be inevitable. If they have not already done so, companies will take steps to retain their older workers or get them to come back.

In addition, with fewer young workers paying into the Social Security Trust Fund (or contributing to the equivalent old age pension system in other countries), what is called the "old age dependency ratio" changes. This is the proportion of non-working dependents (under age fifteen, over age sixty-four) per one hundred individuals in the working-age population. In the United States, the ratio is currently twenty-four retirees to one hundred of the working-age population (roughly four younger workers "supporting" one retiree). Across all thirty-four member countries of the Organisation for Economic Co-operation and Development, the average that was twenty-eight per one hundred in 2015 is expected to be nearly twice that (53.2, or roughly two younger workers "supporting" one retiree) by 2050. In Japan the ratio is already forty-six per one hundred. (The United States and Japan are Organisation for Economic Co-operation and Development members.) The widely held presumption that adults ages sixty-five and older are "generally economically inactive" will have to be revisited by economic forecasters when measuring the amount of financial stress on the productive population that supports the dependent population.

One strategy for addressing the problem at the institutional level is promoting age diversity in the workplace, because generationally diverse companies are better and stronger, according to AARP and other sources. However, developing a workplace with age-friendly policies depends on corporate leaders, particularly personnel directors, "walking the walk" as well as "talking the talk" about recruiting, supporting, and retaining an intergenerational workforce. A lot has changed in the past decade: instead of depicting a "tsunami" of older, skilled knowledge workers, economists are predicting a drought of younger replacements and employers are waking up to a new reality—they can ill afford to lose their mature workforce.

Even so, cross-country studies reveal a wide gap between what employers say about supporting older workers and the policies and programs they actually have in place. For instance, when the aforementioned Transamerica survey asked employers whether their company is supportive of its employees working past age sixty-five, more than three-quarters of employers at small (five to ninety-nine employees), medium (one hundred to 499 employees), and large companies (more than five hundred employees) strongly agreed or somewhat agreed that the company *is* supportive (small companies: 82 percent; medium companies: 81 percent; large companies: 76 percent). Yet collectively over one-third of those same companies actually have *no* work-related programs in place to help their older employees transition into retirement. There is obviously a mismatch between organizational rhetoric about fostering engagement and retention of older workers and on-the-ground practices, such as flexible arrangements and working conditions, employee training and development, intergenerational teamwork, transition planning and support, options for continued employment,

and training of managerial and human resources staff to dispel mispercep-
tions and outright ageism.

NOTES

1. Irving, Paul H., and Rita Beamish, eds. *The Upside of Aging: How Long Life Is Changing the World of Health, Work, Innovation, Policy, and Purpose.* Hoboken, NJ: John Wiley & Sons, 2014, 93.

2. Van Dam, Andrew. "A Record Number of Folks Age 85 and Older Are Working, Here's What They're Doing." *The Washington Post*, July 5, 2018. Retrieved from: https://washingtonpost.com/news/wonk/wp/2018/07/05/e-record.

3. Chang, Michelle, and Dan Kopf. "The Number of Americans Working in Their 70s Is Skyrocketing." *Quartz at Work*, June 3, 2019. Retrieved from: https://qz.com/work/1632602/the-number-of-Americans-/.

4. Stewart, Janet Kidd. "Older Workers Are Staying on the Job; Here's Why." *Star Tribune*, July 3, 2019. Retrieved from: http://strib.mn/2XyZ8UY.

5. Hannon, Kerry. "Reaping the Benefits of an Aging Work Force." *New York Times*, Special Section on Retirement, March 4, 2018, 7.

6. Simon, Ruth. "Booming Job Market Can't Fill Retirement Shortfall." *Wall Street Journal*, December 21, 2018, A1, A9.

7. Quinn, Joseph, Kevin Cahill, and Michael Giandrea. "Early Retirement: The Dawn of a New Era?" New York, NY: TIAA-CREF Institute, 2011.

8. Merrill Lynch/Bank of America. "Work in Retirement: Myths and Motivations." June 2014. Retrieved from: www.ml.com/retirementstudy.

9. Society for Human Resource Management. "The Aging Workforce." Alexandria, VA, June 2014. Retrieved from: https://www.shrm.org/resourcesandtools/hr-topics/behavioral-competencies/global-and-cultural-effectiveness/documents/7-14%20roundtable%20summary.pdf.

10. Stanford Center on Longevity. "The Cognition and Retirement Study: Is Working Longer Good for You?" September 2014. Retrieved from: http://longevity.stanford.edu/the-cognition-and-retirement-study-is-working-longer-good-for-you/.

11. DeSilver, Drew. "More Older Americans Are Working, And Working More Than They Used To." Pew Research Center, June 20, 2016.

12. Fry, Richard. "Baby Boomers Are Staying in the Labor Force at Rates Not Seen in Generations for People Their Age." Pew Research Center, July 24, 2019.

13. Bosworth, Barry, Gary Burtless, and Kan Zhang. *Later Retirement, Inequality in Old Age, and the Growing Gap in Longevity Between Rich and Poor*. Washington, DC: Brookings Institution, January 2016, 12–13.

14. Goldin, Claudia, and Lawrence F. Katz. *Women Working Longer: Facts and Some Explanations*. National Bureau of Economic Research, 2016. Retrieved from: http://www.nber.org/papers/w22607.

15. Transamerica Center for Retirement Studies. "18th Annual Transamerica Retirement Survey." TCRS 1364-0618, June 2018. Retrieved from: https://www .transamericacenter.org/docs/default-retirement-survey-of-workers/tcrs2018_ sr_18th_annual_worker_compendium.pdf.

16. Erdheim, Jesse, and Michael A. Lodato. "Generational Differences in Older Workers and Retirement." In *The Oxford Handbook of Retirement*, edited by Mo Wang. New York: Oxford University Press, 2013, 573–87.

17. Beier, Margaret E., and Ruth Kanfer. "Work Performance and the Older Worker." In *The SAGE Handbook of Aging, Work and Society*, edited by John Field, et al. Los Angeles: SAGE, 2013, 97–117.

18. Toossi, Mitra, and Elka Torpey. "Older Workers: Labor Force Trends and Career Options." *Career Outlook*. Washington, DC: Bureau of Labor Statistics, U.S. Department of Labor, May 2017. Retrieved from: https://www.bls.gov/ careeroutlook/2017/article/pdf/older-workers.pdf.

19. Toossi, Mitra, and Teresa L. Morisi. "Women in the Work Force Before, During, and After the Great Recession." *Spotlight on Statistics*. Washington, DC: Bureau of Labor Statistics, U.S. Department of Labor, July 2017. Retrieved from: https://www.bls.gov/spotlight/2017/women-in-the-workforce-before-during-and-after-the-great-recession/home.htm.

20. The Current Population Survey is a national monthly survey of approximately sixty thousand households conducted by the U.S. Census Bureau for the BLS.

21. U.S. Bureau of Labor Statistics. "Labor Force Characteristics by Race and Ethnicity, 2017." Bureau of Labor Statistics Report no. 1076. Washington, DC: U.S. Department of Labor, August 2018.

22. Munnell, Alicia H., and Steven A. Sass. *Working Longer—The Solution to the Retirement Income Challenge*. Washington, DC: Brookings Institution Press, 2008, 14.

23. Barnes-Farrell, Janet L., and Russell A. Matthews. "Age and Work Attitudes." In *Aging and Work in the 21st Century*, edited by Shultz, Kenneth S. and Gary A. Adams. Mahwah, NJ: Erlbaum, 2007, 139–62.

24. James, Jacquelyn B., et al. "Optimizing the Long Future of Aging: Beyond Involvement to Engagement." In *The SAGE Handbook of Aging, Work and Society*, edited by John Field, et al. Los Angeles: SAGE, 2013, 477–92.

25. Burke, Ronald, et al. "The Aging Workforce: Individual, Organizational and Societal Opportunities and Challenges." In *The SAGE Handbook of Aging, Work and Society*, edited by John Field, et al. Los Angeles: SAGE, 2013, 1–20.

26. Irving, Paul H., and Rita Beamish, eds. *The Upside of Aging: How Long Life Is Changing the World of Health, Work, Innovation, Policy, and Purpose*. Hoboken, NJ: John Wiley & Sons, 2014, 4.

Demographic Profile of Older Professionals

1. Presents an array of demographic data, including findings on race and ethnicity, gender, and educational attainment, drawn from the author's survey of older working professionals
2. Distinguishes among different definitions of "age" in the workplace
3. Presents current and projected rates of U.S. labor force participation and growth
4. Stresses the relevance of educational attainment and continued learning to employment

This chapter introduces the 168 individuals—seventy-three men and ninety-five women—who took my survey in 2017 and presents demographic data, including where they live and their age, race and ethnicity, marital and family status, and educational attainment. (Respondents' income levels will be discussed in chapter 5.) It describes the ways the genders are similar or different and the extent to which respondents conform to or deviate from national trends.

Respondents come from twenty-four states, plus Washington, DC, and Bermuda. Massachusetts, New York, and California predominate. The men's ages range from sixty to ninety years. The women's ages range from sixty to eighty-nine years. A total of 42 percent are in their sixties, 45 percent are in their seventies, 13 percent are in their eighties, and one man is ninety. There are more than twice as many men as women among the eighty year olds, which is unusual. Collectively, they belong to the two oldest generational cohorts, "Traditionalists" and "Baby Boomers," that were referenced in the introductory chapter. The median for working men (seventy-three) is two years older than it was in the 2013 survey; the median for working women (seventy) is four years older than it was in the 2010 survey. (Sixty years was set as the minimum age in all three surveys; there was no upper limit. The median—the mid-point in a distribution above and below which lie an equal number of values—is a truer measure than the average, which can be skewed by extreme values.) Because 62 percent of the men and 75 percent of the women were brand new survey respondents, the higher medians cannot be discounted on the basis of the small number of repeat respondents who added birthdays between surveys.

It is useful to bear in mind that "older" connotes different things to different people. Whereas "older" in this study refers to workers sixty years of age and older, some studies and reports start with fifty or fifty-five years, and others begin with sixty-five years. The U.S. Department of Labor's Bureau of Labor Statistics (BLS) defines older workers as those ages fifty-five and over. ADEA, the U.S. age discrimination law (reviewed in chapter 7), sets the bar at forty. Moreover, chronological age is just one way to talk about aging and work, and it does not capture important distinguishing characteristics of individual workers. For this reason, Sterns and Doverspike have conceptualized five interrelated definitions of age in the workplace, including *chronological* (calendar age, a legal term).[1] *Functional* age addresses worker capabilities, skills, and performance. *Psychosocial* age refers both to *self*-perception (how old an individual feels or wants to be) and to society's norms and attitudes (often stereotypes that influence personnel decisions). *Organizational* age encompasses career stage/seniority and tenure in a job or an organization. The *life span* concept of age refers to behavioral change in various developmental and career stages across the life cycle.

As stated previously, a problem with chronological age is the way it slots people into arbitrary categories that do not reflect the great variation within each category. Seventy year olds, for example, do not all feel the same (subjective age), and they also have different capabilities (functional age). Take Heather Lee, for instance, who was recently featured in the news. At ninety-two, she holds five world records in race walking for her age group (female athletes who are ninety to ninety-four) as well as eight Australian master's titles. She was named the 2019 New South Wales Senior Australian of the Year. With so few competitors in her age group, breaking her own world records is the goal of her training regimen. "I have become very competitive with myself," she declares. "Age is no barrier to anything, really."[2]

Social, cultural, and scientific descriptions of "old" persons have been revised over the centuries, and we still have no universally agreed upon definition. According to one British historian, as far back as the eighteenth century in England when the law directed local parishes to provide assistance to the elderly poor, "the very status 'old' was described by chronological, functional, and cultural markers, the application of which depended on where and for whom the designation was being made. But, even beyond that, there were several stops along the way from entry, or 'green old age,' through various stages of diminished ability to function, and on to decrepitude."[3] Thus how long elderly people could remain independent was "an ongoing negotiation" between their ability to function and various sources of social welfare.

As the expert career coach Dr. Helen Harkness advises in *Don't Stop the Career Clock*, "Functional age combines and integrates the biological, social, and psychological measures into one active package."[4] Barbara Morris, age eighty-nine, shares the active aging philosophy espoused by Dr. Harkness. Barbara describes herself as an anti-aging activist. She rejects the word "senior" because of its association with conventional and unhealthy retiree behaviors. As she explains in her profile in chapter 5, "outlier" with its connotation of spirited independence suits her much better.

Common sense tells us that ability to perform is a much better gauge than chronology when considering an older worker's suitability or fitness for a job. The near-wholesale elimination of mandatory retirement (with the exception of certain jobs with physical requirements and safety considerations, such as firefighting, bus driving, and commercial airplane piloting) follows that logic. Take Dr. Margaret Kivelson, for example, the ninety-year-old American space physicist, planetary scientist, and distinguished professor emerita of space physics at the University of California, Los Angeles. Her primary research interests include the magnetospheres of Earth, Jupiter, and Saturn. The October 9, 2018, *New York Times* science section devoted two full pages to significant discoveries in celestial science that are credited to her and her team. She is currently working on the plasma instrument for the National Aeronautics and Space Administration's next voyage to the outer solar system.

(Like solids, liquids, and gases, plasma is a common state of matter; it consists of ions and electrons.) What does Dr. Kivelson's chronological age have to do with it? Then again, to ensure that patients are treated safely and effectively, it would seem that age-based competency screening of physicians is in order. The American Medical Association reported that nearly one-quarter of U.S. physicians were age sixty-five or older in 2015 and that the age cohort had more than quadrupled between 1975 and 2013. These findings prompted serious consideration of national standards for screening physicians at a certain age as well as push back: assertions that the effect of age on any individual physician's competence can be highly variable. There are lawful job-related reasons known as bona fide occupational qualifications for considering performance or attributes reasonably necessary for normal operations of a particular business or when making personnel decisions. The bona fide occupational qualification for commercial airline pilots has been moved from age sixty to sixty-five, and work rule changes are under consideration for air traffic controllers and for evaluation of driving skills and relicensing.

As to the race and ethnicity of the older workers who responded to the survey, 96 percent are white and 4 percent identify as black, Asian/Pacific, or mixed race. These figures can be compared with data taken from the BLS's Current Population Survey indicating that labor force participation is becoming more diverse. According to the BLS report on labor force characteristics by race and ethnicity for August 2018, whites comprise the majority of the civilian, non-institutional labor force at 78 percent, blacks at 13 percent, and Asians at 6 percent. Workers of Hispanic/Latino ethnicity (who can be white, black, or any other race, which explains overlap in the count) are at 17 percent. Hispanics have the highest labor force participation rate (per percentage of the Hispanic population).[5] BLS projections for the decade 2014 to 2024 show Hispanics, Asians, and other minority groups increasing their numbers in the labor force the most rapidly. Hispanics are projected to be nearly one-fifth of the labor force by 2024 as their population is growing faster than all the race and ethnicity groups. The participation rate of non-Hispanic whites is expected to decrease to 60 percent in the same period.[6] (Depending on fluctuations in federal immigration policy and practices, the labor force may or may not see greater numbers of non-white participants.)

Labor force diversity also includes gender. Men continue to outnumber women in the workforce (across all age groups) as they have historically, but women's share of the labor force is projected to increase from 46.8 percent in

2014 (when it was already at a record high) to 47.2 percent in 2024, whereas men's share of the labor force is expected to decrease from 53.2 percent to 52.8 percent in the same time period. Simply put, fewer women than men are leaving the labor force.[7] In 2016, 56.8 percent of all civilian, non-institutionalized women (across all age groups) and 69.2 percent of all civilian, non-institutionalized men (across all age groups) were participating in the labor force.[8] Other BLS projections offering a gendered view show black women with the highest labor force participation rate (referring to percentage not number) among women across all age groups, followed by Hispanic women, whereas the rates for white and Asian women are expected to decline by 2026.[9]

Overall, however, the labor force is growing at a slower rate (0.5 percent on average) than in the previous ten-year period when it averaged 0.6 percent. In contrast to the projected slowdown in labor force growth, the participation of one group stands out: *older adults are participating in the labor force at three times the growth rate of the labor force as a whole.* The percentage of workers age fifty-five and older is expected to increase from 21.7 percent in 2014 to nearly 25 percent in 2024. And, as discussed in chapter 1, the rates for younger women and men in the working cohorts following the Baby Boomers are expected to decrease, owing to the smaller size of the age groups and their declining labor force participation. In a 2018 report from the Summit on Business and the Future of Aging, Paul Irving and colleagues assert,

> Older employees can help mitigate slippage in overall workforce size and it will be increasingly imperative that companies enlist their full potential. A de facto shift has begun. In the United States, the portion of the 65-plus cohort that is working grew from less than 13 percent in 2000 to 19 percent in 2016. And the 65-plus group also is increasing as a percentage of the overall workforce, from 19 percent in 2015 to a projected 29 percent in 2060—approaching the share of younger age segments.[10]

Two interrelated trends are responsible for the labor force growth: changes in the demographic composition of the population and changing labor market choices.[11] In other words, demographic trends alone—Americans' greater longevity and Baby Boomers swelling the senior ranks—are insufficient to explain the increasing numbers of older women and men working in the retirement years.

Three-quarters of my survey respondents are married, and more of the men are married (85 percent) than the women (67 percent). This conforms to life span patterns for older adults in the United States that show people living longer but men tending to die before women. For similar reasons, more of the women are widowed: 11 percent of the women compared to 3 percent of the men. A total of 9 percent of the women are single, and just 3 percent of the men. A total of 10 percent are divorced, with little difference between the genders. A very few of the respondents described themselves as "partnered." It is often assumed that the retirement decision of a spouse, partner, or close friends influences the retirement planning of pre-retirees so much that they expect to synchronize their exits from the workforce, and research shows that it can be an important factor. Yet it did not appear to hold much sway with the professionals I surveyed. Just under 80 percent of the men and women are adamant about not being ready to retire. As to the rest, a few men in their sixties say they might retire in four or more years and four men in their seventies might retire "in a few years." Not one of the men in their eighties wants to retire. The target date for eleven women in their sixties who want to retire ranges from one to twelve years in the future. For six women in their seventies, the target date ranges from one to four years. One eighty-year-old woman did not specify when she plans to retire. Not one of the women over eighty wants to retire.

Taken all together, four out of five respondents to my survey have children or stepchildren. However, there is a large difference between the genders: 90 percent of the men have children or stepchildren compared to 77 percent of the women. The difference can be partially explained by the greater number of singles in the sample who are women. Another possible explanation is belonging to an age cohort with a predilection for putting career ahead of family. Men have between one and four kids; women have between one and six kids. Two is the median for both genders.

As expected, the educational achievement of the current survey respondents is on a par with the education level of my previous survey respondents. A total of 6 percent of the current respondents have less than a college degree; 18 percent have a bachelor's degree; and 39 percent have a master's degree, master's plus, or A.B.D. (which means that all doctoral coursework was completed but not the dissertation). Another 37 percent completed a doctorate or other advanced degree, such as the J.D. or M.D. In combination, fully three-quarters have a master's, doctorate, or other advanced degree, with no gap between the genders.

Apart from higher earnings, better job security, and the prestige factor, what difference does greater educational attainment make with respect to employment? Less educated older Americans tend to retire prematurely, which almost always makes them worse off financially.[12] And, if they have retired, would they be interested in returning to the workforce if the right job opportunity presented itself? When a RAND Corporation survey of American working conditions asked that question, 60 percent of college graduates who had retired answered in the affirmative; only 40 percent of those who lacked college degrees were interested in returning to work.[13] And a new study by the McKinsey Global Institute foresees that workers with no post-secondary education, both young and old, will be the most vulnerable to displacement by automation technologies.[14]

According to the BLS, higher levels of educational attainment correlate with higher levels of labor force participation. Fully 53 percent of working Americans aged sixty-five and older had at least a college degree in 2019, compared with just 25 percent in 1985. The gap between the participation rates for men and women shrinks as educational attainment increases, and it disappears entirely at the doctoral degree level. Typically, an advanced degree is required for entry to the professions, for performing more interesting, stimulating, complex work, and for being offered leadership positions. The BLS says that increased education is also associated with lower unemployment, although during the Great Recession and for several years afterward even well-educated older workers who decided to leave their job or were terminated found that getting a new job was very difficult.[15]

The good news is that the U.S. labor force has become better educated over recent decades. From 1992 to 2016 alone, the portion of the labor force made up of people with a bachelor's degree grew by 7 percent and the portion with a master's, professional, or doctoral degree grew by 5 percent. Fully two-thirds of the labor force had at least some college experience as of 2016. Educational attainment data disaggregated by race and ethnicity reveal considerable variation: Asians and whites in the labor force have earned at least a bachelor's degree (60 percent and 43 percent, respectively), compared to 28 percent of blacks and 20 percent of Hispanics.[16] Women between the ages of twenty-five and sixty-four have been attaining higher levels of education and are more likely to work full-time and year round than in earlier decades. The proportion of women in what are conventionally called the "prime" working years who held a college degree more than tripled from 1970 to 2016, increasing from 11 percent to 42 percent; the proportion of men with a college degree about doubled over that time.[17]

Among the academic all-stars participating in this study is Dr. Ying L. Becker. Starting in China during the Cultural Revolution and continuing after she moved to this country, Ying Becker's story epitomizes self-directed learning, individual initiative, anticipation of and preparation for change, adaptability, and fulfillment on her own terms. The term "protean" is apt. It describes a self-directed career, one managed by the individual, instead of by employers or companies. Douglas (Tim) Hall introduced the term in *Careers in Organizations* and *Careers In and Out of Organizations*, his 1976 and 2002 analyses of career development. Protean career development is primarily characterized by individual initiative and by openness to frequent change. Managing one's own career on one's own terms can lead to self-fulfillment or subjective success, as well as success according to external measures. Such a self-aware approach to one's career depends on having a "learning orientation" and the ability to adapt to new or different workplace and employment conditions. Ying Becker's educational achievements underpin what is truly a protean career.

PROFILE: DR. YING L. BECKER, FINANCE PROFESSOR

Ying Becker is a Beijing-born American who has demonstrated throughout her life what a determined and focused person can achieve through forward thinking, continuous learning, and hard work. She has encountered many obstacles in her life but is a "survivor." Her parents ingrained in her thinking, "Knowledge is strength, and knowledge is power." She used this to reach high levels of achievement in corporate America and in the academic field.

In Beijing Ying attended a government-run experimental school for gifted children. "My classmates were the children of the intellectual elite and high-level communist officials. It was difficult to get into that school." In 1966 when Ying was twelve years old Chairmen Mao Zedong started the Great Proletarian Cultural Revolution in China. All formal schooling was canceled, and this continued for ten years until Mao's death. Ying and other children were sent to local district middle schools where they learned about Mao's thought and how to participate in the Cultural Revolution. During this time, Ying and a childhood friend conducted their own unguided study by reading Chinese classics and Western classics in Chinese, books by famous authors such as Tolstoy, Hugo, Maupassant, Hemingway, Sholokhov, London, Dickens, and Shakespeare.

In 1969, at the age of fifteen, Ying, along with millions of youths, was sent to the countryside to be "re-educated" to learn from the peasants and "to answer the call from Chairman Mao." Ying remembers it was called "going up to the mountain, down to the countryside." She was assigned to a semi-military agricultural production unit in Inner Mongolia that mandated organized work in the fields, preparing the ground (which was basically desert) and digging ditches, as well as other physical training. A year later she went to Qinghai, the steppes of the Himalayas, to join her parents who were sent there from Beijing to answer Mao's call of providing medical service for the peasants in the countryside instead of caring for the bourgeoisie in the city. Later on, she worked in a local oil pump factory first as an apprentice then as a machine electrician. All during this time in the plant, Ying continued her reading and study, teaching herself mathematics, basic chemistry, and physics. "Even if I never had a chance to attend school again, I never lost hope of gaining knowledge by my self-study!" In 1976, three Chinese leaders, Mao Zedong, Zhou Enlai, and Zhu De, died and the Cultural Revolution came to an end. When Deng Xiaoping took command, he reinstated nationwide entrance exams toward the end of 1977 and re-established formal higher education.

In that same year while at Qinghai, Ying achieved the highest academic score in the province on the re-established entrance exam, which entitled her to attend Tsinghua University, the top Chinese university, with a thousand other young people. This was the university's first class to be selected based on academic merit after the decade-long school drought created by the Cultural Revolution. For every ten thousand applicants, one was accepted. "I was one of the lucky ones," Ying said. Students ranged widely in age; some were as much as eight years older than Ying, who was almost twenty-four, and some were eight years younger. "Our cohort was so different from all that followed," she notes. "We were truly driven to learn and we were self-motivated—that comes from narrowly avoiding illiteracy!" Ying completed her bachelor's and master's degrees in chemical engineering at Tsinghua University in 1982 and 1984, respectively, then worked for the Sino-Petrochemical Corporation for two years as a research engineer. She clearly survived the effects of the Cultural Revolution.

Tsinghua University has a history of preparing leaders for the country. The current leader, Xi Jinping, is a graduate of Tsinghua, as were many other leaders before him.

> We, in that very first Tsinghua class, were known as the "77ers." Freshly educated with real-life experiences, we were expected to help make our country better, stronger. But we found China "too heavy to turn." The residue of the Cultural Revolution made it hard to change anything. Believing science and technology would lead to the bright future, we decided to seek opportunities and greater freedom to learn elsewhere. Many of my friends and schoolmates went to the United States, Great Britain, and Japan.

Thus, instead of doing her doctorate in Beijing, Ying took the Test of English as a Foreign Language and the Graduate Record Exam (which measures verbal reasoning, quantitative reasoning, analytical writing, and critical thinking skills) and earned a scholarship to Worcester Polytechnic Institute in Massachusetts. "I came here well prepared and completed a Ph.D. in chemical engineering in 1992." It was also here that she met her late husband, Lee Becker, who was a professor of computer science at Worcester Polytechnic Institute, and they were happily married for fifteen years before he succumbed to leukemia in 2004.

The Polaroid Corporation's Research and Development Center in Waltham, Massachusetts, hired Ying in 1991 even before she officially earned her doctorate. As a senior principal researcher and development manager for nine years, she led an advanced research group designing innovative manufacturing processes. However, Polaroid was not doing well financially. Like many other companies at that time, it failed to make a transition to emerging technologies. "Employees working in jobs where they had been comfortable found the tech environment changing and themselves facing layoff. Polaroid and similar corporations that used to take care of people until their retirement no longer would do so. I was too young to retire, so I had to do my homework and figure out how to re-engineer myself. Where should I go? In which field could I grow and thrive—management? technology?" It was time to look beyond Polaroid. Another strategic decision to be made.

With her expertise in advanced mathematics, computer simulations, and problem solving, Ying decided to pursue a systematic study of finance. She did not need a general MBA because Polaroid had already sent her to Simmons College's executive program for female managers. While working full-time at Polaroid, she earned a master's degree in finance at Brandeis University's International Business School, where she focused her study on quantitative investment.

Before her graduation from Brandeis, Ying was hired by State Street Global Advisors (SSgA) to work in the company's newly established Advanced Research Center, which focused on research and developing asset management strategies and products for institutional investors. She began at SSgA in 2000 as a quantitative research analyst, then became a senior quantitative research analyst and head of U.S. Active Equity Research, and then the head of global and North American Active Equity Research and managing director and member of SSgA's Senior Management Group. In her many years at SSgA, Ying built and directed quantitative research teams to develop active equity selection models and investment strategies for North American and Global Active Equities, overseeing research for multi-billion dollar investor funds in the United States, Canada, and global markets.

But the handwriting was on the wall—SSgA was closing down the Advanced Research Center in 2013 and shifting the firm's emphasis from active asset management to index investing. In anticipation of her eventual departure from industry, Ying had begun to teach, specializing in linking students' academic learning to industry applications. Unfortunately, during this time, Ying's beloved husband Lee died of leukemia. Another difficult time and another moment of survival and change.

Thus, while still working full-time at SSgA, Ying was teaching one course a year at Brandeis. She started teaching there in 2007 to cover a graduate course for a professor who was going away on sabbatical, Blake LeBaron, a Sachar professor of international economics in the Brandeis International Business School and program director for the master of science in business analytics. Although six years had elapsed since Ying completed the finance program at the university, LeBaron easily recalled the earnest master's student who convinced him she knew enough advanced mathematics to enroll in his Ph.D.-level course without first taking any of the usual prerequisites, and proved it by acing the course. He knew he could entrust the course to her. Again, a strategic decision in preparation for a future change.

Five years of experience as an adjunct finance professor at Brandeis prepared Ying to be hired in 2014 at Suffolk University's Sawyer Business School in Boston, where she became an assistant professor of financial practice. Her multi-faceted background in industry, finance, and technology made her particularly valuable to the business school. She taught a full load of courses in Financial Statement Analysis and Valuation, Principles of Investment, Money and Capital Markets, Business Finance, Applied Risk Management, and Risk Assessment and Simulation. She also conducted and published research, coached students, and consulted with quantitative asset management startups. Coming full circle, so to speak, in 2019 she rejoined the Brandeis faculty as professor of the practice of finance in the university's International Business School.

Through a mutual friend, Ying met Hal, a healthcare industry consultant whose spouse had also died of cancer, and she married again five years ago. Hal was sixty when he enrolled in the radiologic technology training program at Massachusetts Bay Community College. Years earlier he had earned a bachelor's degree in mathematics and joined the high-tech workforce. He spent many years in computers and communications at Fortune 500 companies and at startups, first as a systems engineer, then, having earned an MBA, as a director of marketing. When he began to realize that the field he was in was age biased toward younger people, he determined that he was still vital and capable of acquiring new skills and making a big change. "I chose the medical field since it would be expanding along with population growth. It was either go to nursing school or study for an associate's degree in radiologic technology, and I opted for the latter," Hal explains. He really enjoyed providing diagnostic imaging services to hospital patients but reluctantly left his job after four years when standing on his feet for hours and hours every day became excruciating.

Teaching in Boston allows Ying time for travel once or twice a year to see her aging parents in Beijing as well as to visit other parts of the world with Hal. Perhaps the biggest difference associated with her current job is that Ying does not need to plan for yet another career move at this stage in her life. She works hard and feels that she is making a difference and giving back to society by influencing and mentoring young people. She has no plans to retire. Early on her mother impressed upon her that a woman needs to prepare herself with knowledge and skills and has to do better to be successful in our male-dominated world. And, her mother advised, like the victorious character in the fable about the tortoise and the hare, she should set off in the right direction, keep going, and never give up. In this way she would survive.

⚬⚭⚬

The frequency with which respondents attest to the importance of continued learning, no matter one's age, is striking. A learning orientation fosters successful aging at work across many dimensions, including acquisition of new skills, ability to participate on intergenerational teams, and productivity. Learning outside of work can be equally productive and satisfying. Even after completing years of formal education, more than one-third of the women who completed my survey are taking not-for-credit adult learning classes, far outnumbering the eight men doing so, and two men and one woman are in advanced degree programs for credit. Here are several more lifelong learners who are acquiring new knowledge and skills as part of their work or for another purpose:

- An eighty-five-year-old professor is "constantly studying, growing, learning new things about life, people, and the educative process. My students and I teach one another. It is a reciprocal arrangement."
- An eighty-two-year-old public art consultant continues to learn and problem solve.
- An eighty-year-old psychiatrist is learning French to improve communication with his grandchildren who live in France.
- A seventy-eight-year-old author, speaker, and career coach has "an insatiable desire to learn more about the future of work."
- A seventy-seven-year-old specialist in aging, employment, and the new retirement is "constantly learning and intent on contributing to the dynamic field of aging."
- A seventy-six-year-old market researcher is "always learning new things and keeping my skills fresh."
- A seventy-three-year-old professor values "the opportunity to keep learning and to build new programs."

- A sixty-eight-year-old consultant to higher education institutions gets the greatest satisfaction from "staying intellectually and socially engaged, learning new knowledge and skills in research and practice, and supporting younger colleagues in the field."
- A sixty-five-year-old in the field of communications enjoys "learning new things and staying up to date on technology."
- A sixty-four-year-old professor of epidemiology is "open to learning new methods and approaches to research."

Eighty-year-old composer Joan Tower also exemplifies the learning orientation. Recognized as "a force in contemporary music," she was recently commissioned by the New York Philharmonic for a new work. As she told a *New York Times* interviewer, her "goal is to keep learning. There's so much still to learn—the bass, the piccolo, I'm still working on, and the horn. Those are weak areas for me. . . . What you try to do is write the best piece you can at whatever level of experience and voice that you are at. I know that if I take more risks, I'll get there. It's in the risks."[18]

PROFILE: JO-ANN NEUHAUS, URBAN PLANNER

Urban planning and development is more than a job to Jo-Ann Neuhaus. It has always been "a commitment and a learning experience." Her turf is a downtown neighborhood of embassies, archives, theaters, museums, office buildings, businesses, residences, and more in Washington, DC, where she is the full-time executive director of the Pennsylvania Quarter Neighborhood Association (PQNA). In this profile, she describes her long tenure in the realm of public improvement programs as "an evolution from one thing to another," all the while stimulated by new opportunities and innumerable problems to be solved.

Jo-Ann, now seventy-six, says that she will retire "only when the work no longer interests me. I'll work as long as I am able to and can contribute to the betterment of this community." Association members include government entities in the Pennsylvania Avenue neighborhood, such as the Canadian Embassy, National Archives, and Smithsonian Museums, as well as businesses, residential condominium associations, theaters, museums, restaurants, places of worship, hotels, office tenants, non-profit organizations, and cinemas.

The PQNA was founded in 1988 by the Pennsylvania Avenue Development Corporation, where Jo-Ann was on staff as director of project development, and several developers who were required to build residences as part of their mixed-use development projects in the area. Initially, the association's goals were to find a name for the neighborhood, ensure basic services, and make the area attractive to residents and businesses. By 1993, the PQNA was producing the city's first and largest arts festival "Arts on Foot" with some assistance during the early years from a member of the Shakespeare Theatre Company's staff. The PQNA also organized and co-sponsored an annual neighborhood Holiday Gala that benefited underprivileged children. The Penn Quarterly newsletter introduces residents throughout the city to an emerging, revitalized downtown through short articles featuring the growing list of museums, shops, theaters, and restaurants located in the Penn Quarter. As email became more widely used, the newsletter segued into regular announcements of member events, activities, special offers, openings, and performances. Breakfast meetings, held regularly in various locations, help people living and working in the area to develop a sense of community and to learn of proposed changes in the neighborhood. They also provide a forum for appointed and elected government officials in the District of Columbia.

Over the years, the revitalized Penn Quarter has become a thriving downtown neighborhood, winning national awards and serving as a model for other DC neighborhoods as well as for other cities wishing to revitalize their downtowns. Among the PQNA's major accomplishments was obtaining funding for and completing a residential and arts-use feasibility study of a vacant historic structure, the city-owned Mather Building, which resulted in development of market-rate housing, below-market-rate artist live/work space, and arts space. Banding together gave residents and property owners a voice regarding legislative and development proposals that would affect their quality of life, such as licensing of nude dancing establishments in the neighborhood. The PQNA lobbied successfully for the Penn Quarter name to be added to the Archives-Navy Memorial Metro station and suggested changes to proposed truck vending regulations that could negatively affect neighborhood restaurants. PQNA is the neighborhood's watchdog when it comes to zoning regulations and Alcohol and Beverage Control legislation.

It is easy to understand why Jo-Ann says that "life is an evolution from one thing to another," for her career evolved in just that way. While an international relations major at George Washington University in the early 1960s, her international law professor asked her what she planned to do with her degree. Upon being advised that she would need a master's degree to get the job she envisioned at the United Nations, Jo-Ann went to graduate school at George Washington University at night and worked full-time during the day for the next six years. However, she was no longer studying international relations. Solving problems at her day job in urban development proved utterly fascinating and she opted to take her master's in urban and regional planning. In so doing, she was the very first person admitted to the master's in urban planning program and the first to graduate.

Jo-Ann joined the staff of the Redevelopment Land Agency (RLA) in DC, the agency responsible for implementing downtown urban renewal plans developed by the National Capital Planning Commission. ("Washington, DC, is a city of alphabet agencies," she reminds me.) For her last five years there, she was the RLA's downtown urban planner working on future development sites and a program of public improvements, later called Streets for People. With DC's Metro system under construction in the 1970s, she convinced the transit authority to install an additional Metro station exit at an RLA-owned site across the street from one of DC's major department stores, thinking that both the development site and the department store might one day want to connect directly to the Metro station as was being done elsewhere downtown. In support of private revitalization efforts, she also oversaw the planning and design study for a pedestrian mall—both literally and figuratively groundbreaking accomplishments.

Meanwhile, in 1972 Congress had created and funded a federal entity, the Pennsylvania Avenue Development Corporation (PADC) that was charged with developing a "Plan for America's Main Street" between the White House and the Capitol. John Woodbridge, the PADC's executive director, hired Jo-Ann in 1976 to implement the plans her predecessor had written. A significant achievement during her twenty years with PADC was renovating the historic Willard Hotel that was designed in 1901 in the Beaux Arts style by noted architect Henry Janeway Hardenbergh. (The original hotel, six row houses located at the corner of Fourteenth Street and Pennsylvania Avenue, dated to 1818. In 1861, President-elect Abraham Lincoln was in residence. In

1862, Julia Ward Howe penned "The Battle Hymn of the Republic" there.) In 1968, however, the hotel had to close its doors, and it remained vacant for more than a decade. Fortuitously, in 1977 PADC obtained funding to execute the congressionally approved Pennsylvania Avenue Plan, including funding to purchase the Willard Hotel. After many delays, the Willard reopened as the Willard InterContinental Hotel in 1986. As an insider to the process, Jo-Ann described the numerous decisions and legal approvals needed to get the Willard and adjacent properties ready for development. Development of the adjacent land, for example, required demolishing two parking garages and the long-closed Occidental restaurant and hotel buildings. Also, closing an alley that provided service access to another hotel on the western portion of the block required negotiation of an easement agreement to provide for that hotel's use of the Willard's loading facility. Zoning, design, and historic preservation review of the architectural plans and specifications followed.

At the eastern end of the area under PADC's jurisdiction, the Pennsylvania Avenue Plan required housing and cultural venues as part of mixed-use development. "At the time," Jo-Ann notes, "no one had heard the term 'mixed-use development' and no new housing had been built downtown for one hundred years." Bringing developers into discussions about the area gave rise to the idea of forming a neighborhood association for the Penn Quarter; hence PQNA was born in 1988. In lieu of financial support, which as a federal entity PADC could not provide, it instead donated staff support until Congress closed PADC. "Essentially, one entity morphed into another." Several years after PADC folded the PQNA's membership had grown significantly, thus requiring more of Jo-Ann's time on PQNA matters.

Solving problems—and urban living certainly presents myriad problems—remains "the joy of the job" for her. For example, it took thirty years but her attention to detail and perseverance paid off in 2017 when the city finally fixed the drainage in the "grungiest" alley in DC, then lit and paved it. Residents in a nearby building were especially grateful, which helps Jo-Ann to build and maintain the all-voluntary membership of PQNA and to obtain contributions to special projects. Although there is never enough time for family (two sons and three grandkids) and friends, her work does bring invitations to press briefings at museums and opening nights at several theaters. "This is more than just a job to me," she declares, "it's a commitment and a learning experience."

❧

Clearly, Jo-Ann Neuhaus has contributed greatly to the revitalization of the Penn Quarter while nurturing a sense of community among the downtown area's government and cultural institutions, business owners, and residents. Her know-how, diplomacy, persistence, and enthusiasm for the work are invaluable assets. As argued in Coleman's *Unfinished Work: The Struggle to Build an Aging American Workforce*, "Boomer brains" with those characteristics are hard to replace. "Boomers who were educated and trained in the decades when the United States became the world's pre-eminent industrial, financial, and technological power hold the knowledge and skills that keep whole sections of the economy running." Obviously, Coleman concludes, "the last thing we want to do is hustle Boomers with bachelor's and master's degrees out the door into retirement."[19]

NOTES

1. Sterns, Harvey L., and Dennis Doverspike. "Aging and the Training and Learning Process in Organizations." In *Training and Development in Work Organizations*, edited by I. Goldstein and R. Katzel. San Francisco: Jossey-Bass, 1989, 299–332.

2. Weiss, Bari. "Australia's Fastest 92-Year-Old Woman." *New York Times*, Sunday Review, January 6, 2019, 9.

3. Fideler, Paul A. *Social Welfare in Pre-Industrial England—The Old Poor Law Tradition*. New York: Palgrave Macmillan, 2006, 150.

4. Harkness, Helen. *Don't Stop the Career Clock—Rejecting the Myths of Aging for a New Way to Work in the 21st Century*. Palo Alto, CA: Davies-Black Publishing, 1999.

5. U.S. Bureau of Labor Statistics. "Labor Force Characteristics by Race and Ethnicity, 2017." BLS Report no. 1076. Washington, DC: U.S. Department of Labor, August 2018. Retrieved from: https://www.bls.gov/opub/reports/race-and -ethnicity/2017/home.htm.

6. Toossi, Mitra. "Labor Force Projections to 2024: The Labor Force is Growing, But Slowly." *Monthly Labor Review*. Washington, DC: U.S. Bureau of Labor Statistics, December 2015. Retrieved from: https://doi.org/10.21916/mlr.2015.48.

7. Ibid.

8. U.S. Bureau of Labor Statistics. "Women in the Labor Force: A Databook." BLS Report no. 1071. Washington, DC: U.S. Department of Labor, November 2017. Retrieved from: https://www.bls.gov/opub/reports/womens-databook/2017/home.htm.

9. Toossi, Mitra, and Leslie Joyner. "Blacks in the Labor Force." *Spotlight on Statistics*. Washington, DC: U.S. Bureau of Labor Statistics, February 2018.

10. Irving, Paul, Rita Beamish, and Arielle Burstein. "Silver to Gold—The Business of Aging." *Report from the Summit on Business and the Future of Aging*. Santa Monica, CA: Milken Institute Center for the Future of Aging, 2018.

11. Toossi, Mitra. "Labor Force Projections to 2024: The Labor Force is Growing, But Slowly." *Monthly Labor Review*. Washington, DC: U.S. Bureau of Labor Statistics, December 2015. Retrieved from: https://www.bls.gov/opubs/mlr/2015/article/labor-force-projections-to-2024.htm.

12. Munnell, Alicia H., et al. "Does Socioeconomic Status Lead People to Retire Too Soon?" Issue Brief no. 16-14. Chestnut Hill, MA: Center for Retirement Research at Boston College, August 2016.

13. Maestas, Nicole, et al. "Working Conditions in the United States: Results of the 2015 American Working Conditions Survey." Santa Monica, CA: RAND Corp, August 2017. Retrieved from: https://www.rand.org/pubs/research_reports/RR2014.html.

14. Lund, Susan, et al. "The Future of Work in America: People and Places, Today and Tomorrow." McKinsey Global Institute, July 2019. See: www.mckinsey.com.

15. Brundage, Vernon Jr. "Profile of the Labor Force by Educational Attainment." *Spotlight on Statistics*. Washington, DC: U.S. Bureau of Labor Statistics, August 2017.

16. Ibid.

17. U.S. Bureau of Labor Statistics. "Women in the Labor Force: A Databook." BLS Report no. 1071. Washington, DC: U.S. Department of Labor, November 2017. Retrieved from: https://www.bls.gov/opub/reports/womens-databook/2017/home.htm.

18. Robin, William. "Becoming a Force While Trying to Avoid Disaster." *New York Times*, Arts, November 10, 2018, C2.

19. Coleman, Joseph. *Unfinished Work: The Struggle to Build an Aging American Workforce*. New York: Oxford University Press, 2015.

Reasons for Working in the Retirement Years

1. Reviews the literature on age-related attitudes, behaviors, and motivation to remain active in the workforce
2. Explores survey respondents' top-ranked and lower-ranked reasons for staying on the job in the retirement years
3. Examines factors contributing to job satisfaction, engagement, sense of purpose (meaningful work)

Early studies by McNeely[1] and by Eichar et al.[2] of age and job satisfaction found that older workers were more job satisfied than younger workers, and *intrinsic* rewards, not extrinsic, had the greatest effect on job satisfaction. Those findings have held up. For example, nearly twenty years ago, a study attempted to clarify why the "elderly" continue to work, specifically the extent to which they work out of financial necessity and how job characteristics influence the propensity to work at older ages. The data came from Asset and Health Dynamics Among the Oldest Old (AHEAD), an auxiliary to the Health and Retirement Study (HRS), with a nationally representative sample of more than seven thousand individuals aged seventy and up. The researchers identified "stayers" in the labor force and "leavers." Stayers who held the same job for at least ten years, compared to individuals working but not in their longest-held job, were more educated, wealthier, and healthier, and their reasons for working were largely *non*-pecuniary. Their jobs offered flexible working arrangements and a level of responsibility the stayers desired, even when the jobs paid less. Longer-term stayers worked more hours, were more likely to be in a professional occupation, and were somewhat more likely to be self-employed. They tended to be younger (still in their seventies!) than leavers and still married. Deteriorating health or mortality accounted for most of the leaving.[3]

In 2007, six years after AHEAD and the HRS (and on the brink of the Great Recession), with the publication of *Aging and Work in the 21st Century* Shultz and Adams commented on the scarcity of research into older workers' reasons for staying on the job. What they saw instead was a preponderance of research asking about the productivity of older workers, their ability to learn new skills and to work effectively on intergenerational teams, and factors influencing their retirement-related decisions, such as economic incentives and disincentives and preparation for retirement or lack thereof.[4] Moreover, as one review of the Shultz and Adams book noted, the economic impact of aging and work on low-income older adults was addressed in a chapter contributed by Taylor and Geldhauser, but the editors omitted a similar discussion of middle-class older adults' experience of aging and work. The volume you are reading fills in those missing elements with its focus on middle-class older adults and their reasons for extending work life.

Soon after publication of the Shultz and Adams book and coinciding with the onset of the recession came a very useful literature review examining the influence of the "age factor" on older blue-collar and white-collar workers' attitudes, behaviors, and motivation to remain active in the workforce.[5] Kooij and colleagues employed as a lens the five interrelated categories posited by Sterns and Doverspike to conceptualize age in the workplace (as discussed in chapter 2), particularly chronological, functional, and life span age. Among the limited number of available (mostly empirical) studies was one that attributed the work motivation of older knowledge workers to enjoyment of work, satisfaction from using one's skills, sense of accomplishment, and opportunities to be creative. Still others attributed decisions to persist in the workforce to insufficient income for retirement—wages, savings, pensions, and benefits (i.e., need-based motivation)—and decisions to terminate work largely to the appeal of leisure-time activities. In sum, whereas the reviewers' findings in the literature were inconclusive and often inconsistent, they nonetheless revealed a need for more "age-awareness" regarding the complexities of older workers' motivation to continue work, particularly on the part of human resource managers.

The current volume on working in the retirement years contributes to the literature on aging and work by enhancing and updating my earlier findings about older workers in the larger socio-economic context that were presented in *Women Still at Work* and *Men Still at Work.*[6] And the focus of this work, too, is uncovering my respondents' reasons for staying on the job.

Like nearly 80 percent of the men and women whose surveys are part of this study, Abe Peck, age seventy-two, is certain that he does not want to retire. A part-time writer, editor, and educator, Abe tells me he never uses the word "retired." Instead, he shares his list of acceptable "r" words: "re-invented, re-grooved, re-located, renaissance, and relevant." Here's why Abe and the others want to keep working.

Table 3.1 presents the reasons older men and women give for continuing to work. (Reasons are in rank order, based on combining men's and women's

Table 3.1.   Survey Respondents' Reasons for Staying on the Job (in rank order)

Reasons	Men	Women	Combo
Satisfaction, find meaning in work	92%	93%	92%
Use abilities, skills, training	77%	85%	82%
Help others, contribute, make a difference	74%	71%	72%
Enjoy clients, patients, students, or customers	75%	69%	72%
Love my work	59%	79%	70%
Enjoy colleagues and co-workers	70%	58%	63%
Enjoy good health, high energy	52%	65%	60%
Mentor younger workers	53%	33%	42%
Keep busy, get out of the house	42%	42%	42%
Need the income	42%	42%	42%
Peak of career, high earning power, authority, experience	29%	32%	30%
Save in 401K plan, other retirement plan	33%	26%	29%
Boost Social Security benefits	19%	29%	25%
Changed career field	19%	23%	21%
Expanding business, new opportunities	15%	18%	17%
"Age-friendly" company	14%	18%	16%
Other financial pressures	15%	12%	13%
Rising health insurance costs	16%	7%	11%
Opportunities for training, retraining, updating skills	5%	16%	11%
Accrue pension benefits	10%	9%	10%
New job in same career field	10%	5%	7%

Note: n = 168. Activities are in rank order based on combining men's and women's responses. Respondents could check multiple reasons and add others.

responses). Respondents could check multiple reasons for continuing to work and add others.

The top five reasons given for continuing to work in the retirement years were: 1) satisfaction, finding meaning in work; 2) using my abilities, skills, and training; 3) helping others, contributing, making a difference; 4) enjoying clients, patients, students, or customers; and 5) loving the work. Reasons one through four are the same as the priorities established by my 2012 survey but with even higher percentages. Self-explanatory "love my work" edged out "enjoy colleagues and co-workers" and "enjoy good health and high energy" in the number five and number six spots.

PROFILE: DR. MERRY "CORKY" WHITE, ANTHROPOLOGIST
A love of her work only begins to explain why professor Merry "Corky" White has no intention of leaving Boston University's anthropology faculty any time soon. As she makes clear in her profile, she also really enjoys her university colleagues and co-workers and has good health and high energy, too. At the age of seventy-seven, the professor relishes researching, writing books, and teaching courses on such subjects as Japanese society, food, and culture. Her work in the social sciences brings her to Japan nearly every year. Remarkably, in 2013 the Japanese government gave her one of the highest honors for which a non-Japanese person is eligible, making her not quite a National Treasure, but a treasure for sure. For Corky White, *need* and *enjoy* go together. "I wouldn't quit working even if I had a windfall!" she declares. "My financial advisor tells me to keep working and I love what I do, so *need* and *enjoy* are both true for me." Corky not only teaches courses on Japanese society, women in Asia, food and culture, but also anthropology of travel and tourism. Although her career has taken her in several directions over the years, the main focus has always been Japan. She has been a caterer, cookbook author, columnist, restaurant reviewer, and food anthropologist. "Food takes you into every aspect of life and culture," she explains.

Interest in cultural matters runs in the family. Corky's mother was studying at the Corcoran Institute of Art in Washington, DC, when she gave birth to her daughter. That helps to explain how she got her nickname. "Since my parents expected a boy, they did not have a girl's name ready. When the director of the Corcoran called to see how the new parents were doing, he said that the baby girl should be Corky, and that stuck."

Raised in the Midwest, Corky attended a private high school in Boston whose graduates were encouraged toward "ladylike" activities such as becoming docents at the Museum of Fine Arts. That was not her goal. Yes, she loved French and, yes, she loved art, but the curriculum was too narrowly focused on Western civilization for her taste. Couldn't she get farther away from Boston than Europe? In the school library she devoured everything she could find about Japan. Corky went on to earn degrees in Japanese studies and anthropology from Harvard, a bachelor's degree in 1963 and a doctorate in 1980. (In between she also studied at Oxford toward a master's degree in Victorian literature, completed at Harvard.) Corky wanted to try everything—that included learning Russian as well as Japanese.

The day after she graduated from college, Corky made her first trip to Japan. She had never been outside the United States or on an airplane. "With my first passport, I took my first plane ride to my first foreign country. The exchange rate between the dollar and the yen was great for a student on a budget." Another early step for Corky was marriage two days before the trip to Japan. Although a second marriage took place during graduate school, she has been single and self-supporting for many years. (The children from those marriages are Jennifer White Callaghan, a lawyer with a London-based international firm, and Dr. Benjamin Wurgaft, a writer and intellectual historian.) Harvard's Graduate School of Arts and Sciences approved half-time status for Corky while pursuing her Ph.D. and raising two children—it was the very first time the school granted half-time status to a female graduate student needing childcare time, she notes.

Between 1963 and 1980, Corky was a journalist, writing pieces on travel and food topics for magazines like the *Atlantic* and a food column and restaurant reviews for newspapers. She went to graduate school when she realized that she was "at the edge of her expertise" and needed to learn more about Japan. To earn money for graduate school, she started a catering business in the kitchen of her apartment. "I was catering for Harvard's Center for European Studies, whose members had very sophisticated tastes, and for various luminaries. So I had to come up with unusual foods they didn't know." This experience produced two cookbooks: *Cooking for Crowds* (with illustrations by cartoonist Edward Koren) in 1973, plus a fortieth anniversary edition in 2013, and *Noodles Galore* in 1976. While working on her doctorate, Corky also administered and taught in the East Asian Studies undergraduate program at Harvard College.

She spent 1980 to 1985 as director of the international education program at Harvard's Graduate School of Education and as director of a research project on human potential, a multi-national study of learning in Japan, India, China, Egypt, West Africa, and Mexico. "I was the most junior person by far on the research team that included such distinguished faculty members as Howard Gardner, Israel Scheffler, Gerry Lesser, and Bob LeVine." In 1987, she moved to Boston University to teach in Japanese social science. Tenure followed in 1989, as did several more books on a variety of topics, including Japanese adolescence and popular culture, education, coffee and café life in Japan, and family and social policy.

Corky enjoys good health and high energy. "Why would I quit?" she asks, in her frank way. She is taking it one year at a time. Her department at Boston University is a convivial place. "Some of my best friends are my colleagues. They are interesting, supportive, funny and kind. Some are closer to my age, some junior." She would, however, like more space in her busy schedule for travel and for writing. "I know I am lucky to being doing what I want to do, but there is not enough time for all of it!" Her current research, a study of Japanese food workers—artisanal, domestic, and industrial—brings her to Japan almost every year.

In June 2018, Corky co-curated an exhibit called "Objects of Use and Beauty: Design and Craft in Japanese Culinary Tools" at the Fuller Craft Museum in Brockton, Massachusetts, with Debra Samuels, food educator and author of *My Japanese Table*. On opening day, the museum hosted a reception and tasting of Japanese delicacies. The implements on display included bento boxes, knives, graters, rice tub and baskets, vegetable cutters, chopstick rests in the shape of origami cranes, ceramic bowls, ceramic and cast iron pots, and a tea ceremony box. Many are from the collections of the co-curators, and all are of uncommon beauty. The Japanese do not make a strong separation between museum art and functional craft, as Merry explained in her curatorial talk at the reception. Holding up a knife, she told the audience that it is the most important culinary tool used by any "knife-person" or chef. An excellent knife "cuts with the fluidity of a river current," is made by a master craftsman using techniques hundreds of years old, and can cost up to a thousand dollars. A Japanese craftsman is trained by his father, serves an apprenticeship under another craftsperson, then returns to his family. Some Japanese craftsmen are considered Living National Treasures because of their commitment, skill, and attention to detail.

Although non-Japanese are not eligible for National Treasure status, Corky has received a high honor from the country. In April 2013, the Japanese government bestowed the Order of the Rising Sun, Gold Rays With Neck Ribbon on Corky in recognition of her significant contributions to the development of Japanese studies and introduction of Japanese culture in the United States. Another first for the dynamic professor.

⌒⨯⌒

Men and women are in complete agreement (92 percent) about job satisfaction and finding meaning in their work. They surely would endorse the message in this Ralph Waldo Emerson quote: "The purpose of life is not to be happy. It is to be useful, to be honorable, to be compassionate, to have it make some difference that you have lived and lived well . . . to know even one life has breathed easier because you have lived. This is to have succeeded." The quote was sent to me by a veteran social worker and university educator who has worked for some fifty years. He lays out his reasons for working this way:

> I have worked a long time to get to a point where people ask me to do really interesting things that I want to do. Why would I stop? I love working with incredibly bright, engaged, and dedicated students. The staff and programs I work with outside the university are making a difference in the lives of hundreds of people. I came up during the '60s. I can tell you without irony that I (still) want to change the world—making a difference in the part around me will suffice. One of the programs I work with is Asian Human Services, an agency that provides services to immigrants and refugees from all over east, south, southeast, and central Asia. When I started it was to 'work off some karma' from participating in the Vietnam misunderstanding. Over time that has shifted, and we adopted each other. Now, they are family, and I treasure my monthly visits.
>
> In recent years, I have narrowed my efforts a bit, focusing on services to veterans, immigrants, refugees, and older adults, and on the integration of spirituality and social work practice. I have been incredibly fortunate—blessed even. I

see that as a gift and a responsibility. At one time my wife and I thought of retiring and moving back to Portland, Oregon. At this point, I would have a hard
time moving since I would not have the opportunities to do what I do now. Or,
it would take a long time to build up those opportunities. Besides, what else
would I do? Take up golf? Good Lord, if it comes to that, just shoot me.

Job satisfaction is a very broad term that can be interpreted in a wide variety of ways. Top reasons two through five on the ranked list in Table 3.1
contribute to satisfaction, as well as positives like favorable working conditions; opportunities to learn; sense of personal efficacy, accomplishment, or
fulfillment; and sense of purpose or meaningfulness of the work. According
to aging and work authorities Smyer and Pitt-Catsouphes, "Employees who
find meaning in their work, who find it engaging and report high levels of job
satisfaction, are more likely to want to keep working."[7] A study by Harpaz and
Fu affirmed the centrality of meaningful work over time to a sample of Israeli
workers representing different age groups, education levels, genders, and
occupations. More than 90 percent of the participants said they would work
even in the absence of economic reasons if the work was meaningful. Similar
studies of workers in a variety of occupations in different countries produced
basically the same result with respect to commitment and longer tenure on
the job: most of the participants stated that they would continue to work
even if they won the lottery or inherited a fortune.[8] The RAND Corporation's
labor and population research underscores these findings about relishing the
job when the work is meaningful: more than two-thirds of older workers in
a recent RAND survey get satisfaction from doing useful work and doing it
well. Meaningful work is "a key reason" for delaying retirement. The obverse
would hold true if the older workers surveyed by RAND were in the kinds of
uninteresting, unfulfilling jobs that often drive people into retirement. And
what matters to older workers, even more than benefits that come with the
job, is having some control over how they do their work.[9]

Hard as it may be to believe, Harvard MBAs and their elite brethren can be
wealthy, successful, and professionally discontent, even *miserable*, when they
lack a sense of autonomy, work without a true sense of purpose, and feel that
their efforts do not really matter, says investigative business reporter Charles
Duhigg.[10] Former First Lady Michelle Obama, for one, reveals just this kind of
professional dilemma in her memoir, *Becoming*—the realization that "fancy"

academic degrees from Princeton University and Harvard Law School and status as a high-powered corporate lawyer in Chicago did not come with a guarantee of fulfillment in her work.

Reviewing the reasons in Table 3.1, it comes as no surprise that four out of five respondents to the survey consider using their abilities, skills, and training to be a very high priority, because they had invested significant amounts of time and money acquiring advanced degrees in order to succeed in their careers. There is, however, an interesting gender difference: 77 percent of the men and 85 percent of the women consider this a very important reason. It is quite possible that the women encountered greater obstacles to achieving professional status and are less likely to take it for granted.

As to reason number three, there is little difference between the men (74 percent) and women (71 percent) when it comes to the value they put on helping others and making a difference in their respective fields. A doctor, age seventy-five, at the peak of his career, has "an enhanced sense of competence and internal identity based on being a physician and healer." Several other men and women emphasize the importance of making a difference, being useful, and "doing good." All in their seventies, they work in such fields as business consulting, social work, gerontology, and real estate. Four altruistic individuals are: an Episcopal priest who works so she can "be of use by God," a recruiter of volunteers for school literacy programs who is dedicated to helping her inner-city community, the executive director of an inner-city non-profit who loves solving problems and is committed to the revitalization of her part of the city, and a financial officer at a non-profit organization whose reason for working at age eighty-two is simply "belief in the mission."

∽⧢∾

PROFILE: HAROLD R. CUTLER, BUILDING AND FIRE SAFETY CODE CONSULTANT

Altruistic also describes Hal Cutler, who knows that helping others and making a difference in the lives of less fortunate people is an important part of his professional work in building and fire safety code consulting and is the *raison d'être* of his volunteering. Even when he was working full-time he was on call as a paid firefighter/emergency medical technician in his local community. He also devoted several hours a week to volunteer work there and in Boston. Self-employment and working in a home office enable Hal to set his own schedule. Now that he is in his mid-seventies, he is taking on consulting projects of shorter duration, continuing the volunteer work, and adding some travel to the mix.

Hal Cutler wanted to be a fireman when he was growing up, so he is happy with the profession he did choose, fire protection engineering. The closest he came to experiencing the adrenaline rush of emergency calls was a sideline job as a paid on-call firefighter/emergency medical technician responding to fifty to sixty fire or ambulance calls per year in his hometown of Sudbury, a suburb west of Boston. He served as a firefighter from 1966 to 1975 and as a firefighter/emergency medical technician from 1975 until in 2015 he was forced out when the town's insurer refused to cover him as a public safety officer because he was seventy years old.

Hal took his undergraduate degree in physics from Clarkson College of Technology in 1966 and his master's degree in physics from Tufts University in 1969. "What I studied was 'high-falutin' physics, and what I wanted was more practical stuff. Fire protection is a very practical business," he informs me. At the same time, it is not at all physically challenging and that's a plus for a seventy-four-year old consultant. Hal draws on a thorough knowledge of building and fire safety codes to review construction plans, schemes, specifications, and reports so he can tell builders and architects what they can and cannot do in compliance with those codes. Fire protection is also a "registration profession," comparable to architecture or mechanical engineering, that requires continuing education for an engineer to remain registered.

In his first job as a test engineer and then testing engineering supervisor at the Fenwal Incorporated fire and explosion test facility in Ashland, Massachusetts, Hal applied physics and chemistry to evaluating and testing industrial equipment for its fire suppression capacity and danger of explosion. He moved on to work at a fire protection engineering firm called FirePro Inc., where part of his job was investigating fires for insurance companies. By 1983 Hal decided he was ready to go out on his own as a consulting fire protection engineer. He was confident in his abilities, had a strong client base, and he and his wife Betsey were getting ready to pay college tuitions for their two daughters.

Hal's clients are architects and contractors who are designing buildings and operations within buildings, projects mainly located on the east coast. He spends zero on advertising his services. "I can rely on word of mouth. I have many repeat customers, and they don't want me to retire!" Nevertheless, at the peak of his career, Hal is winding down the business very gradually. He no longer takes on huge projects that would require a commitment of his time for four or five years until construction is completed. He does do smaller projects on an ad hoc basis for clients with whom he has a longstanding relationship.

Apart from supporting his family, what has motivated him from the start is the challenge of solving tough problems. He really enjoys helping others. Hal learned from the example set by his mother, who was a nurse in addition to being a housewife. While home from college on vacation, he would work as an aide in the nursing home where his grandmother resided. He liked earning spending money, but of greater importance was discovering how much he enjoyed helping people. That reason (along with the excitement) was also his motivation to become an emergency medical technician.

Together, Hal and Betsey have been performing volunteer work for many years. From 1996 to 2016, they coordinated a ministry at Rosie's Place, a sanctuary for poor and homeless women in Boston. Members of the Memorial Congregational Church (where they worship) joined the Cutlers in serving meals at the shelter. Rosie's Place nominated Hal for a Patriots Foundation award in 2013 in recognition of his long service; he was honored on the football field before a game and Rosie's Place received a donation from the foundation. After Hurricane Katrina, Hal and Betsey organized five trips to the Back Bay Mission in Biloxi, Mississippi, to assist in recovery efforts. They currently participate in Friends in Service Helping by driving people to their medical appointments, and they support Open Table in the nearby town of Maynard once a week for three to four hours, helping in the food pantry and using their van to pick up surplus goods from area supermarkets. One of their volunteer gigs entails standing in costume at the front door of Longfellow's Wayside Inn to greet dining room patrons and overnight guests. They do earn a free dinner at the inn for this work.

The Wayside Inn is where Sudbury Companies of Militia and Minute hold their meetings. (Minutemen refers to the farmers who grabbed their rifles and other weapons and marched to Concord on April 19, 1775, to drive the British Regulars back to Boston at the start of the American Revolution.) Hal and Betsey are active company members who participate in re-enactments of the 1775 march. As a descendant of the Goodenows, who sailed from England

and settled in Sudbury in 1638, Hal also gives presentations on local history for the Sudbury Historical Society. The Town of Sudbury was incorporated within the boundaries of the Massachusetts Bay Colony in 1639. The spelling of the family name has changed many times since then. His grandmother preferred Goodnow, and it can be Goodnough or Goodenough and other variations. However you spell it, *doing good* is what's most important to Hal.

⚭

The fourth-ranked reason listed in Table 3.1 mirrors the third when responses for men and women are combined, though when the responses are separated it appears that the men (75 percent) enjoy their clients, patients, students, or customers somewhat more than the women do (69 percent). "It's a privilege to work with children and adolescents who have learning challenges and their families, helping discouraged youngsters become confident, independent learners," declares a board-certified educational therapist, age seventy-eight. She doesn't want to retire because "seeing youngsters blossom" is so rewarding. A part-time high school track and field coach, age eighty-two, is "inspired by daily interaction with amazingly talented young adults from around the world. I love what I do!" A seventy-nine-year-old part-time management and leadership development consultant in the field of conservation gets great satisfaction from "reaching young people and supporting their growth, energy, and commitment to protecting our earth. The work is intensive and the hours are long, but I love it! Showing up with integrity, passion, and clarity keeps me on my toes. I am able to be more vulnerable and tap wisdom I didn't have at a younger age."

The reason ranked number five in the list is one of the very few new items in my 2017 survey, added because so many respondents wrote "Love my work!" somewhere on their surveys in 2010 and 2012. This time responses from the women exceed those from the men by twenty points: 79 percent of the women love their work compared to 59 percent of the men.

⚭

PROFILE: DR. MARION NESTLE, NUTRITION SCIENTIST
Dr. Marion Nestle (pronounced like "trestle," not like the Swiss food giant to whom she is not related, or as she puts it, "like nestle the verb, not the

multinational food company") is one of many older women who really love their work. Her work, at first glance and purely by coincidence, appears to resemble Corky White's in that the careers of both women revolve around food, authoring many books, and university teaching and administrative positions. There the similarity ends, however, because Corky is an anthropologist focused on Japanese society and Marion is a nutrition scientist focused on the American diet. As the Goddard Professor of Nutrition, Food Studies, and Public Health, *emerita*, at New York University (NYU), her research and writing address food additives, marketing practices, and dietary habits that have proved harmful to health, as well as food and beverage industry politics and related controversies. At age eighty-one, Marion is in demand as visiting lecturer, blogger, and keynoter at professional conferences.

Despite getting a late start on her career, Dr. Marion Nestle has managed to rise to the top of her profession. In 2011 *Forbes Magazine* designated Nestle as "number two of the world's seven most powerful foodies," calling her "an indispensable voice on the problems of the American diet and their roots in industry's marketing and government policy." (Number one was First Lady Michelle Obama and her "Let's Move" campaign.)

Pushing back against that voice, Activist Facts called the eighty-one-year-old professor one of the country's "most hysterical anti-food industry fanatics" and "the anti-pleasure nutritionist." Nestle is amused by such claims. She knows that Activist Facts' website is a project of the Center for Organizational Research and Education (formerly the Center for Consumer Freedom), an American non-profit that lobbies on behalf of "consumer freedom" and the fast food, meat, alcohol, and tobacco industries, and which does not disclose the names of its industry donors. Nestle drew additional criticism from the website by proposing a simple-to-understand food labeling system that would indicate bad (nutritionally suspect) and good food choices by means of red, yellow, and green traffic signals.

The website also scorns Nestle's involvement with the Center for Science in the Public Interest, a financially and politically independent non-profit organization whose Nutrition Action Healthletter calls out ingredients (like food dyes, sodium, and trans fats), marketing practices, and dietary habits that research shows are harmful to health. Although no longer on the Center for Science in the Public Interest's board, Nestle supports the group's efforts to improve the American diet, and shrugs off criticism from food industry lobbyists. "Consider the source," she might say. "The food industry doesn't like challenges; corporations want to sell products. And government agencies like Health and Human Services and the Agriculture Department knuckle under to industry pressure and water down the government's dietary advice." Even though Michelle Obama made really good progress in removing junk food from school meals, for example, powerful forces opposing her work are undoing it today.

Nestle is the Paulette Goddard Professor of Nutrition, Food Studies, and Public Health at NYU's Steinhardt School, although she took *emerita* status in the fall of 2017. She still teaches part time at NYU and remains affiliated with the Department of Sociology and the College of Global Public Health at NYU and with the Division of Nutrition Sciences at Cornell. She has had visiting appointments at the University of California, Berkeley, as well as in Mexico, Australia, and elsewhere.

Nestle earned three degrees from the University of California, Berkeley: a bachelor's degree in bacteriology in 1959 (Phi Beta Kappa), a doctorate in molecular biology in 1968, and a master's in public health nutrition in 1986. She also has two honorary doctoral degrees. "I started my college studies in dietetics with the best of intentions because I was interested in food even then. But the program was more home economics than science and science was what fascinated me," she explains.

Starting in 1968, Nestle did post-doctoral research in cell biology and taught at Brandeis University for eight years. When assigned to teach a course in introductory nutrition, she discovered that there were disagreements about even the most basic information about human nutritional requirements. That piqued her interest in nutrition. "The Brandeis experience was formative, actually life changing," she observes.

Over the next ten years at the University of California, San Francisco's School of Medicine, where she held faculty and administrative positions, she gradually moved away from biochemistry and biophysics toward health policy. And there she met Dr. Philip Lee, a former Assistant Secretary for Health who had founded the Institute for Policy Studies and was instrumental in helping her to redirect her career. "I owe a great deal to him. I took his advice and went back to school to study public health at Berkeley. And this was twenty years after my doctorate, two children, and two husbands!"

That led to a relatively brief stint in the Department of Health and Human Services, Office of Disease Prevention and Health Promotion in Washington,

DC, where she was senior nutrition policy advisor and managing editor of the *Surgeon General's Report on Nutrition and Health*. Government experience was invaluable: "I learned things I didn't know I didn't know." Other professionals might have been content to rest on those laurels, but not Nestle. She says her career did not really take off until she became professor and chair of what is now NYU's Department of Nutrition, Food Studies and Public Health but was Home Economics in 1988. Being in her early fifties at the time made it, in her view, a late start.

Keeping up a fast pace, the professor still blogs about food politics and talks to journalists every day.[11] "It's an enormous part of my work, and my university loves it!" She is working on her tenth book, which will be (no surprise) about the food industry: *Unsavory Truth: How Food Companies Skew the Science of What We Eat*. Recent books include *Soda Politics: Taking on Big Soda (and Winning)* in 2015 and *Eat Drink Vote: An Illustrated Guide to Food Politics* in 2013. An earlier book, *Food Politics: How the Food Industry Influences Nutrition and Health*, came out right after Eric Schlosser's 2001 bestseller *Fast Food Nation* and greatly helped sustain the drumroll against food industry marketing of harmful foods. She has also made a dozen film appearances, from "Super Size Me" in 2004 up to "Holy Chicken" in 2017.

Invitations to lecture and keynote on food and nutrition policy development and analysis continue to come Nestle's way. Topics focus on dietary guidance, social and environmental influences on food choice, the politics of food safety, the effects of food industry marketing on diet and health, and conflicts of interest introduced by food industry sponsorship of food and nutrition research. Her primary goal is to communicate information about the links between agriculture, food, nutrition, and health to students, professionals, and the public. "Nutrition is complicated, and it's difficult for people to understand. So, the challenge is to strike a balance between simplifying information and keeping scientific rigor in everything I write." Evidently, she has succeeded: honors and awards for her work pour in, favoring terms such as "game changing," "most influential," "best," "top," and "must read."

It becomes obvious why Nestle insists on making up for that so-called late start: "I am not done yet. I have a lot of work to do and more books to write! I am never bored." *Emerita* status has not made any difference on a day-to-day basis. She loves teaching, writing, blogging, tweeting, and traveling to professional meetings. She admitted that it was nice to hear from colleagues that no one wanted her to retire, but she felt at eighty-one that she ought to get out of the way of younger academics. Fortunately, NYU allowed her to keep her office, which is near to her apartment in Greenwich Village. She stays fit by walking everywhere; she hasn't owned a car since moving to the city thirty years ago.

Before drawing the interview to a close, I had one more question for the hard-charging foodie that seemed pertinent based on all she had said: Is she a vegan or a vegetarian? "I'm an omnivore. I love food!" she shot back.

Looking at the next four reasons listed in priority order in Table 3.1, we can see that the men (70 percent) apparently enjoy their colleagues and co-workers more than the women do (58 percent). A full-time symphonic choral director and educator finds joy in "making music with wonderful, talented, dedicated people. I have wonderful colleagues and my work is greatly appreciated by them and by the community at large." A major goal for her in the coming years is protecting her legacy by ensuring a stable transition for the incoming music director who will be selected as her replacement.

Sixty percent of the women and men cite enjoying good health and high energy as a reason for staying in the workforce. And, because health status *is* such an important criterion for working later, it gets in-depth treatment in chapter 6.

Mentoring younger colleagues, another benefit of working, often contributes to mature workers being genuinely engaged. Another term for mentoring now in vogue is "generativity," the act of grooming the next generation. A new book, *How to Live Forever—The Enduring Power of Connecting the Generations*, encourages purposeful engagement through intergenerational programs. In his book, the founder and chief executive officer of Encore.org Marc Freedman argues that nurturing and mentoring the next generation brings fulfillment and happiness in later life and solves vexing social problems in the process. He quotes a Greek proverb that reads, "Society grows great when older people plant trees under whose shade they shall never sit." Then he elaborates on that message: "Planting, tending, bequeathing to the next generation—it's the essential human project, one we've long understood yet let slip over the past half century. It is our role as older people to plant those trees under whose shade we shall never sit. Our task is not to try to be young, but to be there for those who actually are." It is unclear why the men who responded to my survey (53 percent) cite the opportunity to mentor younger workers as a reason far more often than the women (33 percent), as four-fifths of all the respondents had experienced mentoring or positive role models when they themselves were just starting out. It could be that more of the men are farther along in their careers and want to ensure the integrity of the professions to which they are dedicated.

⟨✕⟩

PROFILE: DR. GEORGE CANELLOS, ONCOLOGIST

Mentoring, Dr. George Canellos believes, has been and continues to be a very important part of "moving the field" of medical oncology. At the National Cancer Institute (NCI), where he got his start after years of medical training, George was mentored by senior doctors and participated on NCI teams discovering chemotherapy drugs that, over time, were accepted as effective alternatives to surgery and radiation. Later, as professor of medicine at Dana Farber Cancer Institute (DFCI) and Brigham & Women's Hospital in Boston, he and his colleagues pioneered many life-saving therapeutic treatments in cancer care. All the while, George made sure to mentor several generations of Dana Farber oncology fellows who themselves have gone on to lead the profession to new heights. Now in his eighties, moving the field remains his full-time preoccupation.

In addition to his positions at DFCI and Brigham & Women's, George Canellos holds the William Rosenberg Chair in Medicine at Harvard Medical School. He works full-time in patient care, teaching, mentoring, and editing. His primary interests are chronic lymphocytic leukemia and Hodgkin's and non-Hodgkin's lymphoma.

Among his many recent awards and honors was recognition as an "Oncology Luminary" in 2016 by the American Society of Clinical Oncology for his role in the development of two of the most influential treatments in cancer care. Ever modest, George hastens to point out that research is a team effort; researchers think about and devise ways to benefit patients as a group. "Teamwork is essential. Trusting in colleagues, valuing their opinions, doing everything by consensus." Notably, when he served as president of the American

Society of Clinical Oncology in 1993 and 1994, he endeavored to reconcile the split between that group, which was practice based, and the American Association for Cancer Research, which was science based.

Born in Boston, George attended Boston Latin School and Harvard College, where he earned a degree in biology in 1956. His took his medical degree at Columbia University College of Physicians and Surgeons. During an internship at Massachusetts General Hospital he was inspired by a famous surgeon, Dr. Oliver Cope, known especially for innovative work on the thyroid. George jokes that he decided against surgery because he "had the manual dexterity of a seal." He was not really bad at surgery; the problem was being left-handed when the tools were for righties. He was drawn to internal medicine by the intellectual challenge, an insatiable curiosity about cancer, and the potential of chemotherapeutic agents. He was beginning to realize that the field of cancer was not going to move ahead via surgery and radiation, so he read what little literature about early chemotherapy was available in the hospital library and set out to find some form of systemic medicinal therapy to attack tumors.

George made a discovery inadvertently while a medical senior resident responsible for a patient who had advanced ovarian cancer. He knew of a drug that could help her. He administered the dose himself—chemotherapy nurses were unheard of in those days—and left a note in her chart. The next resident on duty missed seeing the note, administered another dose by mistake, and to everyone's surprise, the patient improved! This only reinforced George's thinking.

With U.S. intervention in Vietnam beginning to heat up in the early 1960s, George had to report for military duty as a commissioned officer in the Public Health Service. Fortuitously, he was assigned to the NCI, part of the National Institutes of Health. Senior doctors there mentored him, including Drs. Emil (Tom) Frei and Emil (Jay) Freireich, who were pioneers in combination chemotherapy. Dr. Vincent DeVita, who went on to head the NCI in 1980, was a colleague. They worked together on combination chemotherapy for Hodgkin's lymphoma and other lymphomas. "It was an era of great productivity," George recalls. "Ideas flourished. Money was not a problem. It was thrilling to be part of the team, working with the best and brightest fellows, like Bruce Chabner.[12] We knew disease, we knew medicine and which drugs were coming along at the time."

Among the team's milestones was developing treatments for large cell lymphomas: C-MOPP (mustargen, oncovin, procarbazine, and prednisone) and a modification of the original MOPP regimen to treat and cure Hodg-kin's lymphoma that substituted cytoxan for one of the drugs. They also published the first papers about using C-MOPP and about a combination chemotherapy called CMF (ciscytoxan, methotrexate, and fluorouracil) used with breast cancer.

Despite these exciting breakthroughs, however, George saw that the medi-cal establishment was suspicious of the word "oncology." As inconceivable as it seems today, in the 1970s chiefs of medicine were "put off" by cancer treat-ment. Therapeutic options for patients were so limited that it seemed best to concentrate on what doctors knew how to do. "Getting full recognition of the oncological discipline, convincing hospitals that radical mastectomy and radical thyroid surgery were unnecessary, was a very slow educational process." As a result, the NCI's first randomized controlled trial of a drug for early breast cancer patients who had had surgery was led by Dr. Gianni Bonadonna at the Instituto Nazionale in Milan, Italy, and not in this country.

In 1974, George declined a tempting appointment as acting clinical di-rector of the NCI in favor of an offer from Tom Frei to establish a medical oncology program at DFCI. (Frei had become director following the death of the founder, Sidney Farber.) Although George knew Frei was an enthusiast for the field of medical oncology, Frei was new to Boston and to the high de-gree of skepticism about drugs so prevalent at the time. Boston surgeons and patients understandably feared toxic side effects that were difficult to tolerate. Undaunted, Tom Frei and George agreed, "We're here to move the field."

George was chief of the division for the next twenty years (1975 through 1995). Dana Farber built a new, spacious building, yet it remained underuti-lized. "We started with a few patients who were hospitalized at the Brigham and moved them over to the Farber. Then we had to beat the bushes for patients. We gave talks at medical schools and at other hospitals. It took a long time!"

Several significant breakthroughs on George's watch included using a new drug called cisplatin and testing its efficacy in testicular cancer in collaboration with the head of urology at Brigham & Women's Hospital; leading a DFCI team to establish treatment for central nervous system lymphoma; and forming a multi-disciplinary team of medical oncologists, surgeons, and radiation oncologists focused on breast cancer. "Until there is a 'magic bullet' for ending disease, it takes a lot of brains working together," he says. Eventually, the field of cancer "came out of the closet." Treatment for Hodgkin's lymphoma attained an 80 percent cure rate. Two forms of acute leukemia became curable or indefinitely manageable. "When medical science enables us to understand the molecular features of a disease, the genetic abnormalities, the right drugs can be designed, often by small, clever biotech companies."

Moving the field has also involved mentoring several generations of DFCI fellows. George knows his oncology fellows are the future of the field. "We are now able to attract the best and the brightest in our fellowship program. This time around we had 450 inquiries, interviewed fifty-two and selected fourteen. Half of them are M.D.s with Ph.D.s; many trained in Boston." Earlier, there were few good training programs in the United States. Now DFCI gets well-trained fellows from top-notch programs at, for example, Washington University in St. Louis; Northwestern; University of California, San Francisco; and Seattle University. The current head of the NCI is a former DFCI fellow. Three of the major cancer programs in New York City—NYU, Mt. Sinai, and Memorial Sloan Kettering—are headed by former DFCI fellows. "The people we train are our best product: they go out and do great things!"

Editing is another facet of George's work. As editor-in-chief of the American Society of Clinical Oncology's *Journal of Clinical Oncology* for more than a decade, George introduced a new section of the journal in 1990 to which oncologists, physicians, cancer patients, family members, nurses, chaplains, and allied health workers have been contributing reflective and narrative essays, poems, and images relating to their personal experiences ever since. Currently, he is editor-in-chief of *Oncology UptoDate*, which combines synthesis of the latest research with actionable recommendations and bills itself as "clinicians' primary resource for medical knowledge at the point of care."

George, his wife Jean, and their three sons look forward to the establishment of an endowed chair at Harvard to be called the Dr. George and Jean Canellos Professorship in Medicine. In addition to contributions from the Canellos family, donations have come from large foundations, patients, fellows, and hospital staff. The first recipient, whether a researcher or a clinician, is likely to be a former DFCI fellow and a good scientist. What could be more fitting for a doctor who was there from oncology's beginnings? George Canellos is the "walking history" of the field he has helped to move.

⸦⟨⟩⸧

There is no disagreement between the genders about the next reason for working that is listed in Table 3.1: both older women and older men want to keep busy and get out of the house! A part-time concierge, age seventy-seven, doesn't want to retire because she enjoys having a place to go every day. A freelance writer, age sixty-three, gets right to the point: "No hobbies, not sure what else I'd do."

All of the above reasons ranked higher than reasons associated with financial gain except for "mentoring younger workers" and "keeping busy and getting out of the house," which are on a par with responses for "need the income." This was true of responses to my earlier surveys as well. The moderately lower rankings for men and women (in combination) when it comes to needing the income from work, having high earning power at the peak of a career, saving in a retirement plan, and boosting Social Security benefits go a long way to refuting the oft-repeated assumption that older workers are staying on the job just for the money. There are sizable gender differences regarding saving in a retirement plan and boosting Social Security benefits. By seven points, men are more attentive to growing their retirement plans than are women (who may not have a retirement plan), and by ten points, women are more concerned about increasing what they will eventually collect from Social Security. Both items indicate the greater financial insecurity women generally face as they age.

Three remaining reasons with clear-cut monetary implications fell toward the very bottom of the list in Table 3.1: other (unspecified) financial pressures (13 percent), rising health insurance costs (11 percent), and accruing pension benefits (10 percent). Although employer-provided pensions for many have become a thing of the past, the cost of health insurance and other financial pressures are here to stay. Money worries trouble more than a few older workers. Some examples: an accountant, age sixty-seven, needs the income to pay very expensive clinic fees for his son (for which insurance benefits have run out) and to keep his own health insurance. A psychologist and coach, age seventy-one, is paying for her son's college tuition. Paying off a mortgage is the goal of a higher education project director, age sixty-four. A research scientist, age sixty-one, works in order to keep his health insurance coverage and to pay alimony to his ex-wife. A woman, age sixty-five, who first worked in lower-paying jobs that offered no benefits is working now "to prepare for her older years." Another woman who got a late start to her career and was underpaid is a technical editor, age sixty-eight. She and her husband, who also got a late start and was unemployed for several years during the recession, are delaying Social Security and are trying to build up their retirement savings. At least three others are doing the same.

⌒⊗⌒

PROFILE: BARBARA BLAIR, GARMENT DISTRICT ALLIANCE PRESIDENT

Barbara Blair, age sixty, is upfront about wanting to save for her retirement. She says it is priority number one for the foreseeable future. She has helped to transform one of the city's most storied neighborhoods into a thriving area. Still midtown Manhattan's fashion center, it is also a multi-purpose business innovation hub, arts mecca, and residential neighborhood that draws many thousands of visitors every day to enjoy its hotels, restaurants, retail shops, sightseeing tours, and cultural happenings. Barbara and her staff juggle economic development initiatives and sensitive political matters, all while protecting the quality of life and meeting the diverse needs of property owners, businesses, and residents. It is very fulfilling work that comes with big responsibilities . . . and income and benefits. Income is the number one reason Barbara Blair will be working for at least twelve more years. She is president of New York City's Garment District Alliance, a non-profit organization with a staff of seventy-five and a budget of eight million dollars.

Barbara started out with a bachelor's degree in sociology from the College of New Rochelle and New York City as her destination. (A master's degree in public administration and urban planning from NYU came much later in 2010.) With great reluctance she followed her mother's advice about learning to type and landed a secretarial position. From 1983 to 1986, she was events coordinator for the Museum of Modern Art. Someone from the Airbus Industries of North America noticed her talents and hired her as public relations coordinator for the international consortium. She loved the job, but after one year Airbus relocated from Rockefeller Center to Herndon, Virginia, which cut short her tenure with the company. Barbara next became administrative director of Fashion Group International, a worldwide association of executive women in fashion and fashion-related industries. Then in 1995 she became president of the Garment District Alliance.

In "A Stitch in Time," the commemorative history of New York's fashion district, a reader learns that the area was once known as "The Tenderloin" because of the sex trade, bootlegging, betting, and racketeering that flourished there in the nineteenth and twentieth centuries. Impervious to efforts by police vice squads, social reformers, and priests to clean up prostitution and squalor, the midtown area was finally transformed by an influx of immigrant garment workers—predominantly Eastern European Jews and Puerto Ricans—whose workshops around Fifth Avenue had been closed down by an association of wealthy Manhattan property owners.[13]

The district could soon boast of being "the living center of American fashion design, home to the greatest concentration of fashion designers in the country." In 1993 midtown Manhattan property owners, residents, and businesses established the Fashion Center Business Improvement District as a public-private partnership "to improve the quality of life and economic vitality in this authentic New York neighborhood." However, apparel manufacturing was already in decline. As of 2018 there were merely forty-six hundred such jobs where there used to be more than two hundred thousand; designers, marketers, and sales representatives comprised just under half of the district's tenancy. Local property values and rising labor costs make clothing expensive, no match for stiff competition from global labor markets that can mass produce cheaper goods. Once work started going overseas on a large scale in the 1980s and 1990s (the North American Free Trade Agreement was signed in 1994), the industry was "in a pickle" in New York City and across the country, as Barbara puts it.

Compounding the problem is special restrictive zoning that was introduced by Mayor Ed Koch's administration in 1987 to protect apparel manufacturing plants in the district's side street buildings. Well-intentioned then, the zoning has outlived its original purpose and no longer makes sense, Barbara explains. Buildings in the zone house far more small businesses than apparel manufacturers. If those non-compliant businesses were to be evicted, the vacancy rate would be terrible. Although it seems obvious that the special zoning should be lifted, city officials are resisting the change. Barbara realizes that the situation has become "complicated and politicized." Moreover, emotional aspects associated with the district's storied history make talking about it even harder.

Taking another approach to stabilizing the apparel manufacturing sector, the Alliance is collaborating with the New York City Economic Development Corporation and the Council of Fashion Designers of America on a multi-million-dollar investment package. It will be available to factories in the five boroughs willing to relocate to a huge, city-owned building in Sunset Park, Brooklyn, that has machinery for modern manufacturing.

According to Barbara, about ten years ago the Alliance realized it "could no longer remain fashion-centric" and had better embrace the varied users and uses of the district. Indeed, where textiles and apparel once reigned supreme, a Kite and Rocket Research space has opened, a "laboratory of ideas" for engineers, artists, designers, and scientists. Tourism is huge. Thirty-seven new hotels have opened, along with the repurposing and rebuilding of Hudson Yards. The Alliance offers free walking tours and guides to local resources: architecture, restaurants, bars, theaters, art galleries, and artist studios. Retail stores, including fabric and trim shops, are listed in the guide. There is an annual arts festival in the fall and a Fashion Walk of Fame. Exhibits, sculptural installations, and activities are held on pedestrian plazas year-round for adults and youngsters alike. One of the newest exhibits, the LOOP, opened in February 2018 and was an immediate hit with tourists. Co-sponsored by the Alliance and the New York City Department of Transportation, it was a six-week interactive art installation on a pedestrian plaza on Broadway that invited the public to create electrifying light shows and bring animated musical movies to life by activating large, futuristic cylinders. (Visitors sat inside the cylinders and worked together to pump activation levers that caused the cylinders to spin and light up with a flickering strobe effect.) In April 2018, the third annual "Car-Free Earth Day" featured environmental programming for pedestrians on thirty blocks of Broadway in midtown that were closed to automobile traffic. And Nap York, a wellness club located at 480 Seventh Avenue, began offering yoga and meditation classes, a café, co-working space, and pods for resting, meditating, napping, and recharging.

A major portion of the Alliance budget now goes to sanitation and public safety, beautification programs, horticulture, and capital improvement projects. The Alliance "Clean Team" is responsible for street and sidewalk sweeping, general maintenance, and trash pickups day and night. Public safety officers are always on patrol. Urban Pathways outreach workers (paid by the Alliance) try to coach homeless men and women who are camping out on pedestrian plazas to accept help and shelter. The Garment District Lighting Program, an extension of the side street lighting program, is improving pedestrian security and illuminating building facades on Sixth, Seventh, and Eighth Avenues and Broadway. A planned Seventh Avenue sidewalk expansion will help to alleviate pedestrian congestion and increase safety. "Parklets" with seating and greenery are being created on side streets. Information services are part of marketing and promotion: an information kiosk located on Seventh Avenue at 39th Street, a newsletter, website, map, and social media presence.

Barbara describes herself as a "Virgo": hardworking, well-organized, goal-oriented, one who likes working on projects with Plan A and Plan B in mind. "If we haven't figured it out with Plan B, I reassess and change direction," she says. She always loved earning her own money, keeping her own checking account and credit cards. She liked her independence. She was not a woman on an allowance. Until her recent divorce, she did not fathom the extent to which she was supporting the household. The divorce was hard on her three children, and Barbara thought everything might fall apart. Eventually, she realized how much she was already doing and knew that she could carry on. Although saving for a decent retirement has become her priority for the foreseeable future, she does have other reasons for staying on the job at least until age seventy-two. "My Alliance responsibilities give me a sense of value. I'm asked my opinion. I'm out in the world, involved in the life of the city. My colleagues are smart, dedicated people. I love my work! Actually, I always wanted to work. Ever since I was in middle school I wanted to be a career girl. I really wanted to be Mary Tyler Moore, but that didn't happen. Maybe I didn't have the right hat!"

Other plausible but lower-ranked reasons listed in Table 3.1 for staying in the workforce include changing one's career field or taking a new job in the same field (discussed fully in chapter 5), expanding one's business or taking advantage of new business opportunities (also discussed in chapter 5), working in an "age-friendly" company, and having opportunities to train, retrain, or update one's skills. (Although employers obviously intend job training to increase organizational productivity, it also can be a big contributor to job satisfaction, according to Leppel et al.[14] Greller's study of college-educated men ranging in age from twenty-three to seventy supports this: late career workers are no less likely to invest "in professional development and in maintaining work-relevant social networks, job satisfaction, and career motivation" than younger workers.[15])

Respondents to AARP's Work and Career Study (1,502 male and female mostly full-time workers, ranging in age from forty-five to seventy-four) rated "the opportunity to learn something new" and "on-the-job training" as essential elements of an ideal job. However, as my survey respondents also indicated, the AARP study found that "doing something worthwhile" and "using skills and talents" in a friendly work environment were even more powerful predictors of older workers' job enjoyment and sense of fulfillment.[16]

A total of 16 percent of the women in my study gave skills training opportunities as a reason for working, compared with just 5 percent of the men. Without knowing whether skills training and updating was available to fewer of the men than the women or whether women were more willing to be trained, it is hard to explain the discrepancy. More women (18 percent) than men (14 percent) in my study also indicated working for an "age-friendly" company as a reason. Because companies that offer training opportunities as well as flexible work arrangements are considered age-friendly, this gender discrepancy, although not large, is consistent with the previous one.

These older workers tacked on many other reasons for working in the retirement years. Their afterthoughts are often quite revealing. For example, a psychotherapist, aged seventy-five, confides two reasons. First, "If I'm home all day, I'm afraid I'll gain weight." And second, looking back over the years of working with factory workers from the plants in a midwestern state, she recalls that men who retired often died within three to six months. "Subconsciously, I'm afraid to retire. Silly, I know, but that thought is in there." A psychiatrist, aged seventy-five, says he is "afraid of isolation and mental dullness after retirement." Others with the same concern are a business executive, aged seventy-two, whose work keeps her mind alive and enables her to keep up with technology changes and social trends, and a management and leadership consultant, aged seventy-nine, whose work keeps her engaged and stimulated. Many seniors are becoming aware of what science is telling them about the rapid decline in brain function when people stop working, interact with fewer people, and lose their sense of purpose. A major British study that tracked thirty-four hundred civil servants found their short-term memory loss accelerated nearly 40 percent faster once they retired: "the lack of regular stimulation takes a heavy toll on cognitive function and speeds up memory loss and dementia."[17]

PROFILE: CHRISTINE LUNDGREN COTÉ, BUSINESSWOMAN

Chris Coté works to stay mentally stimulated, healthy, useful, and not socially isolated. She also likes to make bold moves. When married to her first husband and raising three children she was working as a certified public accountant. Then she met and fell for Paul Coté, an irresistible fellow who was an expert sailor, a successful businessman, and a co-founder of the Greenpeace environmental movement. Sailing adventures all over the world with Paul replaced her job. After a hiatus of almost twenty years, however, Chris realized she had to go back to work to support the family when Paul became ill. Chris landed a good job with a renewable energy company where she excelled at corporate decision making, technology, sales, and finance. After Paul succumbed to his disease in 2013, she also joined the University of California at Irvine Mind Study to monitor her own levels of cognitive function. Recently, after ten years with the renewable energy company, she made another bold decision. Having reached her early seventies, Chris decided that she was ready to give her notice to the energy company and start taking classes to prepare for her next job.

Chris grew up on a sheep ranch in Utah. Her father worked hard all his life, *much too hard* in his daughter's opinion. He was still working with her brother on the family ranch when he passed away at age ninety-seven. "While I was growing up, I decided that I was not going to be like him. And now? I'm just like my dad! He loved working; it gave his life meaning. The acorn doesn't fall far from the tree," she chuckles. Like her father, Chris wants to have a good influence on her children and many grandchildren. She is not only setting an example; she also knows that work gives her credibility with the younger generation and gives her interesting things to talk about with them.

Chris was already married and the mother of two when she graduated first in her class in the University of Utah's accounting program in 1967.

Her husband was an accountant who became vice president of Fleetwood Enterprises, a major manufacturer of mobile homes and travel trailers. Over the next several years they had a third child and she did not work outside the home. In 1975 Chris went to work for the Coopers and Lybrand accounting firm (known today as PricewaterhouseCoopers, owing to a 1998 merger). At first, she worked part-time because one of her children was still in need of supervision after school, then she became a certified public accountant and worked full-time.

In 1989 she had what she calls her mid-life crisis: leaving her husband and accounting job to marry "an amazing guy" with whom she sailed around the world on and off for the next ten years. Her second husband "had saltwater for blood," says Chris. Paul Coté was a Canadian lawyer who competed in the 1972 summer Olympics and won a bronze medal in sailing. He went on to be a successful businessman and father of three children from his first marriage. He was also a member of the "Don't Make a Wave Committee," a small group of British Columbia environmental activists who founded Greenpeace in 1970 to protest against nuclear testing at Amchitka in Alaska.

Unfortunately, Chris's husband became very ill in 2004 and was diagnosed with Lewy body disease, a type of dementia that affects behavior, cognition, and movement. The doctor advised Chris not to let Paul make financial decisions. Too late, she discovered that he had invested heavily in a Ponzi scheme. Between the investment fraud, reversals during the Great Recession, and the cost of round-the-clock nursing for Paul, by 2008 Chris knew she had to go back to work. Paul's connections included people very concerned about renewable energy. Thanks to Paul, she met and was hired by Richard Langson, an inventor and head of ElectraTherm and then Langson Energy, Inc., both innovative renewable energy companies based in Carson City, Nevada. Langson claims to be the world leader in modular, pre-packaged, steam and gas letdown generators that efficiently convert industrial facilities' waste energy into clean electric power. Even after the nineteen-year gap between jobs, Chris did so well in sales that she was eventually promoted to executive vice president.

Ten years later, at age seventy-two, Chris made another major career change when she resigned from her position at Langson Energy. She did this in part to allow for more time to travel, especially to be with her grandchildren. She remained very close to her three step-children after Paul died in 2013 and adores their offspring as much as her biological grandchildren. The grandkids all call her "Mor Mor," which is Swedish for "mother's mother."

She created "Mor Mor's Investing 101" to teach them about the stock market and review with them the stock accounts she opened in their names.

Her latest career decision also resulted in part from a desire for new challenges. Having seen what dementia did to her husband, Chris is anxious to keep her mind sharp. She participates in the University of California at Irvine Mind Study. And she has put herself in "learning mode" to get prepared for her next objective: selling medical equipment. She is presently taking an online course in anatomy and physiology that is offered by Khan Academy, a non-profit organization founded in 2005 "to provide a free, world-class education for anyone, anywhere."

Chris will stay in the workforce to keep supporting herself—southern California is a very expensive place to live and it helps to share her apartment with a roommate. Yet working means more to her than that.

> I feel more mentally stimulated, healthier, [more] useful, and less isolated when I work. Why shouldn't someone with so many years of experience share the knowledge they've gained to benefit others and get paid for it? Working allows me to make a contribution to this incredible planet on which we are so privileged to live and for which I have a deep respect and appreciation. We need to be sure that we bequeath it to our children and grandchildren in good condition.

A smattering of additional afterthoughts penned by respondents to my survey includes "enjoying the travel opportunities associated with my work," "being able to structure my own time," and "do as much or as little as I choose." For a self-employed management consultant, working at age seventy-five is all about fighting age discrimination, saving for retirement, and remaining vital. She explains her reasoning this way:

> I was one of the first women to get "a man's job." Now I intend to be one of the first "old people" to do work young people do. Also, the Great Recession took most of my savings, and interest rates have remained low. It is difficult to rebuild one's nest egg through earnings. Moreover, working for pay gives intellectual, social, emotional, and educational rewards, especially working for mission-driven organizations. What I learned from *Aging Well*, George Vaillant's book based on the Harvard Study of Adult Development, was that those adults who kept working lived longer and healthier lives.

Displaying a similar mindset are the afterthoughts of two other women: the sixty-five-year-old activist and writer whose mission is to raise awareness of ageism (a description of her work concludes chapter 7) and a college administrator, aged sixty-four, who thinks "older people, particularly women, 'disappear' when they no longer have authority, an acknowledged place." She can take heart knowing that a "wave of women, older and in power," is "rejecting invisibility." Not only by dint of their growing number, but also because they enjoy good health, are working longer, and have more income than their predecessors, older women are experiencing "modest but real progress in their visibility and stature," observes a front-page article in the *New York Times*.[18] The article posits that "the arc of women's working lives is changing, as is the broader perception of them," and goes on to highlight the explanation proffered by seventy-eight-year-old and newly elected Florida congresswoman Donna Shalala, former university president and Secretary of Health and Human Services in the Clinton administration: the women's movement developed generations of strong women with professional careers who became achievers in their fields—and society is finally noticing.

NOTES

1. McNeely, R. L. "Age and Job Satisfaction in Human Service Employment." *The Gerontologist*, *28*, no. 2, April 1988.

2. Eichar, Douglas M., et al. "The Job Satisfaction of Older Workers." *Journal of Organizational Behavior*. December 1991. Retrieved from: https://doi.org/10.1002/job.4030120705.

3. Haider, Steven J., and David Loughran. "Elderly Labor Supply: Work or Play?" Working Paper no. 2001-04. Chestnut Hill, MA: Center for Retirement Research, Boston College, September 2001. Retrieved from: https://ssrn.com/abstract=285981.

4. Shultz, Kenneth S., and Gary A. Adams, eds. "In Search of a Unifying Paradigm for Understanding Aging and Work in the 21st Century." *Aging and Work in the 21st Century*. Mahwah, NJ: Erlbaum Associates, 2007.

5. Kooij, Dorien, et al. "Older Workers' Motivation to Continue to Work: Five Meanings of Age." *Journal of Managerial Psychology*, *23*, no. 4, May 2008, 364–94. Retrieved July 21, 2019, from https://doi.org/10.1108/02683940810869015.

6. Fideler, Elizabeth F. *Women Still at Work: Professionals Over Sixty and On the Job*. Lanham, MD: Rowman & Littlefield, 2012, 2017; *Men Still at Work: Professionals Over Sixty and On the Job*. Lanham, MD: Rowman & Littlefield, 2014.

7. Smyer, Michael, and Marcie Pitt-Catsouphes. "The Meanings of Work for Older Workers." *Generations, 31*, no. 1, Spring 2007, 26. Retrieved from: http://hdl.handle.net/2345/763.

8. Harpaz, Itzhak, and Xuanning Fu. "The Structure of the Meaning of Work: A Relative Stability Amidst Change." *Human Relations, 55*, no. 6, 2002, 639–67.

9. Maestas, Nicole, et al. *The American Working Conditions Survey Finds That More Than Half of Retirees Would Return to Work*. Santa Monica, CA: RAND Corp., 2017. Retrieved from: https://www.rand.org/pubs/research_briefs/RB9973.html.

10. Duhigg, Charles. "Wealthy, Successful and Miserable." *New York Times Magazine*, February 24, 2019, 26–27, 60.

11. See www.foodpolitics.com and tweets @marionnestle.

12. Dr. Bruce Chabner was profiled in *Men Still at Work* by this author in 2014.

13. See www.garmentdistrict.nyc.

14. Leppel, Karen, et al. "The Importance of Job Training to Job Satisfaction of Older Workers." *Journal of Aging Social Policy, 24*, no. 1, 2012. Retrieved from: https://www.ncbi.nim.nih.gov/pubmed/22239282.

15. Greller, Martin M. "Hours Invested in Professional Development During Late Career as a Function of Career Motivation and Satisfaction." *Career Development International, 11*, no. 6, October 2006, 544–59. Retrieved July 21, 2019, from: https://doi.org/10.1108/13620430610692944.

16. AARP Research. "Staying Ahead of the Curve 2013—The AARP Work and Career Study." January 2014. Retrieved from: http://www.aarp.org/research.

17. Knapton, Sarah. "Retirement Causes Brain Function to Rapidly Decline, Warn Scientists." *The Telegraph*, News/Science, January 22, 2018. Retrieved from: www.telegraph.co.uk.

18. Bennett, Jessica. "Older and in Power, Unwilling to Remain Unseen." *New York Times*, January 9, 2019, A1, A17.

4

Changing Views of Retirement

CHAPTER OBJECTIVES

---

1. Presents the ways "retirement" is being reconceived as a process, including bridge employment
2. Introduces the phenomenon of *un*retiring
3. Contrasts gains in longevity with inadequate retirement preparedness
4. Highlights gender differences, particularly regarding financial security and Social Security benefits
5. Discusses employer investment in recruitment, training, and retention of older workers

---

Aging, Work, and Retirement was not principally conceived of as a book about retirement, but if we're going to talk about working in the retirement years, we also have to talk about retirement and pre-retirement.

The average retirement age in the United States has now reached sixty-five years for men and sixty-three years for women, reflecting a steady rise that Gallup's annual Economy and Personal Finance Survey has tracked for more than two decades. Noting the trend, in 2013 Gallup observed that "most of the uptick came before the 2008 recession," thus the rise "may reflect more than just a changing economy. It may also indicate changing norms about the value of work, the composition of the workforce, the decrease in jobs with mandatory retirement ages, and other factors."[1]

These observations are fairly consistent with findings from one of the Family and Work Institute's nationally representative studies of the U.S. workforce. The 2008 National Study of the Changing Workforce report linked demographic changes in the workforce with "a new cultural phenomenon related to aging and work," referring to "the emergence of new attitudes and expectations about aging, in general, and about the relationships between aging and work, in particular." As a result of these developments, says the National Study of the Changing Workforce report, "old definitions of retirement no longer apply—*retirement has been redefined*" (italics added). The evidence: 20 percent of workers ages fifty and older were working for pay in retirement, primarily for financial reasons and to avoid boredom. The other 80 percent, who had never retired, said they expected to work for pay after they retired.[2]

In the decade post-recession, the older worker trend continued to strengthen. Insights into labor force trends and career options from the U.S. Bureau of Labor Statistics showed that 40 percent of people ages fifty-five and older were working or actively looking for work.[3] By 2019 when the Associated Press and the NORC Center for Public Affairs Research conducted a new poll of 1,423 adults representative of the U.S. population, researchers found one in four expecting to work well past sixty-five if not prevented by illness, injury, layoffs, or caregiving responsibilities, and one in four with no intention of retiring *ever*.[4] The typical explanation for the decision to keep working was money: the so-called three-legged stool of Social Security, pension, and savings can no longer be relied upon.

We are deluged with television ads, direct mail pieces, website banners, and other formats asking, often in ominous tones, "Are you financially prepared for retirement?" The answer frequently is: No! "The majority of American workers from all backgrounds aren't on a path to retire full time at age 65 under their pre-retirement standard of living," announced an October 2018 Sightlines Special Report from the Stanford Center on Longevity. In the report, Sightlines researchers concluded that people who are less educated, those belonging to ethnic minority groups, and women are moving in the wrong direction, especially with regard to financial security.[5] Among topics covered in the Sightlines report are 1) savings for retirement, 2) generational differences in retirement preparedness, and 3) gender inequalities with respect to financial security. First, the verdict on savings for retirement: although roughly half of American workers ages twenty-five to sixty-four contribute to a retirement plan at work, most are not contributing enough to meet their savings goals. In the future, they will either have to lower their standard of living and make do with less or work beyond traditional retirement age to build up financial resources, or do both.

Second, examining retirement preparedness by mid-Baby Boomers (ages fifty-five to sixty) and the Silent Generation (or Traditionalists, born before the early 1940s), Sightlines researchers find that mid-Boomers have fewer financial assets and save less, including in retirement plans, than previous generations did at the same age, and they carry more debt. The 2008 financial crisis and slow recovery aggravated but overall did not precipitate the situation, they note.

Third, as to gender inequalities and preparedness for retirement, Sightlines researchers reiterate what has long been known: "Women are . . . at a disadvantage when it comes to achieving financial security." Women accumulate less wealth than men. They earn lower salaries and pensions than men of the same age. And because they typically live longer than men, they require more financial resources in order to support themselves. An underlying problem for married women, says the report, is poor financial literacy: women lack confidence because they make fewer major financial decisions than their husbands.[6] Whereas investments, savings, and cost-cutting measures are all worthwhile, other studies agree that working longer and augmenting annual Social Security income is the very best way for women to become more financially secure and maintain their affordable standard of living in retirement.[7]

Despite recommendations to build up financial resources by working beyond traditional retirement age and to delay drawing Social Security benefits, about half of all Americans retire between the ages of sixty-one and sixty-five, if not earlier. The Social Security Administration applies an earnings test when beneficiaries are below full retirement age (sixty-five to sixty-seven, depending on one's year of birth). The earnings test reduces benefits by one dollar for every two dollars in wages over a certain amount. As an incentive to wait before claiming benefits, the Social Security Administration no longer applies the earnings test once beneficiaries reach full retirement age, thereby allowing them to collect benefits and, if desired, also keep working without penalty. Older workers who delay claiming benefits enjoy another financial incentive, a retirement credit that increases every year between full retirement age and age seventy.

The Center for Retirement Research at Boston College reviewed studies of *non*-financial factors affecting the decision to retire or remain in the labor force—for those who have the choice—factors such as a worker's on-the-job experience and the allure of retirement activities. Overall, it seems, "non-pecuniary considerations drive the labor force decisions of older workers." Healthy, well-educated workers with higher incomes who enjoy their jobs are more likely to keep working, as shown in the previous chapter. In contrast, poor health, stressful working conditions, or age discrimination can *push* people out of the labor force; interference with their personal life or ability to do "other things" is what more often *pulls* them into retirement.[8]

Financial advisors are not the only ones asking forty, fifty, and sixty year olds about their preparation for retirement. Life coaches, career coaches, and therapists of various stripes, who are often members of the Life Planning Network, prod clients to think about their emotional or spiritual readiness, because retirement, whether phased or abrupt, can trigger bouts of self-doubt. Leaving behind work roles and responsibilities can feel like the loss of meaning or purpose. Leaving behind the title, structure, and staffing relationships that define a position can invite the loss of identity as well as social isolation. Personal questions such as these can influence the retirement decision as much as or even more than financial considerations.

Increasingly, retirement is viewed as a gradual process, a "moving target," making for a less stressful experience than withdrawing "cold turkey" or "falling off a cliff." There is no longer a single definition. As discussed in chapter 1, in the decade following the Great Recession, *working for pay in the retirement years* has become the "new normal." Oft-times this refers to adults old enough to retire who have nonetheless decided to bypass retirement and keep working at their primary career jobs, full-time or part-time. Sometimes it refers to people who had already retired and then returned to the workforce in some capacity after leaving their longer-term job, perhaps at the same company or in the same industry, perhaps with a different employer or in an altogether different field, on a contractual or a part-time basis. It can also refer to self-employment.

The fairly ungraceful but apt new term "*un*retirement" describes reversing or coming out of "official" retirement to begin working again, also called re-entry or re-careering. For instance, New York City Schools Chancellor Carmen Fariña had been running the New York City Department of Education for four years when in December 2017 she announced her upcoming retirement. She was just shy of her seventy-fifth birthday. In 2013 when she was seventy and retired from a long career in education, newly elected Mayor Bill de Blasio had asked her to *un*retire and join his leadership team. In April 2018 her successor was named and she *re*-retired.

*Un*retirement appears to be catching on—17 percent of the men I surveyed for this study and 11 percent of the women had retired and then *un*retired. That comes to 13 percent of all late-career workers when the responses are combined. In the same year (2017), an analysis of data from a nationally representative RAND survey found a considerably higher frequency of re-entry after an initial period of retirement—39 percent of employed individuals aged sixty-five and older had *un*retired.[9]

⌒∞⌒

PROFILE: DEAN C. MOORE, "AG RADIO IMPRESARIO"

When reaching mandatory retirement age forced Dean Moore from his sales and marketing job with food giant Conagra in 2000, he was sixty-five and still raring to go. His entrepreneurial spirit came to the fore and he pitched an idea for a new agriculture-themed radio program that quickly found its niche. The Market Watch Radio Network he launched in partnership with the AgResource Company grew exponentially, providing listeners with up-to-the-minute grain and livestock research information from the Chicago Board of Trade. Dean has been *un*retired, active and productive ever since. When Dean hit mandatory retirement age at the multi-billion dollar food giant Conagra, Inc. (now called Conagra Brands—think Reddi-wip whipped cream topping, Chef Boyardee spaghetti and meatballs, Peter Pan peanut butter, Wesson oil, Hunt's ketchup, Libby's vegetables, La Choy bean sprouts, and many more products), his boss brought in a well-trained young man to take over the marketing reins, and Dean did not want to stay around watching to see what his replacement would do. Contemplating forced retirement, Dean recalled visiting his mother in a Longboat Key, Florida, retirement community where he noticed a great deal of wasted talent: retired men who had once held impressive jobs were spending their days drinking, napping, or wandering on the beach with a metal detector looking for stray coins or a cannonball left over from the Spanish-American War. That was not for him. He was determined to stay active and be productive.

His retirement party was held, fittingly enough, on the "Challenge" court of a defunct racquetball club in Greeley, Colorado. At the retirement party a guest named Jake Vrabel, a major trader for the Chicago Board of Trade, invited Dean to work for him conducting market research in the midwest with regard to starting an agriculture website. Dean quickly *un*retired, surveyed the area, and told Jake his idea would not fly. What *was* needed, he advised, was a weekly re-cap on "ag" radio of action in the commodity markets—no one was doing that. "Deano," replied Jake, "that's a hell of an idea, but we're not in the radio business." "Jake," Dean shot back, "see those phones on the trading floor? Pick one up and call the KFKA radio station here in Greeley, and we'll have a program."

That conversation led to the launch of Dean's "ag" radio program called "Market Watch." Produced by KFKA, it currently reaches 1.3 million listeners on over five hundred radio stations in twenty-three states and four Canadian provinces. Dean finds sponsors for the time slots—Market Watch Daily is a ninety-second commentary; Market Watch Weekly, Livestock Weekly, and Global Report are two-minute commentaries. The mission is "to help farmer-listeners make better marketing decisions about selling their products." At age eighty-three Dean works full-time managing the network. His greatest satisfaction is knowing that he launched a project with neither assurance of success nor backup from a big company and now has the second largest ag radio network in North America. Outreach to Brazil, one of the world's largest soybean producers and meat exporters, is in the offing.

AgResource Company ("the Tom Brady of the ag radio network") is Dean's partner and the broadcasting "voice" reporting on the latest developments from the Chicago Board of Trade. The AgResource team consists of Dan Basse, president; William Tierney, Ph.D., chief economist; Ben Buckner, grains analyst; and Nate Losey, grain and livestock analyst. Tarso Veloso and Noel Fryer look after the international side. According to Dean, they make his job easy.

According to its website, AgResource "operates at the intersection of economics and agriculture," claiming to be "the world's leading agricultural advisory and research firm." It gives growers "actionable insights" about international markets, telling them "what's happening, why it's happening, what will happen, and how to react" based on the company's own research. In addition to farmers, clients include traders, fund managers, investment banks, governments, grain elevators, processors, millers, food companies, importers and exporters, and meat packers—serving, in other words, agribusiness and agricultural markets around the world.

Dean explains how Market Watch Radio Network differs from the competition. "Other shows pay the stations for air time, while we can use the barter system because of our outstanding delivery of useful information." They are always on the lookout for opportunities to expand the network. "We don't want to do 'same old, same old.' Our niche is 'do it first and do it better.'"

Ag radio is not Dean's only challenge, however. Lee, his wife of sixty years, has Alzheimer's and has been in a memory care unit for a year and a half. Dean spends "respite" time with her every day, sometimes taking her to the grocery store or dry cleaner, sometimes going home to have a snack and listen to her favorite Christmas carols or to dance to the Alabama Boys. She still recognizes Dean, their three children, the grandchildren, and the black lab, Sam. When Dean has to travel out of state, the children step in and take over with Mom.

Work-related travel is another challenge at his age, not only because it's tiring but also because Greeley, the county seat of Weld County in northern Colorado, is located about fifty miles north-northeast of Denver, so he often has to leave at 4:15 am to drive to the airport. Still, he knows that he is most effective when in front of his customers. Dean describes himself as a people person who is good face to face, "a thoroughbred bullshit artist along with solid performance and dependability." His business card simply says "Worker."

Dean studied "ag" science at Ohio State University. After graduation in 1958, he married his hometown sweetheart, Lee Ritterhoff, and the young couple went to Fort Benning, Georgia, for officer training school. (He's a retired army captain, U.S. Infantry.) His father-in-law assured Dean (and himself, no doubt) that people always have to eat, and he would always have a job. Sure enough, he began as a salesman for a poultry business based in South Carolina, and, after proving himself in his territory, was "promoted" to the head office in Ashland, Ohio, where for twenty-two years he wore many hats. Another benefit for the Moores of living in Ashland was raising their kids in a small midwestern town.

In 1989 the Ag Division of the behemoth Conagra acquired the animal health company where Dean worked, United Agricultural Products (UAP), a distributor of fertilizers, seeds, weed control products, pesticides, and over-the-counter medicines and feed medicines for livestock and poultry manufactured by Monsanto, Dupont, and other companies. (UAP's agricultural chemicals are now called "crop protection" products, a fast-growth industry within the global marketplace.) When UAP became a wholly owned subsidiary of Conagra and the ag chemical division moved to Greeley, Colorado, the Moore family moved to Greeley. There Dean first worked out of a Quonset hut doing marketing and advertising of UAP's products. Sales when he started were $180 million; by the time he retired, sales had reached $2.3 billion, and the worker guy known as "Deano" was recognized twice as "Marketing Man of the Year" for Conagra.

At Dean's insistence, I asked his boss at UAP, Charlie Blue, to verify these claims, which he readily did. "Deano was a strong and positive force in our company. It was never necessary to tell him what needed to be done." Charlie also pointed out that Dean was so tenacious and going so fast that sometimes he would "get the cart before the horse," and this would necessitate "a little refereeing" on Charlie's part. AgResource's president Dan Basse also admires Dean's drive and hopes he will keep Market Watch going as long as he can. "He's a true workaholic and salesman. Really good at what he does. We economists love Deano!"

Patsy Comella has known and done business with Dean on and off for some thirty years. She is vice president and media director at the advertising agency that represents one of Market Watch's biggest clients. She believes that Dean "truly hit his stride" only after retirement. He walked into her office in 2004 with an idea for a project he had been working on, an opportunity for her company to consider. "What an idea it was!" she recalls. "Knowing the two things uppermost in a farmer's mind are weather and the commodities markets, he latched onto the one thing a farmer can control—how to maximize what he gets for grain. Dean proposed building a radio network to provide farmers a peek behind the curtain, not only what grain is trading for but *why*. Other radio stations had been reporting grain prices on the air for decades, but there was a void to fill with the *why*. By expanding content from a domestic focus to a global focus, Market Watch has kept my company's client a loyal sponsor for nearly fifteen years." Patsy praises Dean as a force of nature, tenacious, honest, and sincere, then throws in a zinger by saying he's probably the least tech-savvy person she has ever met.

Dean wants me to know that he was originally a "city feller," a midwesterner who grew up in blue-collar Cincinnati, Ohio, which could have made it hard for him and his wife to rub elbows with "sure nuf" Colorado cowboys and Texas "Aggies." Yet he fits in easily with the Weld County T-Bone Club whose members are cattle producers, grain growers, and others in ancillary agriculture-related businesses, such as bankers who make farm loans.

Dean knew from an early age that he wanted to be in the "ag business" someday. An uncle was his role model, his father having died in a car wreck when Dean was five years old. Every year Dean's mother would send him and his two older brothers to stay the summer with their "Uncle Doc," a Missouri veterinarian and entrepreneur who vaccinated hogs and mules for anthrax and other animal maladies. In the 1940s Uncle Doc served stints as his town's mayor, coroner, and sheriff, and was a major cotton grower. Occasionally, he pulled teeth for his workers.

All was not fun and games, however. Part of Dean's stay in Missouri Boot Hill country was fieldwork, hoeing weeds out of rows of cotton. He chopped cotton side by side with two black kids his age, Randal and his brother Dante. Dean recalls how curious they were about schools, swimming pools, rollercoasters, baseball parks, and trains, and how wide-eyed they became as he embellished each description. After finishing the hot fieldwork the threesome would go to the brothers' shack to share sweet iced tea and their mother's homemade molasses cookies. Dean gave Randal one of his old tennis racquets, although Randal had no tennis court to play on. He still wonders what became of his long-ago friends, knowing that they had little chance of escaping the ills of poverty and segregation.

Another of Dean's stories concerns Uncle Doc's annual giant barbeque. One of the guests was heard to say, "I wouldn't miss Doc's barbeque for all the world 'cause he serves the best damn moonshine in all of Missouri!" The guest was Harry S. Truman.

Today, Dean stays busy and makes money to fund his grandkids' college tuitions. A regimen of meeting interesting people and being productive helps to stave off the loneliness resulting from his wife's condition. "Where there is hardship," he tells me, "there's heart, but without my wife it's hard to have heart."

Coping includes some "R and R." Dean enjoys duck hunting (only from a duck blind these days, not out in the open field) especially when he manages to "knock down a green head" (male mallard), which he can bake with red currant sauce and serve with his wife's yellow cheese grits recipe. And he used to enjoy fishing for bass in Canada, stripers in Maine, and red fish and sea trout in Florida. "Old age," he admits, "has caught up with me and my fishing buddies." Still, you will not find him wandering around the park with a metal detector. Dean is right on when he says that *un*retiring has made for "a hell of a good story!"

⸙

PROFILE: DAVID FELDMAN, ANIMAL MASSAGE THERAPIST AND MEDIATOR/NEGOTIATOR

Like Dean Moore, David Feldman also retired from the corporate world and promptly *un*retired. There the similarity ends, for David is in his early seventies, working as a small animal massage therapist and as a trained mediator/ negotiator who helps people resolve their problems. His farm in Ipswitch, Massachusetts, has a variety of horses, dogs, and other animals, but that does not make him the kind of "sure nuf" Colorado cowboy Dean Moore likes to hang out with. (Dean calls me "Boston Lady," a tongue-in-cheek put-down of "effete" Easterners, so that should give you an idea of the different environments he and David Feldman inhabit.) David's journey from performing in magic shows to law school and on to a thriving real estate appraisal business is just the beginning of the fascinating story that comes next. When he says that he has led a "surprising, interesting, and lucky life," David is not exaggerating. "Magical" would not even be a stretch. Here is his story.

David graduated from New York University in 1968 with a degree in psychology and scholarships to attend graduate school in that field. But (and he says this was a "big but") his life took an unexpected turn. He had met a fascinating man in Boston named Cesareo Pelaez (1932–2012), a Cuban exile and psychologist then working under Professor Abraham Maslow (known for his self-actualization theory) at Brandeis University. "I was entranced by Cesareo. I saw him as a mentor, friend, and more experienced traveler who understood me and my adventurous and spiritual aspirations. I was twenty-one, so I dropped the idea of traditional graduate school and went to Boston,"

David chuckles. In 1969, Cesareo was establishing a personal growth center in Dublin, New Hampshire, called Cumbres (Spanish for "peaks"), loosely based on Maslow's ideas about discovering one's inner potential. Cesareo invited David to become an associate at Cumbres, which turned out to be the best "graduate school" for David. In addition to learning how to work with groups, he was introduced to practitioners of various psychological, spiritual, and religious traditions, such as psychodrama, hypnosis, tai chi, Zen Buddhism, Christianity, Yoga, and the Gurdjieff work. This is where David first began to see the common threads among all these traditions.

In 1972, Cesareo became a psychology professor at Salem State College. In addition to teaching, however, Cesareo dreamed of starting a theater and mounting a live stage production modeled on the ones he had enjoyed in Cuba in his youth. His charisma attracted young people like David and his future wife, Catherine. Cesareo told David the theater would need a lawyer, and he suggested that David take on this challenge. "So, I attended New England Law School at night while teaching high school full time in Arlington, Massachusetts. Students loved my course on the law. Becoming a lawyer had an enormously positive impact on my life, more than I could have possibly imagined at that time." In 1976 (a banner year for David), he received his law degree, married Catherine (who was also a teacher), and the members of the group that Cesareo had formed pooled their money and purchased the vaudeville-era grand movie palace called the Cabot Street Theater in Beverly, Massachusetts.

"Le Grand David and His Own Spectacular Company" magic show opened the very next year with a cast of over sixty people, all volunteers. David was a clown, juggler, and manager of the "house" on show days. Catherine was a performer, dancer, and assistant on stage. Within four years the show had become wildly popular, receiving a two-page spread in *Time* magazine, winning awards and accolades, and performing at the White House on eight separate occasions through the 1980s.

David and Catherine "retired" from the company in 1987 after performing in more than one thousand shows. By then, their daughter Liz was ten years old and they wished to devote more of their energies to participating in her life and to provide her with wonderful adventures. They explored the national parks throughout the country together and even went on a "dinosaur dig" sleeping in teepees in the foothills of Montana.

David had already transitioned to working as a real estate appraiser in a small firm and enjoyed the work. After leaving the magic company, he and his business partner dramatically grew their business to one hundred people. Their company extended throughout New England making it the largest real estate appraisal company in the region with eight separate offices. "First American Financial, a multi-billion dollar corporation that wanted to start a national appraisal management company, liked our style and purchased our company in 1997. For the first time in my life I had the possibility of some financial security. I was fifty." David stayed with First American for fourteen years, becoming head of operations and then president of the corporation's appraisal division. With the division's "backroom" in India and Manila, "I got the opportunity to travel internationally and truly expand my perspective. I also learned a great deal about leadership, vision, and getting positive results."

In 2011, David retired from the corporate world. He and Catherine already lived on a small farm in Ipswich, Massachusetts. They got their first dog in 1987, a golden retriever puppy named Shamrock. "He transformed our lives. I had no experience with pets until then. Shamrock opened up the world of animals to me and soon we had several dogs, cats, horses, chickens and ducks." The Feldmans volunteered at a special needs camp in New Hampshire for ten summers helping with their horse program. They trained their dogs to be therapy dogs and visited nursing homes for many years. They also connected with Best Friends Animal Sanctuary in Utah, the largest of its kind in the country and began volunteering there every other year.

Working with dogs and staying in the Ipswich locale were two of David's priorities after retirement, so it is not surprising that he decided to become a certified small animal massage therapist. He paid five thousand dollars to attend the Bancroft School of Massage in Worcester, Massachusetts, learning the essentials of anatomy, physiology, and dog behavior. His business, Skillful Hands Therapeutic Dog Massage, was successful from the start. "People with older dogs, arthritic dogs, as well as post-surgery and hospice situations, find me. I go to their homes, often turn on music and create a peaceful atmosphere. It is quiet and intentional work." He also joined an advisory board of a state-level animal welfare organization and became a volunteer on the Ipswich Open Space Committee.

A third priority was to assist others in expanding their perspective in order to resolve their problems. Consequently, David became a mediator when he unretired. With Harvard Law School's negotiation program under his belt, he enrolled in a mediator training course in Boston. He then joined the North Shore Community Mediation Center in their apprentice program. The North Shore Community Mediation Center offers its services in court cases, divorces, housing issues, and juvenile situations. They use a co-mediation model that fosters learning and teaching.

David soon realized that he could utilize his skills as a mediator/negotiator to assist with animal care and welfare disputes. With this objective in mind, he and an experienced mediator/lawyer from his mediation group started a venture five years ago called Forevercare Mediation. The partners put in a bit of money to launch the venture and designed a marketing plan and website to get the word out to the animal care and dog breeding community in Massachusetts. After two years his partner decided to pursue other interests and David continued with this business.

David refers to two abiding interests that started when he was twenty-one:

> I started out to be a psychologist, and my wish to understand myself and others has stayed strong throughout all these years. I also wondered how the larger universe worked and how everything fit together. I could not phrase it so succinctly then, but I kept studying cosmology and psychology. On the universe side, the wonderful writings of Thomas Berry, Brian Swimme, and others opened me up in ways that have not closed (check out the website, Journey of the Universe). I have a sense of being part of a much larger story, which then influences how I navigate through my daily life.

David felt it was very important to tell me a little about Catherine and their daughter as their lives are so intertwined.

> Over the years, Catherine has developed her own thriving business as an environmental landscape and design consultant. She is also a teacher of the web of life in which all living species are connected and is a master gardener offering courses at Massachusetts Audubon and other venues. The name of her business, "Shamrock Acres," harkens back to our first dog whose impact on us as a family cannot be measured.

As the Feldmans' love and compassion for animals deepened over the years, it was quite natural for them to become mainly vegetarian and create delicious

meals for themselves and sometimes others. They became part of a faith community in the Catholic tradition that celebrates diversity, welcoming, and rec-
onciliation.

Daughter Liz spent her early years within the magic company's environment. She joined the Peace Corps after college, and later became a guide and
therapist in a wilderness therapy program. She then earned a master's in
business administration for a career focused on sustainability. She is one of
the founders of a non-profit (Wild Forests and Fauna) that recently helped
purchase and save from development eleven thousand acres in the Peruvian
Amazon as part of an eco-educational endeavor. This coming year, David and
Catherine are going to join Liz and others in the Amazon at Liz's site where
Wild Forests and Fauna's Peruvian partners obtained the land. Last year, after
David and Catherine had studied Polish for two years, the family traveled to
Poland to experience the oldest remaining and largest primal forest in Eu-
rope, located in Bialowieza, Poland.

And finally for health and additional challenges, David has focused on
fitness. When approaching his seventieth birthday, he wanted to make it a
memorable year. With Catherine's encouragement, he trained for the Crane
Beach Triathlon—a half-mile swim in the ocean, a three-mile run, and a nine-
mile bike ride. He has done three triathlons so far, each a bit faster than the
previous one. He describes himself as "a very joyful and lucky guy right in
the sweet spot." He realizes that aging is part of the life process, but there is a
"window" right now and he is making the most of it. And that is no illusion.

⚭

"Bridge employment" is another term for partial retirement in which
employees may reduce the hours they work and take a reduction in pay as a
precursor to full retirement from a company or agency. Beehr and Bennett
claim the majority of U.S. retirees are working for pay in a wide variety of
modalities prior to permanent exit from the labor force. Like ordinary employment, bridge employment helps to fulfill both financial and psychological
needs of older workers.[10] An analysis of Health and Retirement Study data
by economists Quinn, Cahill, and Giandrea determined that older men and
women at the higher and lower ends of the wage distribution are more apt to
take a bridge job than middle-level earners. It is a lifestyle choice for those at

the upper end and a real necessity for those who depend on the income and health insurance.[11]

Bridge employment also helps to meet employers' staffing needs by keeping older workers in the labor force for a longer time. As mentioned in chapter 1, one result of population aging, falling birth rates, and a smaller age cohort following the Baby Boomers in countries around the world is staffing shortages. Another result is heavier demands on governments' social welfare systems by "pensionable" adults. Prolonged work lives represent one solution to that problem. In a broad review of studies from mainly Western countries that focus on incentives for a prolonged work life, including bridge employment, Swedish researchers note that permanent exit from the labor force has become the exception rather than the rule here in the United States. Their review identifies common factors that enable older individuals to keep working: being in good health, seeing an opportunity for monetary gain, and having "better" education and skills. It also enumerates organizational practices that facilitate extended work lives (for example, supervisors' and co-workers' support for older workers, skills training, flexible working conditions, stimulating work) and practices, like ageism, that create barriers. The review cites a sobering finding from one study of older-worker-friendly organizational policies: in reality, only 21 percent of organizations globally reported having strategies for retaining their older workers.[12]

The head of the Milken Institute's Center for the Future of Aging agrees that corporate leadership is missing the boat when it comes to recruitment and retention of older talent. Too few organizations promote extended work lives, Paul Irving writes, because employers are failing "to invest the time and resources necessary to fully grasp the unprecedented ways that aging will change the rules of the game," too often viewing demographic change as a "looming crisis" and "an expensive drag on society" rather than an opportunity to reap "significant dividends" by building a vibrant multi-generational workforce.[13]

In the state of Maine, Baby Boomers already comprise about one-third of the workforce, and they are likely to be key to easing the state's tight labor market. Maine's unemployment rate averages 3.5 percent statewide. In addition, according to the Maine Department of Labor's Center for Workforce Research, more people have been leaving the workforce than entering. This imbalance results in "churn."[14] Maine has one of the oldest populations in the country and, by 2020, Mainers sixty-five or older will outnumber young people age nineteen and younger. One obvious solution is for employers to retain their experienced older workers who might be thinking about retiring. Another is active recruitment of retired seniors, making a return to the workforce attractive by offering flexible schedules that fit their needs and preferences. The founder of a Portland, Maine, career counseling and outplacement service, Barbara Babkirk, specializes in coaching and placing older job seekers. Despite the state's pressing need for workers, she finds that employers are slow to change their hiring procedures and to offer work conditions that accommodate older workers.[15] Yet Maine businesses are hardly alone in sticking with outmoded employment practices.

Lest workers take for granted the availability of favorable conditions that enable renewal, persistence, and career transitioning, Catherine Collinson, president of the Transamerica Center for Retirement Studies, offers a reality check based on her organization's eighteenth annual survey of workers (discussed in chapter 1). Workers interested in making a phased transition into retirement and who believe their current employer supports working past age sixty-five may be engaging in wishful thinking. They need to be more realistic about the chances for securing part-time work after retirement, she cautions, as "employment business practices haven't caught up with . . . expectations" and part-time workers are often ineligible for essential benefits packages, including health coverage. Pre-retirees thinking about their next move should be networking and meeting new people, keeping their job skills up to date or acquiring new ones, and researching employment opportunities within their current place of employment or elsewhere.[16]

RetirementJobs.com is one resource for older adults (aged fifty and older) wishing to remain active or needing gainful employment. Founded in 2005 by Chief Executive Officer Tim Driver and a team of professionals with senior executive backgrounds in media, recruiting, and human capital management, RetirementJobs.com connects mature job seekers with prospective employers deemed to be age-friendly. The basic service is free to job seekers; premium service adds seminars and "special content" and access to job openings with "pre-certified" employers. Employers pay a fee to post their open positions and to consult a database of qualified mature workers. Claiming a membership of over one million nationwide, RetirementJobs.com provides "opportunity, inspiration, community, and counsel to people over age fifty who seek work that matches their lifestyle and economic security needs."

Career development practitioners employ the term "longevity dividend" for the new and unprecedented life stage between middle age and elderhood in which older adults have many and varied opportunities to grow and develop and make meaningful contributions, whether in the paid workforce or as volunteers (see encore careers, chapter 8), rather than being "put on the shelf." Practitioners, scholars, and writers are coming up with new metaphors that capture the idea of extending a career during retirement.[17] (They might take a tip from Duke University's head basketball coach Mike Krzyzewski, aged seventy-one, whose mantra is "next play": learn from successes and failures, keep going forward, keep learning.[18]) Gerontologist Suzanne L. Cook, for one, uses the term "redirection" to denote the process of transitioning into a new phase of life.[19] Laura L. Carstensen, professor of psychology and public policy at Stanford and director of the Stanford Center on Longevity, writes about finding a good term that aging people can embrace because she knows language matters to them. She credits a businesswoman she met with inventing the word "perennials" to connote older adults blossoming again and again, making new starts, and, given proper conditions like good soil and nutrients, renewing and persisting for decades.[20]

NOTES

1. Brown, Alyssa. "In U.S., Average Retirement Age Up to 61." Gallup Poll. Washington, DC, May 15, 2013. Retrieved from: www.gallup.com/poll/162560/average-retirement-age.aspx?utm.

2. Brown, Melissa, et al. "Working in Retirement: A 21st Century Phenomenon." 2008 National Study of the Changing Workforce. Families and Work Institute, July 2010.

3. Toossi, Mitra, and Elka Torpey. "Older Workers: Labor Force Trends and Career Options." *Career Outlook.* Washington, DC: Bureau of Labor Statistics, U.S. Department of Labor, May 2017. Retrieved from: https://www.bls.gov/careeroutlook/2017/article/pdf/older-workers.pdf.

4. Soergel, Andrew. "Poll: 1 in 4 Don't Plan to Retire Despite Realities of Aging." Associated Press/NORC Center for Public Affairs Research, July 7, 2019. Retrieved July 23, 2019 from www.workinglongerstudy.org.

5. Stanford Center on Longevity. "Seeing Our Way to Financial Security in the Age of Increased Longevity." *Sightlines Special Report*, October 2018. Retrieved from:

http://longevity.stanford.edu/wp-content/uploads/2018/10/sightlines-financial-security-special-report-2018.pdf.

6. Ibid., 19.

7. Bronshtein, Gila, et al. "The Power of Working Longer." Stanford Institute for Economic Policy Research, Working Paper 17-047, January 2018. Retrieved from: www.siepr.stanford.edu.

8. Sass, Steven. "How Do Non-Financial Factors Affect Retirement Decisions?" Issue Brief no. 16-3. Chestnut Hill, MA: Center for Retirement Research at Boston College, February 2016.

9. Maestas, Nicole, et al. *Working Conditions in the United States: Results of the 2015 American Working Conditions Survey.* Santa Monica, CA: RAND Corp, August 2017. Retrieved from: https://www.rand.org/pubs/research_reports/RR2014.html.

10. Beehr, Terry A., and Misty Bennett. "Working After Retirement: Features of Bridge Employment and Research Directions." *Work, Aging, and Retirement, 1,* no. 1, 2015, 112–28.

11. Quinn, Joseph, Kevin Cahill, and Michael Giandrea. *Early Retirement: The Dawn of a New Era?* New York, New York: TIAA-CREF Institute, 2011.

12. Carlstedt, Anita B., et al. "A Scoping Review of the Incentives for a Prolonged Work Life After Pensionable Age and the Importance of 'Bridge Employment.'" *Work,* 60, no. 2, 2018, 175–89. Retrieved from: https://doi.org/10.3233/WOR -182728.

13. Irving, Paul. "When No One Retires." *Harvard Business Review.* The Big Idea— The Aging Workforce. November 2018.

14. Murphy, Edward D. "Workplace Churn Prods More Companies to Consider Hiring Seniors." *Maine Sunday Telegram.* Retrieved March 17, 2019, from: www. pressherald.com/2019/03/17/workplace-churn-prods-more-companies-to-consider-hiring-seniors.

15. Ibid.

16. Eisenberg, Richard. "Working in Retirement: Wishful Thinking?" *Next Avenue,* December 13, 2017. Retrieved from: www.nextavenue.org/working-retirement -wishful-thinking.

17. Mahler, Elizabeth, and John Thompson. "Is It Time to Put Retirement Out to Pasture?" June 2018. Retrieved from: http://rslive.bslcore.com/myArticle .php?aid=44243.

18. Hannon, Kerry. "The Courage to Change the World." *New York Times*, Visionaries. May 27, 2018, F2.

19. See suzannecook.ca.

20. Carstensen, Laura L. "In Search of a Word That Won't Offend 'Old' People." *The Washington Post*, December 29, 2017. Retrieved from: https://www .washingtonpost.com/opinions/in-search-of-a-word-that/2017/12/29/76640346 -b808-11e7-a908.

Job Characteristics and Employment Status

CHAPTER OBJECTIVES

1. Presents survey respondents' choice of occupation, employment sector and location, full-time versus part-time status, and gender and age-related employment patterns
2. Compares self-employment pros and cons, along with the surge in senior entrepreneurship
3. Looks at factors determining number of years on the job and job and career changes
4. Portrays the influence of mentors and role models
5. Discusses sources of income, income levels, the gender pay gap and other disparities, and tangible and intangible benefits of later-life work

Educational attainment may predict the types of work a person can do or job status and ability to move up the career ladder once hired and frequently is also a determining factor in employment decisions. A recent Bureau of Labor Statistics report presents the occupational groups populated by U.S. employees who are twenty-five years and over and who have greater and lesser amounts of education. A total of 63 percent of workers with at least a bachelor's degree hold jobs in management, professional, and related occupations, as do 85 percent with a master's degree, 91 percent with a professional degree, and 94 percent with a doctoral degree. Fewer than one in ten workers with less than a high school diploma are in management, professional, and related occupations. They are more likely to be employed in service occupations (32 percent); natural resources, construction, and maintenance (25 percent); or production, transportation, and material moving occupations (25 percent). Workers with at least a high school diploma but not an advanced degree are most likely to be in sales and office occupations.[1] Faced with the tightening labor market, employers in the traditionally male-dominated fields of mining, construction, and transportation and utilities have begun to hire qualified women for work on the construction site and the factory floor, not only for doing office jobs. These new and unusual opportunities for women come with lower pay and may last only as long as employers cannot find enough men to hire. Only time will tell.[2] Irrespective of their education level, late-career workers tend to concentrate in less physically demanding industries—management and sales rather than manufacturing and construction.[3] In fact, 42 percent of older U.S. workers (aged fifty-five and over) are employed in management, professional, and related occupations.[4]

Given the high educational attainment of my survey respondents, their occupations are consistent with the Bureau of Labor Statistics findings mentioned here. Business is the top career field for forty-nine of the women and men, almost evenly divided by gender. Of the twenty-seven individuals with careers in higher education, seventeen are women and ten are men. Reflecting career preferences that used to be associated with gender, all but one of the eighteen psychologists or other therapists are female and eleven of the fifteen professionals in medicine and dentistry are male. A total of eleven professionals working in non-profit organizations (unspecified as to purpose) are just about evenly divided by gender, and the same split applies to professionals in social work and social services (ten in all), and elementary and secondary education (six in all). Twice as many men (six) as women (three) are in law. Of the eight individuals with careers in journalism and media, all but one are female. Six women and two men are in the arts—photography, theater, music. The slim remainder are scattered across government, engineering, ministry, and science jobs.

Business was the preferred field for the men whom I surveyed in 2013 and was in second place after education for the women who completed my 2010 survey. The current distribution across career fields, particularly business leading all other fields for women and gender parity in several fields that were previously dominated by women, does suggest progress toward ending traditional sex-stereotyping of occupations.

Nearly three-quarters of current respondents' jobs are in the private sector. The remainder are in the public sector or in both. Well over two-thirds of their jobs are located in a metropolitan area where higher-paying professional work is far more available; just under a third are located in a non-metro area or in both. Among the one hundred largest U.S. metropolitan areas, employment is densest in New York City, Boston, and San Francisco, reports the Brookings Institution's Center on Urban and Metropolitan Policy. It is probably not a coincidence that the majority of my survey respondents come from Massachusetts, New York, and California.

After many years of urban centers losing jobs to the suburbs in a process called decentralization, the trend has reversed, largely because more people are choosing to live and work in and near cities, even expensive ones. And, since the Great Recession, recovery in terms of employment gains has been more robust in urban areas.[5] Opportunities for employment in highly skilled, high-paying industries, such as finance and technology, are clustered in major metropolitan areas. Cities characterized by large populations and urban sprawl, like Atlanta, Phoenix, and Los Angeles, also have higher concentrations of jobs in diverse fields. Seniors in the metropolitan areas of the Northeast, particularly in Washington, DC, and some of the nearest northern Virginia suburbs, are working past the age of sixty-five in greater numbers than in other areas of the country, owing to the abundance of jobs in government, finance, law, and academe.[6]

Employment opportunities in rural areas are frequently found in agriculture, drilling, mining, and construction, fields typically requiring physical labor for which older workers are far less suited. To be sure, teachers, librarians, healthcare workers, lawyers, clergy, and providers of social services are always needed in small towns. (Odd and disturbing as it may sound, firefighting and forestry management could become growth industries if wildfires—no longer seasonal phenomena—continue their rampage through back country forests and into residential neighborhoods and commercial districts.) Sadly, however, the rural economy is in decline everywhere across the country. As Eduardo Porter writes in "Abandoned America," the rural population is older and poorer, and it is shrinking. Many small-town and rural businesses have folded since the Great Recession, particularly in one-industry towns that were hard hit. Factory jobs have dried up wherever manufacturing has been automated or outsourced. Today's most innovative companies that depend on highly educated and highly skilled workers prefer urban "mega-clusters" to small-town America. The questions we are left with are how and when the rural economy will recover.[7]

Of course, even New York City's industries are not immune to economic destabilization. Take Manhattan's famed Garment District, where Puerto Rican and Jewish immigrants once made textile and apparel manufacturing flourish. In the 1980s and 1990s, their workshops found it impossible to compete with mass-produced, cheaper goods produced overseas. Rising New York City property values and new zoning laws dealt another blow. Guided by the Garment District Alliance, the area found ways to diversify and prosper once again. Alliance president Barbara Blair's profile in chapter 3 tells the story.

The majority of my survey respondents work for an employer: 60 percent of the men and 54 percent of the women. The rest are self-employed or consulting (or both), which gives them control over scheduling of work along with the advantages and disadvantages associated with being one's own boss. On the one hand, independence, flexibility, and making good use of one's training and experience can give business owners or consultants much satisfaction. On the other hand, the financial risk and responsibility can be stressful. Bureau of Labor Statistics data show higher rates of self-employment among older workers (ages fifty-five and over) than among workers in younger age groups.[8] Although self-employment is not for everyone, a study of Canadian workers finds self-employment "growing in popularity among older workers, often after retirement or for those who are displaced prior to retirement but cannot find other employment." And it seems older self-employed workers stay in the labor market longer than those in waged employment.[9]

When it comes to full-time versus part-time employment, the Bureau of Labor Statistics says 27 percent of workers age fifty-five and older are part-timers. Among the cohort aged sixty-five and older the share in part-time employment jumps to 40 percent.[10] The full-time versus part-time split among respondents to my survey does not conform to the BLS data until gender and age are taken into consideration. At first glance there does not appear to be much difference between the 51 percent (combined men and women) working full-time and the 49 percent working part-time, yet there are big differences by gender and age. A total of 60 percent of the older, well-educated males in this study are working full-time compared to 44 percent of the older, well-educated females. The pattern is similar across three age cohorts: 53 percent of men in their eighties are working full-time, as are 45 percent of women in the same age group; 48 percent of men in their seventies are full-timers, as are 34 percent of women; 81 percent of men in their sixties are full-timers, as are 55 percent of women. The pattern reverses for part-time work, which is preferred by more than half (56 percent) of the women across all three age groups compared to 40 percent of the men. As mentioned in chapter 1, Harvard economists Claudia Goldin and Lawrence F. Katz have written extensively about women at older ages working full-time and year round at a higher rate than part time.[11] Indeed, the Goldin-Katz findings regarding women's increased labor force participation beyond their fifties, disproportionately in full-time jobs, were applicable the first time I took a snapshot of older women in the workforce (a decade ago) and found more than half (53 percent) working full-time and 47 percent working part-time. A likely explanation for the current contrary finding of more part-timers among the women in my study is the prevalence in the sample of self-employed therapists, life coaches, social workers, writers, editors, educators, and women in the arts. They are just as attached to their careers as other professionals are, but full-time, year-round work in their occupations can be harder to come by (or simply not their preference).

∞

PROFILE: PHILISTINE G. WATERS, GENERATIONS INC. RECRUITMENT SPECIALIST

Philistine G. Waters, known as "Phil," is the part-time recruitment special-ist for Generations Inc., a non-profit literacy organization in Greater Boston that helps children in kindergarten through grade three in low-income, high-needs neighborhoods to develop better reading skills. She retired from a long and successful primary career, then *un*retired a few times. Today, Phil recruits and places older literacy volunteers in schools and in after-school settings and gets great satisfaction from knowing that she is doing something important for her community.

Phil grew up in Harlem and started as a mail girl at New York Telephone when she was seventeen. She was part of the first wave of African Americans entering corporate America. (After divestiture of the Bell System took effect in 1984 the company became Nynex, then Verizon Communications.) Phil worked her way up through various positions over the next thirty years, eventually becoming human resources manager. By the time she left the company in 1994 she had married and moved to Boston and, on her employer's dime, earned both bachelor's and master's degrees in education and management through Cambridge College's degree program for working adults. Verizon also offered a good retirement package when it was time to leave. "It's very different today," Phil observes. "Few people stay at one company for their entire career."

Following a short stint working at Bentley College, she was part of the admissions recruiting team at Lesley College for eleven years. She retired again in 2010, tried a bit of unsatisfying retail work, and unretired once more when a colleague told her about Generations Inc., a non-profit literacy organization that helps children "Read to Succeed." Now age seventy-two, Phil is the part-time recruitment specialist for that organization. The intergenerational work environment there is ideal, likewise the opportunity to make a difference in her community. "We say that we want our children to become contributing citizens. To do that they must be educated and well-informed, and that begins with reading!" she contends. As before, Phil worked her way up in the Generations Inc. organization, starting as a volunteer literacy coach at the Martin Luther King School in Dorchester, becoming a team leader, then joining the paid staff as recruiter. "Across the years I navigated my way through trial and error. It wasn't easy. No one person served as a mentor with the possible exception of Bentley College's John Sims, who 'spoke to my spirit' and gave me pointers on business and management."

Generations Inc. serves some thirty-six hundred students in kindergarten through grade three, many of whom live in low-income, high-needs neighborhoods in Greater Boston. Generations Inc. trains older adult volunteers to work as literacy coaches in partner schools and after-school programs. Volunteers in the Classroom Literacy Program spend up to ten hours per week conducting one-on-one and small group sessions devoted to reading aloud, independent reading, writing, and phonics and skills support. Volunteers in the Reading Coaches Program provide individualized tutoring twice per week, focusing on vocabulary acquisition and reading comprehension, for example. The five-week Summer School/Summer Readiness Program combats "summer slippage" (loss of achievement gains) with vocabulary building and reading practice sessions that prepare kindergarteners and first graders for the first day of school in September.

Phil is responsible for outreach to and placement of volunteers, whose ages generally range from fifty to eighty. Recruitment occurs at job fairs, via print and online ads, on cable television and radio shows, and in churches. Volunteers themselves help to put the word out. "It is particularly difficult to recruit men," Phil notes. "Of 260 volunteers only ten percent are men and that means a dearth of role models."

Generations Inc. operates in partnership with the AARP Foundation's Experience Corps, the Boys and Girls Clubs of Greater Boston, and the public school systems of Boston and Revere. Although Massachusetts consistently ranks number one in the nation on standardized testing, some 70 percent of students in the Boston Public Schools are not reading to proficiency by fourth grade. By boosting literacy learning in the early grades, Generations Inc. endeavors to stem the tide of negative consequences typically associated with poor reading skills.

In addition to the core literacy initiatives, Generations Inc. offers an Active Aging component for its volunteers that encompasses health and wellness activities and fosters social and community connections meant to reduce elders' isolation. Activities include movies, a book club, line dancing, and financial literacy workshops. Volunteers donating at least three hundred hours earn an education benefit that can be applied, for example, toward a grandchild's college tuition.

Line dancing at the Masonic Temple and at the Grove Hall Community Center is Phil's favorite activity. "Country-western?" I chime in. "No!" comes the reply. "It's R&B-style line dancing. Look it up." And that is how I learn about "soul" line dancing, which is rooted in the African American experience. One description tells me that it is about *fellowship* as much as dancing. Because most dancers are middle-aged and older women, *sisterhood* seems more apt. Another important pastime for Phil is singing with the Boston Pops Gospel Choir and the Boston Community Choir.

Phil recommends a book called *Disrupt Aging: A Bold New Path to Living Your Best Life at Every Age*, by Jo Ann Jenkins, chief executive officer of AARP and former chief operations officer of the Library of Congress. By *disrupt* Jenkins means creating a new mindset around aging, changing the conversation about what it means to grow older, shifting attention from the burdens to the benefits of living longer. Topics range from health to housing, from finances to working longer. Regarding the latter topic she asks: "What if instead of seeing just dependent retirees we saw a new type of experienced, accomplished workforce?" It is easy to see why Jenkins' positive messages are attracting attention.

While emphasizing the benefits of living longer over the burdens, Phil has nonetheless had her share of challenges. Her mother, whose health was failing, came from New York to live with her in Boston some years back. Phil was divorced and the single parent of a teenaged daughter. The divorce and then the Great Recession both took a toll financially. Working certainly eases the financial shortfall, but that is not the only reason she wants to remain employed by Generations Inc. "I have no intention of retiring from this job as long as I am healthy and able to do it," she tells me. "It's fun and stimulating. I'm always meeting new people. The multi-generational makeup of the staff means we learn from one another, and I get help with my computer skills." And, she reiterates, "I am doing something important for the community."

Being of relatively advanced years, the men and women who responded to my survey can claim an impressive record of attachment to the labor force. The average number of years the men have worked overall is forty-seven (the median is forty-eight years). The average number of years overall for the women is lower at forty-three (the median is forty-three years). An eighty-five-year-old physician told me he has been working for sixty-seven years. An eighty-nine-year-old pharmacist-turned-activist and writer, Barbara Morris, said she started working in her father's pharmacy when she was a teenager and has been working for seventy-two years.

PROFILE: BARBARA MORRIS, ANTI-AGING ACTIVIST AND AUTHOR

Californian Barbara Morris is a former pharmacist and now feisty anti-aging activist. Giving advice has been an important feature of both her primary career as a pharmacist and her subsequent work as a writer of books for women. Nowadays, she tells her readers to strut their stuff; stay strong, growth-oriented, and independent; and not become "little old ladies" conforming to the traditional "senior" mindset. Work of some kind will keep them active and vital and, above all, useful. Her parents taught her to be productive eight-plus decades ago and she has lived accordingly ever since. Barbara is a self-described "ageless activist" who changed her career field, but not entirely. Drawing on her experience as a pharmacist and observer of human behavior for some six or seven decades, she devotes herself nowadays to writing books and publishing the monthly online anti-aging *Put Old on Hold Journal*. She is the author of six books for women: *Put Old on Hold, No More Little Old Ladies, I Don't Wanna Be My Mother!, I'm Not Goin' There, The Expert's Guide To Strut Your Stuff!*, and *The NEW Put Old on Hold*.[12] The foreword to her 2017 *Put Old on Hold* presents this lifestyle choice:

> It starts with the decision to walk your own road and seek your own best version of a life, but again and again, you will do battle with the lame reality that makes us all invisible and assumes we are ineffective once we acquire some gray hair . . . and wrinkles. That cultural mindset accelerates when "we give up work." *Old* is perceived as an inevitable affliction rather than a normal and positive part of a good, long life.

Barbara advises older adults to stay strong, growth-oriented, and productive, and to be of value not just to themselves but to others. The word *productive* resonates: Barbara's parents insisted that their children be useful from an early age; parental love and approval were contingent on the kids' ability to produce. Thus, when she was ten Barbara dusted and stocked the shelves in her father's drugstore, having quickly learned to be useful. As a teenager she knew how to compound prescriptions. "In those days," she recalls, "kids were not allowed to sit around and do nothing, especially in a large family during the Depression."

In a family of seven children, she was fifth in line and practically had to raise herself. "Things weren't done for me." For example, if she was feeling sick, she would cruise the shelves of her father's drugstore to find a remedy. She realizes now that her upbringing toughened her up for whatever life would deliver: "When life is a constant guilt trip because you somehow disappointed your parents, being productive can make a person happy. And that is how I became a joyful workaholic."

A big part of a pharmacist's job is listening and giving advice. "I love giving advice. As a pharmacist I did it all day long. It's part of my personality." There was a large elderly population in the vicinity of the Rite-Aid pharmacy in southern California where Barbara worked. Many folks were lonely; many were barely scraping by. When Barbara told a nearly indigent man who frequented the store that a part-time job might ease his situation, he took it as an insult. He told her that he had worked all his life and was *entitled* to retire.

Barbara earned a bachelor of science degree in pharmacy from Rutgers University and was licensed in New Jersey in 1956. After her husband Marty completed his doctorate in organic chemistry, the couple and their young daughter Pat moved to Maryland where Marty joined the faculty at the University of Maryland and Barbara became licensed by the state so she could work as a pharmacist. After teaching for twenty-five years, Marty took early retirement and decided to become a pharmacist. He and Barbara studied hard and passed the state pharmacy exam in California. Both found positions with the Rite-Aid chain at different drug stores. Much later, when her husband's health began to fail and she was needed at home, Barbara, age seventy-six, left Rite-Aid. While caring for Marty over the next ten years, she was also writing.

In the foreword to *The NEW Put Old on Hold*, Barbara's attitude concerning retirement is described as "feisty." While granting that older adults can and do live however they wish, she stresses avoidance of traditional cultural norms and practices that have become outdated. "Based on my experience and my observations, there are better choices, healthier choices!" Becoming a "senior" is a choice, Barbara insists. In fact, she detests the word "senior" and its usual connotations. Instead, she favors "outlier" to describe an individual who wants more than the traditional retiree lifestyle. For example, retirement communities are, in her opinion, unhealthy. (She calls them "golden ghettoes" because they separate older adults from the *real* world in which several generations mix. True to form, Barbara shares her house with daughter Pat and her husband.) Outliers shun negative mindsets about aging and are vital, curious, and independent, with a desire to learn and grow and healthy self-esteem. They are mature, as in growth-oriented, using their minds and bodies every day, whether going to a job or doing something else. Barbara has been an outlier or "individualist" as long as she can remember.

Barbara is a big fan of Mark Middleton, whose GrowingBolder.com video proclaims, "What the mind believes, the body embraces." Barbara puts it this way: Once accepted, the "senior" mindset leads inexorably to decline and deterioration. Keep your mind and body active. (She exercises every day and does the *New York Times* crossword puzzle.) And keep renewing your professional license! Barbara fulfills continuing education requirements to maintain hers. She enjoys the perks of California pharmacist licensure, such as discounts on vitamin supplements.

Chapter 12 of Barbara's latest book touches on the subject of finding love as an older adult. Here is what particularly annoys her. "If you are single and make it known that you'd like to have a guy in your life, that is sooo unbelievably *cute*. Aren't the cute old gals looking for romance a riot? Those over-the-hill libidinous Lizzies (wink wink) are too cute for words." Even worse is being told how *wonderful* she is *for her age*. In our conversation Barbara tells me that after three years as a widow she is looking for a boyfriend (not a husband) and admits, "It's hopeless for a woman my age." Although she joined a couple of dating sites, she was disappointed to find that men a decade or more younger than herself were "over the hill and they don't even know where the hill is!" What's more, those older guys seem to think they are attractive to younger women. Complicating matters, Barbara has a list of prerequisites for her dating partners: the men cannot have beards or other facial hair (even if they have everything else going for them), and they must still be productive. When asked to define *productive* in this context, Barbara tells me that her date should not merely get by on Social Security; he should have enough money to afford tickets to a show.

Having initially said that her search for a boyfriend is hopeless, the next words from Barbara are "hope springs eternal." And, having told me that she will not relax her dating criteria, she says she is reading a book about relationships and thinking about being more flexible. But flexibility probably won't happen because Barbara insists, "Lucky is the guy (preferably younger) who meets all my requirements. I'm a catch."

The need for extended education and training or raising a family are usually the primary reasons for delayed entry to the workforce, either of which obviously lessens the number of work years overall. A mid-career interruption can also do the same. Less than one-third of the women had taken time out from work for childrearing. Only one man had done so. When asked about childrearing in my earlier surveys, 58 percent of the women and three of the men said they had taken time out. Although fewer of the women in my current survey reported taking time out when they were younger, prime age women today are still far more likely to be juggling childrearing and job responsibilities than men. Time out for adult caregiving, which can easily disrupt or even end a career, appears to have occurred less frequently for both genders participating in my survey: just two men and ten women had taken time off to help an ill or disabled family member. The likely explanation is that family resources were sufficient for placement in an assisted living or skilled nursing facility or for bringing aides or other hired caregivers into the home.

Apart from interruptions, the total number of years in the current job is largely dependent on whether and how often one has taken a new job in the same field or changed career field altogether. An AARP/SHRM survey of workers aged fifty and over who were employed full-time or part-time found that more than three-quarters planned to remain in their current job until retiring completely, about one in ten planned to change jobs but stay in the same field, about one in twenty wanted to find a job in a different field, and a similar number planned to start their own business.[13] When Sanzenbacher et al. looked at the effect of job changes on retirement timing by socio-economic status, they found that 1) workers in their fifties today are more likely to switch jobs voluntarily than were workers of previous generations, 2) job changes lengthen careers, 3) those who switch jobs are much more likely to still be in the labor force at age sixty-five than those who stay put, and 4) the effect is somewhat larger for better-educated workers than for less-educated workers.[14]

The range for the males I surveyed for this study was one to sixty-one years in the current job and for females the range was one to fifty-four years. A seventy-nine-year-old consultant who has worked for forty-two years overall (plus years spent raising three children) says she has been working since she was nine years old making popsicles at an ice cream shop. Women have spent more years in the same job (the median is nineteen years) than men (the median is fifteen years), arguably because for most women getting there was a challenge and once in the job they held on. At the same time, although changing career field was not very common, the women I surveyed have made more changes in career field than the men (23 percent compared to 19 percent). There were various reasons for this. Often, for older women, the change in career field was because the fields open to them when they graduated from college were limited to the all-too-familiar list—teaching, nursing, social work, secretarial work—and they could finally go where their ambitions led. For either gender, it was sometimes the result of stepping away from full-time work and seeking a part-time job, or individuals making a new career move occasioned by a layoff or a voluntary retirement decision that proved unsatisfying (prompting the career move known as *un*retirement, discussed in chapter 4). The career changes were often rather dramatic. An aerospace engineer became a computer instructor in a non-profit job training organization. The director of a non-profit organization began working part-time as a rabbi and a professor. A high school English teacher became a business management consultant. Another high school English teacher became a psychotherapist. A psychotherapist became an art instructor. A marketing specialist took up retirement coaching. An elementary school teacher switched to kitchen and bath design. A social worker began managing a dental office. A technical writer and software editor now works at a garden center. A small fraction of respondents (7 percent) moved into a new job without changing their field.

These days older, well-educated, more affluent individuals whose retirement was involuntary are apt to become senior entrepreneurs, like Dr. Paul Tasner, whose story comes next. The belief that young people have a lock on innovation simply does not hold up. In fact, the average age of startup founders is forty-two, not twenty-something, and the average age of founders of high-growth companies is forty-five, according to a Massachusetts Institute of Technology analysis of U.S. Census Bureau data.[15] Startup activity in the United States only began to rebound from the Great Recession in 2013, but aside from the entrepreneurs themselves, it has not created jobs for people, reports the Kauffman Foundation. There has been a healthy 12 percent rise in the "opportunity share of new entrepreneurs" since 2009, which means startups are increasingly the result of perceived *market opportunity* rather than *necessity* (i.e., the entrepreneur's response to being "downsized," retired involuntarily, or unemployed for another reason and unable to find a new job). Men are much more likely to start a new business than women (61 percent of entrepreneurs compared to 39 percent in 2016). Immigrants, especially Latinx and Asians, comprise almost 30 percent of all new entrepreneurs. Older adults (ages fifty-five to sixty-four) are a growing segment of the U.S. entrepreneurial population, having dramatically increased their share from 14.8 percent in 1996 to 25.5 percent in 2016.[16] And, tellingly, senior entrepreneurs are successful, notes the head of the Global Institute for Experienced Entrepreneurship, Elizabeth Isele: 70 percent are still in business after five years, more than double the success rate of younger startups. By tapping human capital—ideas, skills, knowledge, networks—and collaborating across generations to solve a problem, entrepreneurship is, according to one commentator, "the leading edge of the change in our economy."[17]

PROFILE: DR. PAUL TASNER, COMPOSTABLE PACKAGING MANUFACTURER

Dr. Paul Tasner became a senior entrepreneur for *both* of the reasons underpinning startup activity that were outlined in the Kauffman Foundation study—necessity *and* market opportunity. Paul is a Ph.D. engineer who fell prey to one of the many recession-induced corporate downsizings in 2011. (In the closing words of chapter 2, he was a Boomer with brains who was hustled out the door.) Retirement was not an option for him: he was in his sixties and had major financial obligations. While doing some consulting as a stop-gap measure, he saw a market opportunity and a way to utilize his years of engineering and packaging experience. He and a new partner founded Pulp-Works, Inc., in San Francisco to design and manufacture sustainable, compostable packaging for the consumer products industry. In place of single-use plastic packaging that clogs landfills and waterways, they are using clean technology to produce biodegradable materials. Paul is now a recognized innovator in the global marketplace and has the TED Talk numbers to prove it. At age seventy-two, Paul is doing the most rewarding work of his life. In a mere seven years, Pulp Works, Inc. has become an award-winning company doing innovative design and manufacturing work. PulpWorks uses clean technology to produce biodegradable packaging from paper, agricultural, and textile waste. As claimed on its website, the firm is "molding a better world" by helping to reduce the billions of pounds of single-use plastic packaging dumped in landfills and waterways every year. "I'm passionate about doing something meaningful in the global marketplace," Paul says with evident pride.

Paul found his partner, Elena Olivari, on LinkedIn by searching for an architect based in the San Francisco area who had environmental expertise plus commitment to LEED certification (Leadership in Energy and Environmental Design, a "green" building and sustainability rating system). Paul and his partner had to deal with the usual challenges of a startup—manufacturing, partnerships, outsourcing, patents, job creation, and funding. When they failed to raise the money needed for their own manufacturing plant—investors clearly preferred to give their money to much younger Silicon Valley entrepreneurs—Paul and his partner decided to outsource manufacturing. Overseas partners in China, India, Egypt, and the United Kingdom do the bulk of the manufacturing, each according to its unique capability and the raw materials available; U.S. companies do a small portion. (The Chinese suppliers have proved to be the most accommodating, he notes.) Initially, Paul and Elena invested their own savings in the startup. As revenues commenced doubling from year to year, they re-invested the profits. Paul can work from home, at a WeWork site in San Francisco, or at Plug and Play Tech Center, a so-called business accelerator organization in Silicon Valley that connects PulpWorks and other innovators with potential new clients.

Paul hatched the idea for PulpWorks when he was laid off in 2011 after a career spanning forty-plus years. Here is what led up to that turning point. Although he had earned a bachelor's degree in industrial engineering from New Jersey Institute of Technology, he tried out a series of *non*-engineering jobs after college, meeting interesting people in the arts and journalism along the way. He finally decided to "get his act together" by earning a doctoral degree at Boston University in 1978 in the field of mathematics called topology. "This was a newer branch of mathematics in my experience," he explains, "involving the study of the properties of a space which are unaltered by elastic deformations such as stretching and twisting. It was also known as 'rubber sheet geometry' because of this stretching and twisting without tearing." However, the deeper he delved into mathematics, the more he knew he did not want to earn his living in that field. "It was too solitary a pursuit and inconsistent with my temperament," he realized.

At about the same time, an uncle in Chicago helped Paul out of his dilemma by inviting him to work for him. The uncle owned a big manufacturing facility for packaging, and Paul found the business "pretty fascinating." Unfortunately, the uncle became too ill to continue the business, so Paul moved on to the Clorox Company (one of his uncle's customers) where he managed the company's external manufacturing plants. After fifteen years he did some consulting work then moved again, this time to The California Closet Company, managing the company's supply and distribution chain of wood and metal products for a half-dozen years. Then some of his former colleagues from Clorox presented him with an attractive offer to help make "healthy, natural, non-toxic" products, and he willingly left the larger corporate world to become director of operations at Method Products. The Great Recession struck a few years later, the company laid off employees, and Paul was out of a job. "There I was in my sixties wondering what to do next. Retirement was out of the question. San Francisco is very expensive, and I still had family obligations and a sizable mortgage." As an engineer with manufacturing and packaging experience and a robust network of contacts, Paul was able to get back into consulting. "I had no passion for it whatsoever," he admits. "I simply needed the income." Perhaps it was not quite a "eureka" moment, but the idea for PulpWorks began to take shape at that time. In response to my question about what motivates him to keep working now, Paul says, "I enjoy PulpWorks so much, it is hard to separate *need to* from *like to*. I am really having fun."

Paul's interaction with one PulpWorks customer is illustrative. She is based in India where her company makes medical kits for rural practitioners containing items such as safe, sanitary instruments, diapers, and blankets. Instead of kits made of plastic, she converted to PulpWorks kits made of compostable material called "bagasse," the dry pulpy waste product that remains after sugar cane stalks are crushed and their juice extracted. That businesswoman also happened to be talking with Paul about a shipment one day when he discovered that she was not calling him from India but from New York City where she was participating in a four-month TED Residency. She encouraged Paul to apply for acceptance to the next class, and he did just that.

He knew that TED is "an incubator for breakthrough ideas." What he soon learned was that TED Residents in each class of innovators come from all over the world to New York City to be coached on giving talks that are broadcast online and via traditional media. After extensive preparation during spring 2017 (while living at his daughter's New York home and continuing with his PulpWorks responsibilities), Paul took to the TED stage to deliver his talk in June. "I got to know and learn from the most amazing men and women who had become my twenty-three new best friends," he enthuses. "I would welcome being on a desert isle with any one of them. TED is an amazing platform for ideas worth spreading; there are millions of subscribers!" Indeed, more than 1.7 million people have already listened to Paul's TED Talk; he had a half-million views the very first day alone.

Paul made a point of telling his TED audience that small businesses like his are creating the majority of new jobs in the private sector in this country. And *older* entrepreneurs in the United States have a success rate that is more than twice that of younger entrepreneurs. "Senior entrepreneurs [like himself] are checking in when their peers in essence are checking out." He would like to form a community of bold first-time entrepreneurs from among the rapidly growing ranks of seniors. "Why not make '70 over 70' as commonplace as '30 under 30'?" he concludes with a grin.

⸎

An equal number of men and women identified by my study are working a second job, although the numbers are small. Three among the 14 percent doing so are unpaid; most are paid. In the former group is a private teacher of violin who teaches "for the joy of it," a grandparent providing day care for a grandchild, and a jokester whose second job is "listening to a very nagging wife whom I adore after forty-five years of marriage." The latter group includes various writing, editing, teaching, training, and consulting positions, plus retail sales, bookkeeping for a small business, geriatric care management, creating fabric art, property management, and officiating at sporting events.

Often the choice of education and training leading to a career was influenced by a mentor who gave advice and encouragement or by a role model who provided inspiration. Four out of five survey respondents specified one or more mentors or role models. Senior professionals who mentored were mentioned more frequently than any others—a former boss or supervisor, an older social worker, an academic, a law partner, clergyperson, writer, editor, doctor, researcher, or more than one. Family members, particularly fathers and mothers, were very important influences, as were grandparents and spouses, schoolteachers, college professors, and coaches. Peers, colleagues, and friends gave and still give support. One woman wrote, "Close friends my age and older have functioned as my 'board of directors.' I took advantage of these relationships for career advice and networking in my later working years. Wish I had known about having a mentor in my younger days!" Another woman credited "many dual-career women, including those breaking the glass ceiling." Yet another admired her mom who was always active although she never had a career. Betty Freidan and Gloria Steinem were cited.

PROFILE: JAMES M. BARROWS, UNIVERSITY PUBLIC AFFAIRS AND COMMUNICATIONS ASSOCIATE DIRECTOR

Mentors and role models meant everything to Jim Barrows. His parents had the foresight to move their family out of inner-city Boston to a suburban school district where their kids would have a better chance of getting a good education. Jim's first role models were the older college boys who were his co-workers at a Boston restaurant. They were attending four-year colleges when he was enrolled at Massasoit Community College (MCC), making a name for himself as a top student and soccer player. His first mentor was the Massasoit soccer coach who led his team to national junior college championships. Jim was recruited by selective four-year schools, and on the advice of his restaurant buddies, decided on Amherst. After college he had valuable work experience that led to his current position with Harvard Public Affairs & Communications. As explained in the following, Jim is right in the thick of the university's economic development initiatives, community partnerships, and outreach activities connected to Harvard's expansion into the Allston-Brighton section of Boston.

Absorbed as he is in his work, Jim has always made time to give back. He is determined to use what he learned from role models and mentors and his own experience as an upwardly mobile black male to help future generations of deserving student-athletes. Jim, age sixty-two, already knows what he would like to do when he retires later in his sixties from his job as associate director of Harvard Public Affairs & Communications. He plans to help community college athletes prepare for transfer to a four-year school. Many of them are single parents holding down a job while taking classes. English may not be their first language. "The community college is an untapped resource for diversifying four-year institutions," he observes. "With counseling and mentoring, they can leverage their athletic and academic abilities and make it to the next level."

Jim speaks from personal experience. He was born in Roxbury, Massachusetts, whose schools were the subject of Jonathan Kozol's *Death at an Early Age*. When Jim was in second grade, his parents moved the family to Duxbury, a Boston suburb with better schools. "My parents never went to college, but they had the courage to make the move so their kids could get an excellent education. Several of my cousins who stayed in the city had very different lives."

As a standout high school student and soccer player, Jim "found his way" to MCC in 1975 with the encouragement of co-workers at the Chart House Restaurant, where he worked as a cook and bartender. His restaurant co-workers were slightly older than Jim and already in college. Mike Russo, Jim's junior varsity high school soccer coach, ran a summer soccer camp where Jim worked. The coach recruited him for the soccer program he had just started at Massasoit and became Jim's mentor. Massasoit soccer went on to win national junior college championships. Mike Russo moved on to Williams College where he was named national coach of the year four times. Jim studied business management at Massasoit, made dean's list every semester, and was recruited by top universities. The soccer coach at Amherst College, Peter Gooding, invited him to apply there. Jim had never heard of Amherst, so he turned to trusted advisors, the restaurant buddies who called him "J.B." They exclaimed, "Amherst College is freaking awesome!" and told him he should apply. One even offered to review his application and drive him to visit the campus.

Jim majored in political science at Amherst. Like many of his classmates, he thought he wanted to be a lawyer. Instead, after college he worked as the assistant director at a community center in Roxbury that was run by the United Methodist Church. The pay was low, he recalls, too low to keep talented young people on staff for more than a couple of years, but it was a very good learning experience. He then managed public housing near Kendall Square and the Massachusetts Institute of Technology in Cambridge for four years, and that got him interested in real estate. A few years with a small commercial real estate firm led to a position within John Hancock's Real Estate Investment Group where he did underwriting research on competitive commercial real estate markets and had marketing and communications responsibilities for nearly ten years.

In 2002, Jim landed the job at Harvard through networking. "In a relatively small town like Boston, who you know and how you treat people can make a huge difference. I like people, and the time I spend connecting with them inside and outside of work is well spent. As I tell my nieces and nephews, you never know when someone might be noticing and judging you." Jim brings this attitude to his work connecting Harvard to the business community in the nearby Allston-Brighton section of Boston. The university is carrying out a multi-year plan for a mega-expansion project, the first part of which is construction of a new science and engineering complex in Allston. Jim's primary charge is economic development, managing community partnerships and outreach activities geared to helping small businesses and local entrepreneurs, such as restaurants, auto shops, and attorneys, to develop and grow their enterprises in Allston-Brighton. He connects them with mentors, ideas, and skill-building workshops. For example, SCORE retirees and semi-retirees, under the auspices of the U.S. Small Business Association, lead workshops three times a month on topics including marketing, business development, accounting, and taxes. Harvard Public Affairs & Communications also connects Boston and Cambridge teens with job opportunities through a summer youth employment program. The goal is to develop teens' strong work habits, establish networks, and help them acquire real-world work experience.

Grateful for all the advice and support he received as a young man, Jim has for many years been giving back. He served on MCC's board of trustees for ten years, chairing the board for two years. "MCC is where it all started for me," he says. "MCC changed my life." He has been a Big Brother and has volunteered in soccer programs at the YMCA. Currently, he sits on the public programming committee of the Boston Society of Architects Foundation. He looks forward to being involved with college access programs for underserved students in Boston and Cambridge after he retires. Indicative of how far in the future retirement is, he is still playing outside back, defensive midfield, or striker ("when the team is REALLY desperate") every Sunday on one of the teams in the New England Over the Hill Soccer League.

Several women responded to the question about mentors and role models with comments, such as, "I felt pretty alone." "Boomers were told it's a rat race, get over it." "I made my own way." "I was self-motivated with a strong desire for learning." Several men listed various role models—the Dalai Lama,

Dwight D. Eisenhower, Abraham Lincoln, Abbie Hoffman, Paolo Freire, Georg W. F. Hegel, W. E. B. DuBois, Martin Luther King Jr., Ernest Holmes, Eckhart Tolle, Oprah Winfrey, Dizzy Gillespie, and Whoopi Goldberg. Another man said, "No one, no one in particular." Stephen Holmes, profiled later in this chapter, was inspired by his mother who was still reading to the blind when she was over one hundred (she lived to be 107). A clinical psychologist in her mid-sixties said that she is constantly inspired by her ninety-one-year-old mother who had a full-time practice as a psychologist before she retired, and by her grandmother who was president of a company and lived to be ninety-two.

⧼∞⧽

PROFILE: JOAN RUTTENBERG, PUBLIC INTEREST LAW ADVISOR AND MENTOR

Joan Ruttenberg enjoys providing Harvard Law School (HLS) students with the career advising and mentoring she badly needed and never had. When she earned her J.D. at Harvard in 1982, she knew she wanted to go into public interest law but did not know where to start. The vast majority of HLS graduates jumped on the corporate law fast track, the route that Joan knew was not for her. Over the years, she made some good and some not-so-good career moves. Teaching law and legal studies part-time at universities was particularly satisfying and made it possible for her to be home while raising three young children. When HLS finally established an Office of Public Interest Advising (OPIA), the timing was right for Joan. She became an OPIA advisor and the director of a fellowship program that provides financial support and guidance for students and lawyers exploring and engaging in public service internships and law careers within the federal government. As her profile makes clear, Joan has found work that fits her social justice values, her interests, and her personality, and she is helping HLS students and alumni do the same. At age sixty-one, Joan has been a public interest career advisor in the OPIA at HLS and director of the Heyman Fellowship Program there for fourteen years. She is doing for HLS students who are interested in public service careers what the institution failed to do for her when she earned her J.D. cum laude at Harvard. As a law student with public interest practice ambitions, she made her way through trial and error.

Although I was social justice minded, I had no clear sense of direction for how to make a public interest career in law. I felt pretty alone, and ended up creating a very non-linear path in my career. It was very tough to navigate that path by myself. Now I give students the support I never had. It's super gratifying to help stressed-out, confused students find a path to work that will feed their souls and change the world. The students are lovely and inspiring; they ask such good questions. Each is distinct, and I love getting to know them!

Joan earned her bachelor's degree summa cum laude in political science with minors in economics and French from University of Illinois, Urbana-Champaign, in 1978. After college she took time off to travel and work in Europe where she could use her facility in French, Spanish, and Russian. Although she wanted to be independent and earn a living, she also felt insecure about being out of school, where she had always excelled. She applied to law schools and was accepted at several. "I couldn't say no to Harvard Law. My plan was to get the J.D. and figure out later how to use it."

Most graduates of Harvard Law "roll downhill into a career," Joan explains. Virtually all law schools have a bias toward the private sector, and Harvard is no exception. Thus, although Harvard boasts an impressive minority of students committed to public service careers, the majority of students still enter a system of interviewing and matchmaking with private law firms. During the summer after the first year, students hand in a résumé, indicate the firms they are interested in, put on a suit, and go to a hotel to be interviewed for a second-year summer internship. By the end of that second summer, most students have a post-graduate job offer from their firm. The firm pays bar exam expenses and often moving expenses, and the newly minted lawyer is all set. When Joan was at HLS in the late 1970s and early 1980s, students choosing public interest law experienced none of that and had no comparable support for the public interest search.

In 1990, with the Career Services Office at HLS almost exclusively concerned with the private firm recruiting process, and under considerable pressure from students, Harvard finally established an OPIA to assist law school students and lawyers interested in exploring and engaging in public service internships and careers. The OPIA helps students and alumni to find the type of work that fits their values, interests, and personalities. Public service practice settings include careers in legal services and law reform organizations; courts, labor unions, and political campaigns; government agencies at federal, state, and local levels; charities and foundations; educational and public international organizations; private public interest law firms; and private law firms performing pro bono work. Harvard now provides significant fellowship and financial support for students entering public interest careers. Currently, almost 18 percent of HLS graduates take public service jobs upon graduation or after a clerkship.

One source of support for public interest–minded students is the Heyman Fellowship Program, established by Samuel Heyman, a 1963 HLS graduate and former Justice Department prosecutor under Attorney General Robert Kennedy. Heyman acted on his concern about an impending drop-off in experienced federal government lawyers as Baby Boomers retired by funding a fellowship program for law graduates that provides a network of mentors and some financial support. More than three hundred men and women have now gone through HLS's Heyman Fellowship Program.

Looking back, Joan recalls, "I did find other students in my HLS class with interests similar to mine. The class was 28 percent female. It felt like a feminist accomplishment just to go to HLS. But we were clueless. We didn't know what opportunities existed. We kind of raised ourselves without institutional support. I had no guidance whatsoever. My parents were good, smart people, but they had no idea how to advise me either."

In her first year at HLS Joan didn't realize she needed to start looking for a summer internship only a few weeks after classes began, nor that she should expect to accept unpaid internships in public interest organizations. Luckily, in the spring her property law professor offered her a paid summer job. In her second year she landed a summer internship with a public interest practice in San Francisco. It was unpaid, so she funded the experience by spending the first half of that summer at a law firm. (Although Harvard now funds students working in unpaid summer public interest internships, it did not do so then.) Neither internship was a particularly good experience. After graduation, Joan got a one-year clerkship with a judge on the U.S. Court of Appeals for the Fourth Circuit in Baltimore.

When trying to figure out what might come after the clerkship, Joan thought about teaching and about the field of women's health. She had always liked teaching, and she loved law school. She wondered whether she could teach law, and perhaps health law. "The idea seemed presumptuous; I wanted to get work experience first before teaching others how to be a lawyer." In the meantime, she did a one-year Bigelow Teaching Fellowship at the University of Chicago's law school. As a lecturer in law she taught legal research and writing to first-year law students. The teaching fellowship was designed to allow young lawyers interested in academia to produce legal scholarship while gaining teaching experience. Joan discovered that she did not enjoy the research and writing as much as the teaching. Still trying to find her niche, Joan decided to try out a nuts and bolts public interest law practice, and for the next four years she worked on healthcare and insurance matters as an assistant attorney general in Boston. She had moved back east with her husband, David Abromowitz, a lawyer in private practice. They eventually had three children and Joan took time out to raise them. (With many years of pro bono experience under his belt, David recently became the full-time chief public policy officer of YouthBuild USA, a national non-profit with programs in forty-four states and an international component in twenty-one countries.)

Joan left the attorney general's office after her first child was born. When her daughter was two years old, Joan began teaching law and legal studies part-time at universities in the Boston area. She adored the teaching and, for a long time, was willing to trade off salary and security for the flexibility and intellectual gratification that the part-time arrangements offered. Eventually, though, the adjunct status began to get to her: she was underpaid, undervalued, and isolated—no colleagues, no office. After more than a dozen years "at the bottom of the academic food chain," and with her three children now comfortably in school, she started looking around for another job. It came serendipitously in 2004, partially through the "mommy network." Joan had seen a posting for a half-time fellowship director and career advising position in the OPIA at HLS. One day, she went to pick up her son from a play date and discovered that his little friend was the son of OPIA's director, who encouraged her to apply for the position.

Now she helps students find their own public interest paths. She discusses career plans and options with advisees, answers questions about course selection and ways to build public service experience and skills, suggests job search strategies, invites advisees to meet public interest leaders and potential mentors at campus events, and points them toward OPIA's library of resources and job search database. She also runs the Heyman Program, which keeps her in touch with hundreds of terrific graduates in federal government and lets her connect interested students with mentors throughout the federal government.

> It took me a long time to figure out that most of what was expected of the stereotypical law graduate was not right for me. For starters, I decided that staying home at least part-time when our children were young was right. Moreover, I was neither suited to be on the corporate law fast track nor to be a crusading public interest litigator. But I love working with students, and I love promoting public interest law practice. So, by "midwifing" these HLS students, I have a hand in making positive change in the world.

As a lifelong feminist, Joan did experience some initial cognitive dissonance over choosing to stay home with her children, as well as moving into more traditional female roles of teaching and counseling, at a time when much at least superficial feminist rhetoric was all about women moving into male-dominated workplace roles. But she knew these choices were right for her. "I feel this work plays to my strengths and is a good fit for me, which earlier jobs were not. I love the sense of mission I share with my colleagues, too. Advising and supporting these students to achieve the public interest careers they hope for is important—I know it viscerally."

⌒⬯⌒

Income in the senior years typically comes from Social Security benefits, pensions, investments, and wages, salary, or self-employment. Income depends on many factors in addition to education level, such as part-time versus full-time status (discussed previously); career field; rank or title; experience level; length of service; skills, abilities, and job performance; geographic location; and (often) gender. Socio-economic status accrues over a lifetime, and, scholars say, pervasive inequality often leaves various subpopulations at a disadvantage when it comes to working in their later years.[18] Increasingly, employers are replacing permanent, full-time jobs with less expensive, temporary, freelance, or contract employment, which comes with no benefits and no paid overtime. Labor historian Louis Hyman's new book about the inexorable takeover of the "gig economy" claims that approximately one-third of the workforce is now participating in some type of "gig labor" as a main or supplementary source of income.[19] And, if those freelancers and contract employees are located in a major metropolis, they could very likely be members of the Project Management Institute and working out of shared commercial office space leased on a short-term basis from WeWork or the equivalent, or for free at an Older Adults Technology Services center like Senior Planet.

According to the Bureau of Labor Statistics' report on earnings of all wage and salary workers in the second quarter of 2019,[20] median weekly earnings of full-time workers are $908, a gain of 3.7 percent over the previous year. Women across all categories have median weekly earnings of $814, or 81.4 percent of the one thousand dollar median for men. As mentioned, earnings generally reflect levels of educational attainment—the higher the better— experience, and occupational field. Thus, U.S. workers aged twenty-five and up with less than a high school diploma have the lowest median weekly earnings at $588 and high school graduates earn $751. Median weekly earnings are higher for those with at least a bachelor's degree, $1,357, and much higher still for employees with advanced degrees (master's, professional, or doctoral degree). The highest 10 percent of males with advanced degrees earn $3,997 or more per week and their female counterparts earn $2,822. When looked at by occupational category, median weekly earnings for men and women (all ages) employed in management, professional, and related occupations are $1,540 and $1,117, respectively. The medians for men and women in service occupations come to less than half of those figures. Looked at another way, men dominate the highest-paying job categories and women populate the lowest.

The gender pay gap is typically defined as the difference in median or average gross salary (without overtime) received by men and women in full-time jobs. American Association of University Women's (AAUW's) analysis of U.S. Census data also finds the largest gender pay gap in the *higher-paying* occupations.[21] The gender wage gap starts right after college graduation, says the AAUW, and grows over time, even after many factors are taken into consideration, such as college major, GPA, choice of occupation, hours worked, experience, age, race and ethnicity, region of the country, marital status, and motherhood. Marketwatch.com insists that the gender wage gap starts *much earlier* when boys get larger allowances and higher pay for household chores and girls do more chores for less pay.[22] The unequal division of labor at home persists because of motherhood, says another columnist: women do more of the household chores and childcare even when both spouses are college-educated and working full-time in high-earning careers.[23]

The widest pay gap—54 percent of white men's pay—belongs to Latina women. Depending on their race or ethnicity, women working full time in 2017 were earning about eighty cents for every dollar full-time male workers earned. The AAUW estimates how much this has set women back financially over the years: seven hundred thousand dollars for a high school graduate, $1.2 million for a college graduate, and two million dollars for the graduate of a professional school. Although the gender wage gap in this country is narrower than it used to be, it is important to remember that the figure is an average that obscures great variation, not only by race and ethnicity, but also by state, region, occupation, seniority, and other dimensions of employment. The 13.7 percent gender pay gap in Britain, where women earn 86.3 percent of what men earn for the same work, has narrowed in the past twenty years but not enough to obviate the need for designating an Equal Pay Day each year. Despite laws against paying women less for the same work, the disparity in Organisation for Economic Co-operation and Development member nations, 13.9 percent, is greater than in Britain, and, at 16 percent, it is higher still in the European Union countries.

A 2018 McKinsey & Co. and LeanIn.org joint study regarding promotion of women to higher-paying senior management positions looked at pipeline data from 279 companies employing some thirteen million people. The news from "Women in the Workplace" is disappointing: a majority of the companies claiming that they are "highly committed" to gender and racial diversity have not made meaningful progress. Only one in five senior leaders is a woman, even fewer are women of color. Improvement is "agonizingly slow."[24] A previous McKinsey study of women in the workplace looked at law firms' efforts to improve gender equality and found many impediments to career advancement at the higher (partner) levels. Female lawyers participating in the McKinsey survey said that difficulties with juggling work-life demands present the greatest threat to their professional success.[25]

As mentioned previously, when children enter the picture, traditional male and female roles seem to hold sway, leaving many prime age working women with the lion's share of household chores and caregiving even when a spouse or partner does help out. Moreover, women frequently pay a "penalty" for motherhood when their lifetime earnings later generate lower Social Security benefits.[26] Anne-Marie Slaughter describes a triple whammy: "Plenty of women have 'leaned in' for all they're worth but still run up against insuperable obstacles created by the combination of unpredictable life circumstances and the rigid inflexibilities of our workplaces, the lack of a public infrastructure of care, and cultural attitudes that devalue them the minute they step out, or even just lean back from the work force."[27] Hard as it is to fathom, the United States is one of the only countries in the entire world without family-friendly policies, such as universal paid parental leave and subsidized childcare. Sweden is in the forefront of developed and third-world countries with an array of family-friendly policies. The Swedish government's commitment to dual-earner families, work-life balance, and gender equity is manifest in paid, job-protected, and lengthy parental leave for employed mothers *and* fathers; subsidized, high-quality childcare; temporary parental leave to care for a sick child; nearly free health and dental care; and free education from preschool through university.

Mindful of the financial damage a mid-career interruption for childrearing can cause and learning that less than one-third of the women I surveyed had taken time out from work for childrearing (while only one man had done so) and that the women had worked five fewer years on average than the men, I wanted to get a sense of respondents' current earnings. My survey asked whether their personal annual income from paid work was "modest" (under thirty thousand dollars), "middling" (thirty thousand dollars to seventy-nine thousand dollars), or "higher" (eighty thousand dollars and up). Keep in mind the *average* salary of all U.S. workers is a tad over forty-seven thousand dollars, but the *median* (a truer measure) is close to thirty-nine thousand dollars. When the genders are taken together, nearly half are in the "higher" earnings category. At least ten of the higher-earning women and ten of the higher-earning men I surveyed are working part-time, thus it would be wrong to assume that the income of someone working part-time is always less than the income of a full-time worker. Higher earnings are to be expected for exceptionally well-educated professionals who have been working for a long time. When the earnings data are disaggregated, however, it becomes clear that far more of the men (57 percent) than the women (38 percent) are earning eighty thousand dollars or more. Earnings for the rest of the women fall evenly in the "modest" and "middling" ranges, 31 percent in each category. Earnings for the rest of the men are 20 percent "modest" and 23 percent "middling." No matter that women put job satisfaction way ahead of income as their reason for working in the retirement years, the gender wage gap is indisputable.

The gender gap with respect to earnings is joined by another gender gap in a survey conducted for the *New York Times* in October 2018 asking more than ninety-five hundred adults of all ages whether their own finances have improved since the Great Recession. Just under half of the men said their family finances were in better shape, but the women were far more skeptical, according to *NYT* reporters Casselman and Tankersley. The gender gap widened when respondents rated the U.S. economy as a whole, even between men and women of similar age, race, education, and income. Women are simply less sanguine about the direction of the economy. These gaps in perception, say the reporters, can be explained to some extent by political partisanship and also by inequality—recovery since 2008 has bypassed many families, leaving millions of Americans struggling in part-time and low-paying jobs, especially in communities where the economy is less robust.[28]

A useful snapshot of one area of the Northeast reveals exceptionally strong job growth, particularly in professional and business services, trade, transportation, utilities, education, and health services, whereas manufacturing continues sliding downward. Prepared by the MetroWest Economic Research Center at Framingham State University, the 2018 profile of the economy in the Greater MetroWest area (encompassing communities between Boston and Worcester, Massachusetts) describes a well-educated, highly skilled labor force, low unemployment, and household incomes higher than the state average. Then, too, the cost of living for the region is about 40 percent higher than the national average, there is a shortage of available housing, and housing costs are nearly double the national average.[29] The MetroWest Economic Research Center profile fits the older workers I surveyed who are fortunate enough to live and work in parts of the country where the economy is as robust as that of MetroWest.

Massachusetts bills itself as a leader among states with respect to improving the economic security of seniors and providing other services to the aging. Executive Order 576 established the Governor's Council to Address Aging in Massachusetts in April 2017 to advise Governor Charlie Baker on developmental policies, community resources, best practices, and informal supports that will promote healthy aging in the Commonwealth. The council was charged with formulating a plan for making Massachusetts "the most age-friendly state for people of all ages." The council convened meetings and panels, reviewed documents and data, and held listening sessions in year one, then released an Initial Blueprint in April 2018 containing recommendations, among others, for improving the economic security of seniors by *promoting the employment of older workers*. That, in turn, can be accomplished by supporting training and retraining for older workers and establishing career centers to better serve older job seekers, establishing an "age-friendly employer" recognition program, and promoting the benefits of hiring and retaining mature workers. Implementation strategies will be addressed in year two. Robin Lipson, staff member of Massachusetts' executive office on elder affairs (a department of the executive office of health and human services), notes "a new emphasis" on older workers and what they can contribute: "The conversation has changed."

In addition to salary-related concerns, the availability or absence of employer-provided benefits can be a major reason for taking a job or holding on to one. Three-quarters of current survey respondents have benefits from a previous or current employer (34 percent of the women and 25 percent of the men still have benefits from previous employers; 36 percent of the women and 56 percent of the men have benefits from their current employer). The remaining respondents have no benefits from either source. Savings plans and health insurance are the most common types of employment benefits. Vacation days and sick leave are provided less often. Fewer still get disability insurance, life insurance, or a pension. Many employers have either replaced defined benefit plans with defined contribution plans (i.e., instead of the company "paying out" employees "pay in" and accrue more pension benefits the longer they work) or they have eliminated pension plans altogether. Monetized benefits include:

- A lawyer's subsidized parking
- A physician's dental insurance and profit-sharing arrangement
- A sales manager's car allowance
- Travel reimbursement and retreat time for a clergyperson
- Free admission to art museums for an artist who teaches
- Tme off for caregiving for a director of communications
- A discount on work clothes and tools for a garden center employee
- A semester of paid leave when a university professor retires, and
- Various mentions of flexible scheduling and personal days.

Other benefits that were mentioned are intangible. For a sixty-three-year-old business owner it's his "personal freedom."

PROFILE: STEPHEN V. HOLMES, INDEPENDENT SCHOOL TRACK AND FIELD COACH

An eighty-two-year-old track and field coach values his active involvement with enormously talented young people. Coach Steve Holmes specializes in training the shot put, discus, and javelin throwers at Phillips Exeter Academy in Exeter, New Hampshire. He has devoted almost his entire career to teaching and coaching young people on the secondary school level. "For fifty-seven years I have had the pleasure and unique opportunity to associate with teenagers," he says. "On a daily basis, they provide hope and display goodwill to all around them. I have always been impressed with the clear and rational thinking of our teenage population. Ask them how to solve the problems of the world, such as the need for a ban on assault-type weapons, and they know what should be done!"

Steve was so active as a little kid that he reminded his grandmother of a hummingbird, darting here and there. His grandmother called him "Hummer" and the nickname stuck. These days he is Coach Hummer to students at Phillips Exeter Academy. "I'm having a wonderful time working with amazing students from all corners of the globe," he enthuses, "and I do not want to retire!"

Having worked for years in various public school settings, he finds adjunct faculty status at a place like Phillips Exeter "refreshing, a whole different scenario in which all the students are very strong academically, focused on their interests, and committed to working hard." The heavily endowed private school has a brand new forty-two million dollar track facility where Steve coaches indoor and outdoor track. When he meets students for regular afternoon practices, Steve lifts weights and works out along with the students. He gives extra coaching sessions to the most promising throwers in shot put, discus, and javelin. Naturally, it helps that he is the top-ranked master's level discus thrower in the United States and number two in the world. He has also been the national champion javelin thrower on the master's level a few times recently, and in 2012 was the champion in javelin and discus in Canada. "I have always been active in sports," he says, adding modestly that he was "a Jack of all trades and master of none," when competing in his younger days.

Having worked in summer camps where he enjoyed interacting with kids, Steve opted to earn his bachelor's degree in physical education and youth leadership at Springfield College. In his senior year of college, Steve had a field experience at the Massachusetts Eye and Ear Infirmary in Boston. When an administrator there encouraged him to go for a career in hospital administration, he decided to get a master's degree at the Medical College of Virginia in Richmond. His first administrative assignment was at Mary Hitchcock Memorial Hospital. The best thing about it was the Hanover, New Hampshire, location, which meant Steve could frequently play basketball at nearby Dartmouth College. His next hospital administration position was at Emerson Hospital in Concord, Massachusetts, but his heart wasn't in it. "I realized that I much preferred working with kids, so I 'retired' at age twenty-five and got a job in 1963 teaching biology and coaching soccer, basketball, and baseball at the Buckingham, Browne, & Nichols School in Cambridge."

Throughout the 1960s and 1970s Steve taught and coached at the private Kents Hill School in Maine and at the public Fall Mountain Regional High School in New Hampshire's Connecticut River Valley. Married by this time and with a growing family—his wife Joan was a part-time music teacher in the Keene, New Hampshire, schools—Steve needed to supplement his income. He became an administrator at a YMCA summer camp for a few years and, for a short time in the 1980s, also tried his hand selling orthopedic products, a job he disliked intensely. Luckily, a newspaper want ad caught his eye in 1982 and he soon landed a good job as health educator in Brattleboro, Vermont, where he stayed for the next nineteen years.

By 2001 Steve and Joan had left Vermont and moved to Newmarket, an old mill town that was once home to a thriving textile industry on the Lamprey River in New Hampshire's seacoast region. Steve enjoyed taking his skiff out into nearby Great Bay and he loved building reproductions of Shaker furniture in his state-of-the-art woodworking shop at home, but a life of total leisure was not for him. He soon had signed on to be a full-time substitute teacher and soccer and track coach at the public high school in Exeter. "You really get the pulse of a school when you are a full-time sub: you discover which teachers are well prepared, the various ways kids try to test the sub," he observes.

"Of course, I knew all the tricks!" In 2016, after twelve years of working at the public high school, Steve was offered and gladly accepted the plum track and field coaching job at Phillips Exeter. He quickly found interacting with Phillips Exeter's outstanding students to be the best part of his job.

In his free time Steve sings in the church choir along with his wife. He serves on the property committee, which means the church can call on him to fix things. He also plays the trombone, sometimes at church and sometimes as a "musician on call" for ROTC ceremonies at the nearby Durham campus of the University of New Hampshire. When I asked whether he plays in a band he quipped, "Maybe when I retire I can join a band." Since his dad died "early" at age ninety-five and his mother was active into her hundreds—she died at 107—Coach Hummer will probably not have time to join a band anytime soon.

∽◇◇∾

NOTES

1. Brundage, Vernon Jr. "Profile of the Labor Force by Educational Attainment." *Spotlight on Statistics*. Washington, DC: U.S. Bureau of Labor Statistics, August 2017.

2. Kolko, Jed, and Claire Cain Miller. "As Labor Market Tightens, Gender Lines Blur." *New York Times*, Sunday Business, December 16, 2018, 7.

3. Van Dam, Andrew. "A Record Number of Folks Age 85 and Older Are Working, Here's What They're Doing." *The Washington Post*, July 5, 2018. Retrieved from: https://washingtonpost.com/news/wonk/wp/2018/07/05/e-record.

4. Toossi, Mitra, and Elka Torpey. "Older Workers: Labor Force Trends and Career Options." *Career Outlook*. Bureau of Labor Statistics, U.S. Department of Labor, May 2017. Retrieved from: https://www.bls.gov/careeroutlook/2017/article/pdf/older-workers.pdf.

5. Lund, Susan, et al. "The Future of Work in America: People and Places, Today and Tomorrow." McKinsey Global Institute, July 2019.

6. Soergel, Andrew. "Seniors More Likely to Work Longer in Big Metropolitan Areas." *The Denver Post*, June 10, 2019. Retrieved July 9, 2019, from: https://www.denverpost.com/2019/06/10/metro-area-seniors-working-jobs-retirement/.

7. Porter, Eduardo. "Abandoned America." *New York Times*, Sunday Review, December 16, 2018, 1, 6.

8. Toossi, Mitra, and Elka Torpey. "Older Workers: Labor Force Trends and Career Options." *Career Outlook*. Bureau of Labor Statistics, U.S. Department of Labor. May 2017. Retrieved from: https://www.bls.gov/careeroutlook/2017/article/pdf/older-workers.pdf.

9. Casey, Rebecca, and Ellie Berger. "Enriching or Discouraging? Competing Pictures of Aging and Paid Work in Later Life." Population Change and Life Course Strategic Knowledge Cluster Discussion Paper Series, 3, no. 3, article 3, March 2015. Retrieved from: http://ir.lib.uwo.ca/pclc/vol3/iss3/3.

10. Toossi, Mitra, and Elka Torpey. "Older Workers: Labor Force Trends and Career Options." *Career Outlook*. Bureau of Labor Statistics, U.S. Department of Labor. May 2017. Retrieved from: https://www.bls.gov/careeroutlook/2017/article/pdf/older-workers.pdf.

11. Goldin, Claudia, and Lawrence F. Katz. *Women Working Longer: Increased Employment at Older Ages*. National Bureau of Economic Research and University of Chicago Press, 2018.

12. See www.BarbaraMorris.com.

13. Brown, S. Kathi. "What Are Older Workers Seeking? An AARP/SHRM Survey of 50+ Workers." Washington, DC: AARP, June 2012. Retrieved from: www.aarp.org/research.

14. Sanzenbacher, Geoffrey T., Steven A. Sass, and Christopher M. Gillis. "How Job Changes Affect Retirement Timing by Socioeconomic Status." Brief no. 17.3. Chestnut Hill, MA: Center for Retirement Research at Boston College, February 2017.

15. Azoulay, Pierre, et al. "Age and High-Growth Entrepreneurship." March 23, 2018. Retrieved from: http://mitsloan.mit.edu.

16. Fairlie, Robert W., et al. "2017 Kauffman Index of Start-up Activity, National Trends." Ewing Marion Kauffman Foundation, May 2017. Retrieved from: www.kauffmanindex.org.

17. Farrell, Chris. *Purpose and a Paycheck—Finding Meaning, Money, and Happiness in the Second Half of Life*. New York: HarperCollins, 2019.

18. Gonzales, Ernest, et al. "Increasing Opportunities for the Productive Engagement of Older Adults: A Response to Population Aging." *The Gerontologist*, Special Issue: 2015 WHCoA.

19. Hyman, Louis. *Temp: How American Work, American Business, and the American Dream Became Temporary.* New York: Viking, 2018.

20. U.S. Bureau of Labor Statistics. "Usual Weekly Earnings of Wage and Salary Workers, Second Quarter 2019." Washington, DC: U.S. Department of Labor, July 17, 2019.

21. See www.aauw.org.

22. Paul, Kari. "The Wage Gap Starts at Home: Boys Are Paid More Than Girls for Household Chores." July 15, 2018. Retrieved from: www.MarketWatch.com.

23. Miller, Claire Cain. "The Gender Pay Gap is Largely Because of Motherhood." *New York Times*, The Upshot, May 13, 2017. Retrieved from: www.nytimes.com.

24. Krivkovich, Alexis, et al. "Women in the Workplace 2018." McKinsey & Co. and LeanIn.com. October 2018.

25. Rushton, Charlotte. "Inaugural McKinsey & Co. Women in the Workplace 2017 Legal Study." October 31, 2017.

26. Rutledge, Matthew, et al. "How Much Does Motherhood Cost Women in Social Security Benefits?" Working Paper 2017-14. Boston College, Center for Retirement Research, 2017.

27. Slaughter, Anne-Marie. *Unfinished Business.* New York: Random House, 2015, 14.

28. Casselman, Ben, and Jim Tankersley. "A Booming Economy? Women Don't Share Men's Rosy Viewpoint." *New York Times*, October 28, 2018, 25.

29. Haddadin, Jim. "Economy, Housing Crunch Grow." *Framingham TAB*, May 25, 2018, A3.

6

Health, Well-being, and Longevity

CHAPTER OBJECTIVES

1. Compares survey participants' reported health status and well-being with federal data, including gender disparities
2. Discusses life expectancy, including racial and ethnic disparities, and the pace of increasing longevity globally
3. Poses a correlation between educational attainment, working longer, engagement, and well-being
4. Provides evidence from brain science about types of intelligence

If educational attainment is often a determining factor in corporate hiring decisions, health status is the critical factor for older men and women choosing between extending their work lives in some fashion and retirement. Data from the Centers for Disease Control and Prevention's National Center for Health Statistics show that women still live longer than men on average, and Americans with the most education tend to outlive their less educated countrymen. These facts resonate with the findings from my current and previous studies of older, well-educated professionals' reasons for working in the retirement years. The percentage of women citing good health and high energy as a reason exceeds the percentage of men by thirteen points. That's two-thirds of the female respondents to my survey (65 percent) and just over half of the male respondents (52 percent). A comparison of my latest findings with my earlier surveys in which 66 percent of the women and 63 percent of the men indicated good health and high energy as an important reason for their extended work lives reveals an eleven point drop for male respondents but a barely perceptible change for female respondents across the years. The gender difference with respect to health and stamina may be attributable in part to the men in the current sample tending to be older than the women or simply less motivated to go to the gym. To that point, another current survey item pertaining to older workers' health and lifestyle produced a similar imbalance in the responses: 72 percent of the women but only 58 percent of the men say they try to exercise and keep fit in their spare time.

PROFILE: DON SACKMAN, HI-TECH CONSULTANT

One who keeps fit is Don Sackman, president of a high-tech consulting business. I discovered that his favorite topic of conversation is sports (playing, not spectating). He has been playing tennis doubles for years and is a whiz at softball. He has no intention of retiring from sports or from his consulting business, Sackman Associates, which he formed way back when electronics were just coming to the fore. He had been the chair of the U.S. Department of Commerce's Computer Systems Technical Advisory Committee, the government-industry group that wrote regulations for controlling the export of high tech, a process with political, security, commercial, and operational dimensions that is even more complex today. Many countries seeking to build their technological capacity want access to cutting-edge technical information, know-how, skills, and methods developed by companies and universities in the United States. We frequently hear and read in the news about international technology transfer negotiations involving weighty matters, such as the protection of intellectual property rights as well as potential threats to national security. It is easy to see why Don finds sports far more relaxing. Don has been active in sports ever since grade school in Brooklyn, and now that he is eighty-three he has no intentions of stopping. "For such a skinny kid, I was the best athlete in my class, whatever sport I took up." In his early twenties, when Don was in General Electric's engineering training program, he was invited to join some men who played tennis during their lunch hour. He had never played tennis. He borrowed a racquet and soon was as good or better than the others. GE, like other big companies, had an industrial league for factory workers. Don joined the softball league where he played both shortstop and center field. A bowling traveling team represented GE; with his great eye-hand coordination, Don excelled at bowling, too. His league teammates were factory hands, not professionals. Don quickly learned to get along with everyone.

These days, just like six decades ago, his tennis partners are mainly affluent, well-educated white guys, whereas his master's level softball buddies are typically high school–educated blue collar workers ("Trump guys" in shorthand). "The camaraderie is spectacular! You can't imagine the loyalty of softball league athletes. We are extremely close." And now that Don and his wife Kay are downsizing and moving from Sudbury, Massachusetts, to a townhouse in New Jersey to be near family (the move date coincides with their sixtieth wedding anniversary), he has to find a softball league for seniors and a good tennis doubles game there. "It's the hardest thing for me about leaving Sudbury, harder even than giving up our house," he confesses. One thing is for sure, Don will continue full time in his high-tech consulting business, Sackman Associates, from his new home office.

In 1955, armed with an electrical engineering degree from Brooklyn Polytechnic Institute, Don took some time to bicycle through Europe then headed for GE's engineering training program. GE and Bell Labs were the two powerhouse research organizations offering recent graduates the opportunity to work for three months at a time in different capacities within the company. Although Don badly wanted to go to GE's Electronics Park in Syracuse (headquarters for research, development, and manufacturing of radio, radar, television, and other equipment), he was sent instead to Fort Wayne, Indiana, where small motors for washing machines were made. His next GE assignment was Utica, New York, where light military electronics were made. He finally got to Electronics Park where he could work on early transistors and other semi-conductor products.

On six-month leave from GE to fulfill his ROTC commitment of military service, the second lieutenant learned to drive. "The kid from Brooklyn who didn't have a car and couldn't drive was soon driving a Jeep, a two-ton truck, and a bulldozer!" he crows. After basic training at Fort Dix in New Jersey, the army sent him to process refugees pouring into Camp Kilmer, the intake portal for Hungarians fleeing the Soviet invasion of their country. His next assignment gave him a terrific opportunity to demonstrate his moxie. The town of Owego, located near New York State's border with Pennsylvania, had been pummeled by a major storm and needed help with cleanup. Don led a platoon from Fort Dix, taking the truck convoy right through midtown Manhattan to pick up supplies at Fort Totten in Queens and thence to Owego. "That escapade was my crowning achievement, and I made first lieutenant."

Back at GE, Don undertook another three-month assignment in the company's new Palo Alto computer lab and ended up staying for ten years because he found the work so exciting. The Bank of America contracted with GE to build "ERMA," an Electronic Recording Method of Accounting, to replace the cumbersome manual check-sorting process with a faster, more effective method. (The technology is still in use today.) When GE moved its headquarters to Fairfield, Connecticut, and merged its computer business with Honeywell's in Waltham, Massachusetts, in 1971, the Sackmans settled in nearby Sudbury. GE/Honeywell having acquired both Olivetti (manufacturer of calculators, computers, and typewriters in Milan, Italy) and Bull (a pioneering computer company in France), Don began traveling abroad as the technical liaison between Europe and the renamed entity, Honeywell Information Systems (HIS).

"The U.S. was the supreme technological power in the world at the time, and the Chinese and Japanese were eager to get in on the computer business," Don explains. As the director responsible for all of HIS's international relations, he reported directly to the president of the company. A huge challenge was placating two Japanese companies that were mortal enemies—GE had licensed Toshiba and Honeywell had licensed Nippon Electric—and getting them to cooperate. With the agility of a shortstop, Don helped to establish a joint venture called HIS International and convinced the two competitors to sign on.

The chair of Honeywell's board offered Don an attractive job in London, but the Sackman kids were in high school and the family did not want to relocate. Once again the former kid from Brooklyn showed his moxie: he left GE/Honeywell after twenty years to found Sackman Associates. The risk was great; he had plenty of technological expertise and first-hand knowledge of the electronics sector worldwide but no income other than a six-month retainer. This was when he chaired the government committee that wrote regulations for controlling the export of high tech. (To this day, the Department of Commerce appoints advisory committee members representing government and industries that produce a broad range of U.S.-origin goods, technologies, and software controlled for national security, foreign policy, non-proliferation, and short supply reasons; however, the export laws are broader and far more complicated.) As Don puts it, "Electronics were coming to the fore. The U.S. was being challenged, especially by Japan. I knew tariffs and non-tariff barriers. And I had the right personality for consulting." Digital Equipment Company and Data General were among the first clients needing Don's help securing U.S. technology export approvals. Fortunately, says Don, "I was the only person around who was fluent in three domains—China, following President Nixon's visit in 1972; the U.S.S.R; and Japan—thus enabling expansion of bilateral trade in technology and intellectual property."

And he's still in the game.

⌐∞ͻ

On the subject of fitness, and speaking from personal experience, I find that women at my health club regularly work out *and* enjoy conversing with one another—if not while using the equipment, then in the ladies' locker room. (I have not been able to ascertain whether exercise for men has that social component.) Shortly after my fitness class ended one morning, an attractive, grey-haired woman I didn't know came into the locker room and I heard another woman complimenting her on her recent appearance on "Chronicle," a newsmagazine television program about New England. Naturally, I joined the chorus asking her for more information. The show's hosts were doing a segment on street names in Boston, she explained, and they discovered that she is knowledgeable about the architecture and history of the city. It seems she had joined the cadre of Boston By Foot tour guides in 2013 after retiring from a long career in marketing for high-tech companies. That was also when she started writing a blog aptly called "The Next Phase." With my usual enthusiasm about someone working in the retirement years, I couldn't resist commenting that being a docent and writing social commentary was her encore career. "Yes, it's my retirement job," she replied with a smile. "Boston

By Foot does not pay its tour guides, but I do make money giving ghost tours for Haunted Boston, and great tips, too! That's a new endeavor that I started this year, for which my friends at BBF recommended me. Both keep me very busy during the tour season."

Demographers, economists, gerontologists, and others charting aging in the United States and globally now speak of the pace by which longevity is increasing and its myriad implications for healthcare, housing, transportation, personal finances, labor markets, consumer behavior, and so on, using the expression "longevity revolution." Life expectancy at birth in this country is 78.6 years for the total U.S. population (76.1 years for males and 81.1 years for females). Although the racial and ethnic life expectancy gap has been narrowing, Hispanic males and females still have the longest life expectancy at birth; non-Hispanic black males and females have the shortest.[1] Actually, U.S. life expectancy dropped in 2018 for the third year in a row (the longest sustained decline since World War I and the 1918 Spanish flu pandemic) and now lags behind many other developed countries owing to a spike in opioid deaths, alcohol and tobacco use, obesity, depression, and suicide, plus the usual causes of death from major diseases. According to health statistics compiled by the Centers for Disease Control and Prevention, the average lifespan for Americans was projected to be 79.8 years by 2040, whereas Spaniards and Japanese, ranked numbers one and two, respectively, can expect to have average lifespans of 85.8 years and 85.7 years, respectively, by that date.

Along with greater life expectancy, *The Economist* reports, Japan has a marked age-dependency challenge (not having enough working people to support those who do not or cannot work). The Japanese population is dropping by almost four hundred thousand each year and there are "a stunning 1.6 vacancies for every jobseeker." Faced with such a challenge, Japan is looking to make progress toward creating what the prime minister calls the "100-year-life-society." The country has more over-sixty-fives working than the rest of the highly industrialized economies in the Group of Seven, of which it is a member. It has more women in the labor force than America does. Its parliament is debating whether to allow 345,000 foreign workers into the country by 2025 and whether to adjust the public pension system and ban mandatory retirement to reflect rising life expectancy. Even age seventy may be too early to retire in Japan![2] Cultural differences aside, this scenario provides a preview of emerging aging and work challenges that Americans would do well to watch and learn from.

There is growing evidence that delayed retirement helps to reduce mortality—honestly! Working longer does not *cause* people to live longer, but remaining active and engaged on the job does convey social and health benefits in addition to economic advantages, say Chenkai Wu and fellow Oregon State University researchers. They found healthy adults who retired one year past age sixty-five had an 11 percent lower risk of death from all causes; even unhealthy adults who kept working had a 9 percent lower mortality risk.[3]

Researchers are finding that working in the retirement years can be good for one's mental *and* physical health and adds to life satisfaction. One study by Quinn and colleagues comparing retirees with and without bridge jobs saw better mental health outcomes in the bridge job group, even if they worked part-time, than in those who fully withdrew from the workforce.[4] Along the same lines, James and colleagues found that overall well-being is considerably higher among older adults who engage in paid work, caregiving, education and training, or volunteering. Their study measured levels of engagement, defined as enthusiasm, dedication, and absorption in the activity, as opposed to mere participation or involvement, among adults younger than age fifty, fifty to sixty-four, and sixty-five and older. Those in the older age groups who were actively engaged reported higher levels of well-being.[5] The picture grows darker when the lens is widened to capture the state of well-being in America. Gallup-ShareCare's Index reveals overall decline in the well-being of adults (all ages) across five elements: sense of purpose, social connection, financial security, connection to community, and physical condition.[6]

A career coach attending a June 2019 AGEist Conference in Los Angeles, where the economic and social impact of the fifty and up demographic was examined, reported this takeaway: "People with a sense of purpose live 7.5 years longer. Purpose has more impact than any other intervention, like working out, vitamins, or healthy eating."[7] But can it be proven that working longer makes people healthier and happier, aside from making them better off financially? Esteban Calvo set out to determine the *non*-monetary effects of late-life paid work, specifically its impact on physical and psychological well-being. Building on earlier studies showing that loss of opportunities for active engagement in either paid work or non-paid activities tends to adversely impact overall well-being, Calvo used longitudinal data drawn from the Health and Retirement Study and the RAND–Health and Retirement

Study database to confirm that longer working lives have beneficial effects on individuals' physical and psychological well-being, depending primarily on the type of job and how undesirable (demanding) or satisfying it is.[8]

The exemplar of engagement and well-being (mental, not physical) has to be Stephen Hawking, the brilliant theoretical physicist, cosmologist, and author who died in March 2018 at age seventy-six. He was diagnosed with a rare form of a motor neuron disease in 1964 when he was only twenty-two. He spent years in a wheelchair and depended on technology for "speaking" and writing and on caregivers for everything else, and never gave up. Hawking, who lacked physical well-being but had the other four elements in abundance, especially sense of purpose, believed that "Work gives you meaning and purpose and life is empty without it."

Even if there was no cure for Stephen Hawking, neuroscience has made many breakthroughs about brain function. Although shrinkage in certain parts of the brain caused by aging can affect mental functioning, such as multi-tasking, even in healthy older individuals, there is growing evidence of neurogenesis or "plasticity" of neural cells, synapses, and circuits. This means the brain can adapt to new challenges and tasks because it is capable of making new connections and repairing broken ones, says the National Institute on Aging. The National Center for Biotechnology Information adds more encouraging news for professionals who are prolonging their work life or planning to do so: "Higher levels of education or occupational attainment may act as a protective factor," in addition to healthy diet, regular exercise, social activity, and low-to-moderate alcohol intake. Furthermore, well-educated people who maintain a healthy, active lifestyle appear to have more *cognitive reserve*, which helps offset deterioration of the brain due to aging or disease, like dementia. The more malleable the brain, the higher the level of cognitive functioning, which produces a greater ability to learn new things, improvise, and find alternative ways of doing a job.

Learning new things, challenging oneself, having new experiences *over a lifetime*, and working in more complex occupations all contribute to the acquisition of cognitive reserve. Some of that learning augments our store of "crystallized" intelligence in long-term memory, the ability to use pre-existing knowledge, facts, skills, and information acquired in school or from past experience. In 1987 psychologist Raymond Cattell identified a complementary but different kind of intelligence he called "fluid" because it refers to the process of reasoning, analyzing, and solving new problems creatively, without the benefit of pre-existing knowledge. Crystallized intelligence can be maintained or increased during the aging process, a boon to the performance of older workers. Fluid intelligence, on the other hand, responds to physiological functioning and can begin to decline by age thirty. Psychologists (and the rest of us) would like to discover whether it is possible to improve it.[9]

A more familiar typology compares hard skills with soft skills. Hard skills, such as literacy, numeracy, and technological know-how, can be defined, taught, and measured (much like crystallized intelligence). Soft skills, such as "people" skills, leadership, communication, collaboration, and teamwork, are more elusive and hard to quantify (like fluid intelligence). Both hard and soft skills are valued and can be required for specific jobs, but a 2018 LinkedIn survey of business leaders finds the greatest demand is for soft skills.[10]

A good way to challenge oneself, Gretchen Reynolds reminds readers in her columns on physical fitness in the *New York Times*, is to be physically active. Only about 10 percent of people older than sixty-five in the Western countries exercise regularly, she reports. In January 2018 Reynolds told the story of a *centenarian* competitive cyclist who intensified his training and began to better his own records. This was to make the point that age does not have to be a deterrent to challenging oneself with hard(er) exercise. Two months later she wrote about research on older British recreational (not competitive) cyclists ages fifty-five to seventy-nine who had been pedaling for decades. Compared to a control group of sedentary older people, the cyclists were healthier and had musculature and immune systems that made them *biologically* much younger. In May 2018 she reported that exercising even as little as ten minutes a day can make us happier and thereby healthier.

⌒⧓⌒

PROFILE: JERRY LAMBERT, OCEAN LIFEGUARD

Gretchen Reynolds did not happen to be the reporter who wrote about Gerard Lambert, known as Jerry, in the *New York Times* in 2017, but his story reinforces her point about staying fit. Jerry Lambert has been surfing on Long Island's south shore for about sixty years, and he has been an ocean lifeguard there every summer for forty-four years. He has to be medically fit and pass a series of challenging swimming and rescue tests every year to qualify for the job (the same tests a sixteen-year-old first-time lifeguarding applicant has to take). Jerry's main job for four decades was journeyman electrician. Like his father and grandfather before him, he held membership in the electrical workers' union. One of his regular assignments was maintaining the high-voltage electrical system beneath the World Trade Center in Lower Manhattan. He happened to be off from work on 9/11 when all his buddies perished in the collapse of the Twin Towers. Jerry retired from his primary career in 2004 but comes north from Florida every summer to lifeguard and surf at Tobay Beach. Jerry was about to start his forty-fourth season as a lifeguard at Tobay Beach in Massapequa, Long Island, when I interviewed him. At seventy-four Jerry is the oldest New York ocean lifeguard. Nassau County requires lifeguards to be medically fit and to qualify yearly in multiple categories, including swimming fifty yards freestyle in thirty-five seconds or less, swimming two hundred yards in continuous crawl style in three minutes, performing a cross-chest carry of a struggling victim for twenty-five yards, performing front and back head hold escapes, retrieving a ten-pound weight from ten feet of water, and more.

Tobay Beach (an acronym for Town of Oyster Bay) is on Long Island's south shore just to the east of the much larger, more populous, and better known Jones Beach. Tobay has a gentle bay side and an ocean side that is good for body boarding. Jerry loves to surf, so the surfing beach is his preferred assignment. He has been catching the waves ever since the late 1950s when he was a teenager working in the snack bar at the beach and he would trade hot dogs for the use of an off-duty lifeguard's rescue board.

Lest I become overly impressed by his exploits, Jerry talked about Reggie Jones who lifeguarded at Jones Beach (a New York State park) from 1944 until 2009 when he failed to recertify by a fraction of a second. Reggie was then eighty-two, and the testing standards for state beach lifeguards are even more rigorous than the county's. A Google search turns up a July 24, 2000, *New York Times* article about Reggie when he was merely seventy-three years of age. The article reported that "the dinosaur of the ocean" had made a thousand or more rescues (he had been lifeguarding for fifty-six years at that point) and that the lifeguard shack he shared with his buddies was dubbed "Jurassic Park." Reggie told the reporter that the biggest change he had witnessed was the suits getting smaller and the people getting fatter. When the reporter asked why he refused to retire, Reggie tossed off a well-used lifeguard line: "I'd rather watch the tomatoes walk by than watch them grow in the backyard!"

Today's lifeguard chairs are manned every day from 8 am to 6 pm from June through Labor Day. During the beach season Jerry comes up from his home in Florida in the late spring and stays with one of his brothers (a refrigeration guy in Manhattan) in Seaford, Long Island. Cathleen Lambert, Jerry's wife of fifty-three years, stays in Florida at their seventeen-acre horse farm. They are very proud of their grown daughter Nicole, a pre-K teacher, who was Florida Golden Apple Teacher of the Year in 2008.

Jerry is particularly proud of his family heritage and the strivers he has known. He and his seven brothers and one sister grew up in Massapequa Park on Long Island. (Jerry is the oldest.) "Life is like a marathon. You can never stop seeing how well you can do," he observes, naming some of the successful people who surrounded him as he grew up, people his community nurtured. Peggy Noonan, speechwriter for Ronald Reagan and George H. W. Bush, was a neighbor. Actor Alec Baldwin and his brothers Steven and Billy (also a lifeguard) were familiars, as was comedian Jerry Seinfeld, and several notorious organized crime families. Three brothers who played professional football, the Baldingers, were also lifeguards.

Jerry experienced blatant age discrimination six years ago when the Town of Oyster Bay attempted to get rid of older workers and refused to raise lifeguards' low pay. The lifeguard captain and Jerry's brother were laid off. Jerry, who was under treatment for prostate cancer at the time, was demoted and told not to come back. However, the problem was resolved with the help of the recently formed labor union; the new person in charge restored Jerry's rank as a lieutenant lifeguard.

Following in the footsteps of his father and grandfather, Jerry enjoyed a four-decade career as a journeyman electrician and member of the International Brotherhood of Electrical Workers, Local #3. After high school in Massapequa, he spent two nights a week for five and a half years attending trade school while apprenticing for private contractors. This was around the time that women were accepted in the trade for the first time, he notes. Once he became a journeyman, he could work anywhere. He especially loved high-voltage work, such as maintaining the high-voltage electrical system far beneath the World Trade Center. To take out live 277-volt, five-thousand-amp fuses, he would stand on a certified safety mat dressed in protective equipment. On 9/11 if Jerry had not been recuperating from knee replacement surgery he would have been working in the World Trade Center tower along with seven fellows from his construction company who all perished when the Twin Towers fell. By October he was well enough to return to the Trade Center and was called to work at Ground Zero because his specialty high-voltage training and expertise was needed to check on the electrical situation underground.

Since retiring from his primary career in 2004 when he was sixty, Jerry keeps in shape and keeps busy by doing renovations to his house in Florida, maintaining the trees and fences on his property, and working on his prized automobiles, a 1959 TR-3 and a 2014 Mercedes-Benz Sprinter van. Horses are his wife's passion. Formerly a special education teacher, Cathleen enjoys riding her horses and has always been devoted to health and fitness and living a healthy lifestyle. Jerry admits to some aches and pains, saying that he is not immune to aging. He can no longer "snap and pop" while surfing (jump up from a prone position on the board), owing to some loss of flexibility in his right knee. Yet he can qualify for lifeguarding. In a July 2017 *New York Times* article featuring Jerry Lambert with the headline "Saving Swimmers, Well Into Senior Years," he explained what draws him from Florida to Long Island every year: "Once you develop a waterman's lifestyle, you keep coming back."

Just to be sure that the athletic exploits of older women get equal attention, allow me to present Flo Filion Meiler, who took up pole vaulting when she was sixty-five and set the world record for her age group at eighty. Now still fit and eighty-five, she trains five or six days a week at the University of Vermont in preparation for competing in senior games events, such as the long jump, sixty-meter hurdles, eight-hundred-meter run, pentathlon, and pole vault. Pole vaulting is one of her favorite events because it requires a strong upper core and good timing. She likes the challenge of running hard, planting the pole, flying over the bar, and landing on the mat.[11] At the indoor World Masters Athletics Championship held in March 2019 in Poland, she won seven medals in the eighty to eighty-five age division (five golds, two silvers). With few or no other female athletes in her age group, Flo frequently competes against her own records. And that is fine by her!

NOTES

1. National Center for Health Statistics. "Health, United States, 2017: With Special Feature on Mortality." U.S. Department of Health and Human Services. Hyattsville, MD, 2018.

2. "Coping With the 100-Year-Life Society." *The Economist*, *429*, no. 9118. November 17, 2018.

3. Klampe, Michelle. "Working Longer May Lead to a Longer Life, New OSU Research Shows." Corvallis, OR: Oregon State University, April 27, 2016. Retrieved from: https://today.oregonstate.edu/archives/2016/apr/working-longer-may-lead-longer-life-new-osu-research-shows.

4. Quinn, Joseph, Kevin Cahill, and Michael Giandrea. "Early Retirement: The Dawn of a New Era?" New York, NY: TIAA-CREF Institute, 2011.

5. James, Jacquelyn B., et al. "Insights on Activity in Later Life from the Life & Times in an Aging Society Study—Engaged as We Age." Sloan Center on Aging & Work, Boston College. Chestnut Hill, MA: January 2012. Retrieved from: http://www .bc.edu/content/bc/research/agingandwork/archive_pubs/EAWA_JustDoIt.html.

6. Gallup-ShareCare Well-Being Index, 2017. "State of American Well-Being 2017." Retrieved from: https://wellbeingindex.sharecare.com.

7. Flynn, Diane Johnson. "7 Insights on Ageism That May Surprise You." PBS Next Avenue, Work and Purpose, July 16, 2019. Flynn is a co-founder of Reboot Accel, an organization helping women to get current, connected, and confident to resume careers and companies to create cultures that hire, advance, and empower women.

8. Calvo, Esteban. "Does Working Longer Make People Healthier and Happier?" Center for Retirement Research at Boston College, Issue Brief, Series 2, February 2006.

9. Vinney, Cynthia. "Fluid Versus Crystallized Intelligence: What's the Difference?" ThoughtCo. September 17, 2018.

10. Lewis, Gregory. "The Most In-Demand Hard and Soft Skills of 2018." LinkedIn Survey, January 22, 2018. Retrieved from: https://business.LinkedIn.com/talent-solutions/blog/trends-and-research/2018/the-most-in-demand-hard.

11. Rathke, Lisa. "Pole Vaulter, 84, Sets Her Sights on More Records." Retrieved March 22, 2019, from: https://olympics.nbcsports.com/2019/03/22/pole-vaulter-84-sets-her-sights-on-more-records/.

7

Concerns, Challenges, and Ageism

CHAPTER OBJECTIVES

1. Situates later-life work within a framework of employment-related constraints
2. Describes survey respondents' reported concerns and challenges
3. Discusses organizational climate, workplace ageism—institutional and internalized, federal law (Age Discrimination in Employment Act of 1967 [ADEA]), age diversity, and inclusion
4. Addresses technological change and its implications for workers
5. Portrays manager and co-worker perceptions and stereotypes concerning age, motivation, training, and professional development
6. Presents organizations addressing ageism in the United States and globally

Working in the retirement years certainly presents many of the same challenges experienced by younger workers and also a number of challenges that are unique to seniors. To examine some of the constraints older workers face in their efforts to obtain or retain employment and identify strategies for overcoming those constraints for people who either want to or need to work in later life, a day-long workshop on the theme "Research that Matters to Employers: Overcoming the Constraints of Later Life Work" was part of the November 2018 Gerontological Society of America's Annual Scientific Meeting in Boston. Organized and presented by members of the Sloan Research

Network on Aging & Work, this workshop (and more than a dozen other Gerontological Society of America symposia, papers, and poster sessions) represents a new and broader focus on the aging workforce by the influential Gerontological Society.

One-third of older workers surveyed for this study say they have no challenges or concerns associated with their jobs. "Making my time left on earth really count" is the only challenge for a full-time business consultant, aged seventy-one. For the sixty-seven-year-old chief executive officer of a social services agency, succession planning will be the focus for the coming years. Most of the respondents are open about their "issues," many indicating more than one concern. Fully one-third admit to stress or fatigue. The wear and tear of commuting, institutional dysfunction, and reorganizational battles need no explanation. The biggest worry of an eighty-seven-year-old aquatic instructor in Texas is "not being able to work when I am too old." (In a recent holiday card he sent to my husband and me, he added a note saying that he had turned eighty-eight and still teaches swimming at the local Y.) A sixty-nine-year-old software maintenance engineer confesses that "staying abreast of continually improving and changing technology is starting to outweigh the advantages of working part time, and I'd rather be building boats." An eighty-one-year-old who does physically demanding historic preservation work comes home to piles of office work and financial correspondence in the evening. The sixty-eight-year-old head of a busy private practice in urology is frustrated by the difficulty of hiring younger M.D.s who share his dedication and work ethic. He is also stressed by hassles with insurers and by government mandates. A part-time technical editor, aged sixty-eight, who works remotely feels lonely. The owner of a transportation business, aged sixty-four, faults ride-sharing companies for serious difficulties in her industry. (You will find her profile in the next chapter.)

Stress is an inadequate term for what is bothering a few older men and women. A consultant, aged seventy-seven, who advises financial institutions on social risk management is experiencing "a decreasing sense of discovery." A part-time instructor of English as a second language in a college setting, aged sixty-six, is "getting bored, but reinvention takes energy." And, after many years of doing the same work, a lawyer, aged sixty-one, admits that "some parts of the job feel redundant" and she has "a been there, done that feeling."

Nearly one-quarter (twice as many women as men) say they do not have enough time for all the things they want or need to do outside of their jobs—time for family and friends and pursuing other interests. A sixty-one-year-old manufacturer who leads a sales and management team would like more time for travel and "getting off the grid." He writes of "the vagaries and challenges of running a small, growing business and all that entails, with sales goals, marketing related to achieving those goals, as well as plant and operations challenges regarding new equipment, staying current with manu-facturing technology, and all the [human resources] issues to make sure we have people with the right skills for meeting our strategic objectives." An attorney of the same age would like more time for community activities and for "protesting the Trump regime." Several others would like more time for reading, writing, projects, exercising, or traveling, yet a freelance speaker and writer is stressed by all the traveling that is part of her job. There are "not enough hours in the day to do all the things I'd like to do," says the sixty-two-year-old manager of a non-profit organization. This common complaint echoes several that address work-life balance and the desire to have fewer hours at work and more time for "adventures" or "discovering passions" or "looking for new challenges." Others comment that they are working harder, but tasks take longer.

A total of 14 percent (nearly twice as many men as women) say they or their spouse have physical ailments or limitations. A seventy-five-year-old part-time house painter admits to "getting older and slower." A psychiatrist of the same age says his health is more "precarious," and a seventy-seven-year-old oncologist is thinking about the implications of his "advancing" age. Some women mentioned the pressure of deadlines or late teaching hours causing difficulties with getting enough sleep. An anti-aging activist in her mid-sixties finds that she has never worked harder, but notices that her part-ner and her friends are slowing down. A medical writer, aged seventy-three, worries about "loss of mind and/or body" as she ages. Even if not articulated, it is no secret that loss of mental acuity is a frightening prospect for any se-nior, whether in or out of the workforce.

⸙

PROFILE: FRANCES R. SCHNADIG, LICENSED CLINICAL SOCIAL WORKER

Chicagoan Fran Schnadig is remarkably philosophical about the serious threats to her health. She is seventy-six and urgently needs a lung transplant. That is only one of many problems she has dealt with; yet, in speaking with her, the overall impression one gets is that of resilience in the face of adversity. Fran had always wanted to be a licensed clinical social worker, but four kids, a failed marriage, the fallout from divorce, financial troubles, and alcoholism intervened. She got sober with the help of Alcoholics Anonymous (AA) and was finally able to enroll in Loyola University's social work program. She discovered that her age (she was fifty-three when she went back to school) made her the oldest student in the program, and some of her fellow students were friends of her grown children. "It never occurred to me that age was a limiting factor in social work," she tells me. "In fact, maturity is a real advantage, especially when counseling older adults with substance abuse problems." Fran's work in not-for-profit community social services agencies and, more recently, in private practice has been enormously satisfying. She would never have cut back her schedule were it not for doctor's orders. Her pulmonologist insisted on a reduced work schedule because Fran has "galloping" (Fran's term) chronic obstructive pulmonary disease, an inflammatory lung disease that causes obstructed airflow from the lungs. The chronic obstructive pulmonary disease is advancing quickly and has recently made her dependent on oxygen round the clock. There is no cure. She has already "dodged the bullet" twice: surviving breast cancer in 1995 when she was in graduate school and lung cancer in 2014. Now she is waiting to learn whether she is a candidate for a lung transplant.

"Work is a gift that means everything to me. I have such a fascinating profession," Fran enthuses. "I never considered retiring once I became a social worker. My work is both extremely stimulating intellectually and emotionally satisfying." As a licensed clinical social worker, she provides psychotherapy for adults and older adults in the metropolitan Chicago area. Since 2014 she has been in private practice, following sixteen years as a clinician and program manager in not-for-profit community social service agencies.

Fran did three years of her undergraduate work at Smith College. When she got married after her junior year and college officials insisted that she reside on campus, Fran transferred to Tufts University near Boston and completed her degree there in 1965. She and her husband moved to Chicago where she planned to become a social worker following graduate school. Eleven years later, she had four children ranging in age from two-and-a-half years to eleven years and a failed marriage. Social work was on the back burner, and alcoholism took over. Fran says,

A combination of problems led to my alcoholism: my divorce and all of the tensions and losses involved; the pressures and difficulties of being a single parent; and significant financial difficulties. Alcohol appeared to help me—to be calmer, to deal better with problems, to sleep. But, after thirteen years, it became horribly destructive to me and my children, the negative effects far outweighing the positive. Still, I was one of the lucky ones: I got sober with the help of AA and haven't had any desire for a drink in more than thirty years.

Starting when her youngest child was six years old and in school, Fran began work outside the home. "I had no real work experience other than volunteering for the League of Women Voters and working on the state level on environmental protection issues." Nevertheless, based on her volunteer work, she was hired to design, launch, and manage a human resources function for a small tech company, drinking at night until she finally "bottomed out" on alcohol.

In her early recovery, Fran sold encyclopedias for several months in order to obtain health insurance. She then joined in partnership with a friend from AA, developing a small and quickly successful moving services company for seniors. However, that venture collapsed after two years because the partner withdrew in order to deal with personal credit card debt. At about the same time, Fran's mother fell ill and Fran was glad she was available to be with her until she passed away. "My mom had always encouraged me to do what I wanted and that was to become a social worker. She left me enough money so that I could finally get my master's in social work."

When she enrolled at Loyola University Chicago in the mid-1990s, Fran was the oldest person in the social work program. She often encountered ("with pleasure," Fran says) friends of her children who were in the same program and classes. While she was well aware of her age, it was not a problem in the social work field. "I've never experienced ageism in my profession. In fact, I see lots of gray hair in the office or agency environment and a recognition of the value of older workers who are both mature and really good at what they do."

Starting in 2000, Fran initiated an outpatient adult substance abuse treatment program in a small not-for-profit agency in Evanston, Illinois, called PEER Services, PEER standing for Prevention Education Evaluation Recovery. Then, in 2002, becoming aware of the need for a specialized approach to helping older adults with alcohol and prescription drug addictions, Fran landed a grant from the Dr. Scholl Foundation to start a program for older adult substance abusers. She continued applying for and receiving Dr. Scholl Foundation grants for the next fifteen years to support the program. She also heard her older adult clients' accounts of demeaning and painful experiences with family, social services agencies, and medical workers, and was witness to similar types of destructive incidents in hospital emergency rooms when she accompanied her clients.

As the result of those clinical experiences and her awareness that 17 percent of older Americans are at risk for or suffer from alcohol and/or prescription medication use problems, Fran co-founded the Illinois Coalition on Substance Use and Aging in 2013 with Stanley McCracken, Ph.D., a licensed clinical social worker and a senior lecturer at the University of Chicago's School of Social Service Administration. McCracken's expertise, like Fran's, encompasses mental health, substance abuse, and aging issues. The Illinois Coalition on Substance Use and Aging operates with a highly dedicated, all-volunteer group of older adult services professionals. Membership includes forty-five organizations in the Chicago metropolitan area, including mental health and substance abuse treatment providers and a broad range of senior services providers (the Veterans Administration, legal services, LGBTQ support, retirement communities, hospitals, universities, municipalities, and the State of Illinois). An essential component of the coalition's work is training on effective ways of talking to older adults, helping them, and dealing with family issues related to substance abuse. Fran, who serves on the coalition's leadership and planning group, points out, "Aging brings previously unimagined losses, and older adults who drink have often internalized, been completely alone with, their losses. It's also important to recognize that older adults with substance abuse problems need specialized treatment that also addresses the shame, secrecy, and anger from family members."

After working for nearly sixteen years at not-for-profit agencies, all but two of those years at PEER Services, Fran decided in 2014 to start a private practice so that she would have more time to write poetry and short stories. Her own health problems were not a part of the decision at that time. Before she left the agency, she made sure to train her successor. "Fortunately, I found a talented young woman, a natural."

Fran is still working in her private practice and writing, while awaiting word about getting a lung transplant. (She may be ineligible because of her age and medical history. Lungs are fragile and viable only for a few hours once removed from a body, and they are in short supply.) "I am content. I will accept whatever happens," she tells me. Meanwhile, she has little green oxygen tanks in her office that are noiseless and do not disturb her patients, as well as a portable oxygen concentrator that she walks and travels with to visit her children and ten grandchildren. "I love my work," she wrote to me, underlining love two times. "I have many older clients and it is very meaningful to me to help them have healthier, more enjoyable lives, making changes that they choose to make and can make. Older adults *can* and *do* change, if they wish to do so!" Fran is proof of that.

⸙

A total of 10 percent of the survey respondents (predominantly women) have caregiving responsibilities for an elderly or infirm parent, spouse, relative, child, or grandchild. A sixty-seven-year-old accountant has financial responsibility for his grown son who is in a clinic and for the son's eventual aftercare. A part-time therapist who is sixty-nine years old supports her disabled son. Another therapist, aged sixty-seven, takes care of her ninety-four-year-old mother. A journalist in her mid-seventies is worried about her husband who is nine years older. And a director of sales and marketing, in her mid-sixties, needs the salary because she and her husband are co-parenting their small grandchildren.

Even smaller numbers acknowledge that their skills are not up to date and they need training or retraining to maintain competence (or, avoid *discompetence*, the less familiar term). The seventy-one-year-old manager of a non-profit organization knows she needs to update her computer skills. An academic in his mid-sixties wants to learn new methods and approaches to research. A communications manager in her mid-sixties enjoys learning new things and staying up to date on technology. Her greater worry is "being left out of things when I quit working." Loss of friends or loved ones is not as big a concern as one might expect, nor, surprisingly, is the decreased value of investments or other financial setbacks. Only a handful of these professionals are experiencing a negative organizational climate at work or outright age discrimination.

The question about negative organizational climate in the workplace or outright age discrimination in the section of my survey addressing challenges or concerns of older workers elicited only twelve responses (7 percent). One came from an illustrator, aged seventy, who is paid less than her male peers. Three women in their sixties had similar complaints—a professor believes the new dean is not giving her assignments and feels that she is being "put out to pasture." Another professor is publishing papers but feels that "quality work is not recognized." A journalist finds it harder to get assignments when competing with "trendier" (translation: younger) writers. A man, age sixty-three, who moved to higher education after a long career in finance, is an adjunct instructor at two universities while pursuing a doctoral degree. He sees age, race, ethnicity, religious, and gender discrimination in the academic world and feels that his demographics "are discriminated against increasingly in many institutions of higher education."

Another response came from a woman who sees ageism in the fitness industry where she has one of her part-time jobs. Now sixty-six years of age, she is teaching boot camp and kickboxing classes at gyms and private facilities after a long career in radio program management. She observes that "ageism in the fitness industry has more to do with stereotype-driven limitations that we impose on clients and participants than the ones that are imposed on us as fitness professionals. There is a constant assumption that older people are all deconditioned and need modifications or to be tracked into less challenging specialty programs and that all young people are ultra-conditioned. This could not be further from the truth." Another woman in her mid-sixties doesn't see age discrimination within the non-profit organization where she works full-time as communications director but does detect it from external partners. She says that a strategic decision made by one civic organization to focus on communities of color and young people has, either by design or oversight, left older people out of choice volunteer roles. And some employers use thinly veiled appeals to younger job applicants, such as "We need go-getters," "Energetic," and "Build your career with us."

Apart from these examples, the vast majority of survey respondents did not mention negativity in the organizational climate, perhaps because they have job security or are self-employed. Of course, not everyone is so fortunate. Older workers who leave a job voluntarily or are laid off, often, on average, take many months to land a replacement job, and they may never get one. True, the (average) unemployment rate is currently very low in most parts of the country, but employers continue to prefer younger workers. As shown by studies in this country and abroad, discrimination against older job seekers and workers is, in the words of AARP, "a persistent and common problem."

⚭

PROFILE: E. ETHELBERT MILLER, POET, TEACHER, LITERARY ACTIVIST, AUTHOR, RADIO AND TELEVISION HOST

It was a problem for poet, author, editor, radio host, and activist E. Ethelbert Miller. After serving as director and archivist of Howard University's African American Resource Center for forty years, in 2015 Miller was abruptly terminated along with some eighty other Howard employees. The ostensible reason was budget cuts, but he suspected age discrimination in his case. Many poets, literary figures, and other notable people in the arts and humanities wrote letters vigorously protesting the university's decision and praising Miller. Ironically, Miller is a Howard alumnus, one of the first to graduate from the university's African American Studies program in the early 1970s. What began as civil rights activism for him during and after college morphed into *literary* activism. Three examples of his activism among many: founding and serving as chair of the Humanities Council of Washington, DC, co-editing the oldest poetry journal in the country, and promoting the careers of promising young writers. What happened at Howard is the university's loss: Miller is in greater demand than ever as a teacher, mentor, writer, book reviewer, radio and television host, and producer. He refuses to think "old." He is looking forward to the "seventh inning stretch" and, in the immediate future, celebrating the success of his sixteenth book, a new collection of poems about baseball. *If God Invented Baseball* is intended for wide readership in the baseball community, not the for literati, asserts this devoted Nationals fan.

Extending the baseball metaphor, Miller explains why his "fifth inning" was critical. The long-serving director/archivist of Howard University's African American Resource Center for forty years, in 2015 he found himself locked out of his university computer account when Howard abruptly terminated him and a slew of other university employees, apparently for fiscal reasons. Whereas age discrimination might have been a factor in his case, chipping away at the humanities in favor of the sciences and income-generating research was another troubling possibility. Friends and admirers rallied to his side. Prominent historian and author Douglas Brinkley called him "the heart and soul of Howard University." Award-winning poet, author, and professor Elizabeth Alexander bemoaned his loss to the university. (Alexander, who read an original poem at Barack Obama's first inauguration, has just been named to the presidency of the Andrew W. Mellon Foundation, the nation's largest humanities grant maker.) National Book Award winner and MacArthur Fellow Charles Johnson praised Miller's ability to inspire young writers. In another letter criticizing the university's decision, an accomplished author named Reginald Dwayne Betts stated on Split This Rock (the national network of socially engaged poets) that Miller was "the voice of the Black community that helped me understand and believe in my own worth." A comment following that letter referred to Miller as "a visionary connector of peoples, ideas, art, love, humanity."

Miller does credit his alma mater for getting him on the path to a literary career. It was not until he got to college and met professors who encouraged him and introduced him to the work of luminaries such as Langston Hughes, Countee Cullen, and Claude McKay that Miller started writing. At Paul L. Dunbar Junior High School in the early 1960s in the Bronx no one taught Dunbar's poetry, and Christopher Columbus High School did not have African American studies. However, in the charged political and cultural climate of the 1960s and 1970s, a Black Arts Movement had arisen alongside the Black Power Movement. As African American studies programs began to emerge from curricular battles at universities, in 1969 Ethelbert Miller became one of the first students to major in the program at Howard. With the increase in civil rights activism that followed the voter registration drives from the Congress of Racial Equality and the Student Nonviolent Coordinating Committee during the 1964 Mississippi Summer, inevitably he was "baptized into the black consciousness movement."

Activism for Miller fed into *literary* activism. It is intriguing to discover how much he personifies two of Malcolm Gladwell's *Tipping Point* terms: *connector*, with a knack for making friends and bringing people together, and *maven*, with knowledge, social skills, and the ability to communicate. Some of that knowledge is contained in files Miller has amassed over the years about major writers—he jokes that this reminds him of J. Edgar Hoover, who collected files on everybody. Miller's are archived with his personal papers at George Washington University, the University of Minnesota, and at Emory & Henry College. What's more, he contributes his knowledge and skills to literary boards, often sitting on several at once, helping to decide who should be nominated for prestigious awards because he "knows the territory, how literature is produced and preserved." For example, he became board chair of the Institute for Policy Studies, a multi-issue progressive think tank in Washington, DC (an unusual post for a *poet*, he points out), and he is the founder and former chair of the Humanities Council of DC. From 1997 to 2008, he served as a commissioner for the DC Commission on the Arts and Humanities.

Miller co-edits *Poet Lore* with Jody Bolz. It is the oldest poetry journal in the country. "In fourteen years of volunteering my time as editor, I have seen trends in literature and discovered new voices. Associating with, publishing, and promoting new young writers just beginning their careers keeps me humble, keeps me aware." Previous literary activism included practicing cultural diplomacy for the State Department in the Middle East. "There are things you can do as a writer that you cannot do as a politician."

It is all about *listening to* and *respecting* people. The website of the African American Literature Book Club reports on books written by or about black writers from America, Africa, and throughout the African diaspora. Coupled with Miller's own African American Literature Book Club biography on the website is the announcement of his unique E-Channel project[1] comprising the words and wisdom of the writer and professor emeritus Charles Johnson, eminent scholar of literature and race. For a period of one year, Miller interviewed Johnson about his books, beliefs, and "various matters of the heart and mind." *The Words and Wisdom of Charles Johnson* presents Johnson's responses to questions asked each week by Miller. In the introduction to its companion volume, *The Way of the Writer: Reflections on the Art and Craft of Storytelling*, Johnson's admiration for and appreciation of Miller is clear:

> It is very difficult to find someone in the writing community, here or abroad, who has not been touched by his unselfish contributions to literary culture since the late 1960s. . . . He has devoted himself to the support of other writers, young and old. In the literary world, he is an activist who is as ubiquitous as air—publishing poetry and memoirs, columns and social commentary. . . . For

him art is spirit work aimed at realizing the "beloved community" that Martin Luther King Jr. envisioned. He works as indefatigably as W.E.B. Du Bois, and his work is always in support of social justice and bringing to the community of literary artists . . . a spirit of cooperation, not competition; compassion, not indifference; and idealism, not cynicism. He cares about everyone.

In addition to stints as scholar in residence at various colleges and universities, Miller has been teaching courses in memoir writing at Goucher College and (online) for the University of Houston, Victoria. He "maintains a presence" not only in print by writing and reviewing books, but also on radio and television. As host of a weekly morning radio show called "On the Margin," he makes book discussions interesting, interviewing writers, editors, bookstore owners, and others connected to the literary community. In similar fashion he hosts and produces "The Scholars" on UDC-TV, now in its fourth year. Miller also used to be a regular guest for book reviewing on NPR's Diane Rehm Show. They served together on the PEN/Faulkner Foundation board.

Miller formed an E-Group (the E is for Ethelbert) to create "a sense of synergies" among those who have shown exceptional promise as future leaders. He described his mission in a piece he wrote for "E on DC" in 2015.[2] "In the last innings of life you want to look around at the team you're on. You want a life filled with rookies and seasoned veterans. . . . I try to keep my eyes and ears open to new ideas. We poets have much work to do in our city, nation, and world." In order to "navigate the streets of life," he advises, one must find "small, quiet moments of light." Instead of hatred, racism, and wars, *explore goodness.*

Miller borrows an expression from Langston Hughes to describe all these *un*retirement ventures as "literary sharecropping." That is, he never knows how his myriad initiatives will do each year. So far, production has been "off the charts." He has expanded his network, found new resources, and developed new capabilities. He agrees with his wife and family that he is overextended. "Yet," he enthuses, "it never would have happened while I was on staff at Howard. I can actually get paid for my expertise, since it's no longer part of my academic job." Perhaps what happened in 2015 wasn't all bad: in April of that year he was inducted into the Washington DC Hall of Fame and set his sights on the seventh inning. In sum, he believes what happened to him in 2015 was a kind of "emancipation," releasing him to be "a free person of color in the Frederick Douglass tradition."

⌒⊗⌒

As discussed in chapter 2, there is no commonly accepted definition of "old," no universal yardstick for aging—even though everyone is doing it all the time. And workers in their sixties, seventies, and eighties are not the only ones to feel the sting of ageism. Indeed, an article in the *New York Times* business section revealed anxieties about ageism, personal irrelevance and obsolescence among *thirty-*, *forty-*, and *fifty-*year-old workers in Silicon Valley. The title of the article spoke volumes: "In the Digital World, Midlife Crisis Can Hit at 30." Young as they actually are, thirty- and forty-somethings in tech jobs are often seen as "elders" by co-workers in their twenties, and it can be very painful.[3]

Joseph Coughlin, director of the Age Lab at the Massachusetts Institute of Technology, says "aging unfolds differently for everyone," making socially constructed notions about old age "deeply flawed."[4] What is more, Coughlin continues, society's "dysfunctional narrative" about old people depicts them as burdensome, "needy and greedy." Businesses (other than pharmaceutical companies and financial services firms that constantly pelt seniors with ads for their products and services) too often share that bias. Businesses that ignore old age or mischaracterize it miss out by their failure to market to older consumers who, it is estimated, control anywhere from 70 to 80 percent of disposable household income.

Companies lose valuable assets too when they show experienced, mature workers the door. Productivity has been shown to increase when older and younger people work together in multi-generational teams. However, research by Moody's Analytics economists into older workers and productivity takes a contrary tack, associating the aging workforce with lower productivity growth. Defining productivity as a measure of how much is produced based on the number of people working and the hours they work, these economists are concerned about the rapid increase in Boomer retirements and the shrinking working-age population. They also say that "an older workforce may slow the adoption of productivity-enhancing technologies that require learning," and they offer two explanations: older workers with less time remaining in their careers would reap fewer benefits from new training, and such training may not be worth a company's investment if older workers have a hard time learning the new skills or resist productivity-improving technologies.[5] Essentially, these economists come down on the side of the negative "albatross theory" rather than the positive "wise man theory" when they weigh the contribution of older workers to productivity.

Applebaum and colleagues have identified a number of other commonly held and detrimental "old-age stereotypes" (in addition to difficulty in acquiring new technological skills and resistance to change) that can decrease overall organizational productivity. These include assumptions about decreased learning ability, intelligence, and memory; poor health and propensity to have accidents; higher organizational costs; decreased motivation; and low innovation and individual worker productivity.[6] Organizations that reject such stereotyping when integrating older adults into their workforces can increase productivity in all employees, Applebaum and his co-researchers assert.

Robert N. Butler, M.D., a pioneer in gerontology and the first director of the National Institutes of Health's National Institute on Aging, coined the term "ageism" in 1969 to describe stereotyping and discrimination against the old. (The definition has since been extended to include the young who can be deemed too *in*experienced.) Federal law is supposed to protect certain applicants and employees forty years of age and older from discrimination on the basis of age in hiring, promotion, discharge, compensation, or terms, conditions or privileges of employment. The Age Discrimination in Employment Act (ADEA) is enforced by the Equal Employment Opportunity Commission (EEOC). In 2017 workers filed more than eighteen thousand age discrimination and age-based harassment complaints with the EEOC, but the EEOC received nearly fifteen hundred fewer the following year. Unfortunately, age discrimination can be very hard to prove, especially if it occurs in the hiring process (and much discriminatory and harassing conduct goes unreported). In fact, the U.S. Seventh Circuit Court of Appeals ruled on January 23, 2019, in *Dale E. Kleber v. CareFusion Corporation* that the federal law barring age discrimination in employment does not apply to "disappointed" outside job applicants, only to current employees. (The outside job application of Dale Kleber, a fifty-eight-year-old attorney, exceeded the three to seven years of relevant legal experience stated in the company's job vacancy advertisement for a senior in-house legal position; a twenty-nine-year-old applicant who met the prescribed experience requirement was hired.) Critics of the ADEA legislation say that it is ineffective and inadequate in its treatment of age when compared with Civil Rights Act protection against racism or sexism.[7] An encouraging sign as of January 2020 is the Protecting Older Workers Against Discrimination Act, which would amend the ADEA so suits claiming bias would have a better chance of success in court. Having passed with bipartisan support in the House of Representatives, it awaits deliberation in the Senate.

In a 2018 report characterizing the state of age discrimination and older workers fifty years after passage of the ADEA and ten years after the Great Recession, the EEOC noted that "age discrimination remains a significant and costly problem for workers, their families, and our economy."[8] Despite an unexpectedly robust job market post-recession and favorable conditions for finding jobs, the average older and experienced worker who has lost a job has more difficulty than a younger worker in finding a new job, particularly one on a par with the job previously held. This is, says the EEOC, attributable to prevalent age discrimination, unfounded and outdated assumptions about age and ability in making employment decisions, "one constant" for older workers of all races, ethnicities, and income in all types of jobs and industries throughout the country. Today, more complaints are filed with the EEOC by women than men, more by blacks and Asians than other groups, and more by workers aged fifty-five and older. The EEOC report concludes with recommendations for employers to change ageist attitudes and to institute practices that value a multi-generational workforce.

Occasionally, the alleged victims of discrimination in the discharge (layoff) process are vindicated. In July 2018, a "New Old Age" column in the *New York Times* featured a federal age discrimination lawsuit won by Julianne Taaffe and Kathryn Moon, two teachers of English as a Second Language in the College of Education and Human Ecology at Ohio State University. Both instructors were women not yet sixty who had been teaching effectively at the university for years when a new administrator took over the program they had helped to build and systematically began to weed out all the older staff. It took four years and a great deal of anguish before the two women got a favorable ruling from the EEOC: the administrator's emails that disparaged older staff members as "dead wood" were the clincher. The plaintiffs got their jobs back, plus back pay, retroactive benefits, and a commitment from the university to review within a year its policies and guidelines and train human resources personnel "to recognize, investigate, and prevent age discrimination."[9] (Following up one year later, Taaffe and Moon note that evidence of the university's fulfillment of that commitment has been hard to pinpoint. Represented by a Columbus law firm and AARP, they have sued for public records, communications, and notifications from the university in hopes of learning who is conducting the review and how it is being conducted.)

According to a March 22, 2018, ProPublica exposé by Peter Gosselin and Ariana Tobin, IBM has slid under the ADEA radar despite cutting "tens of thousands of U.S. workers, hitting its most experienced and aging senior employees hardest and flouting rules against age bias." ProPublica says the Fortune 500 company has been systematically shedding its Baby Boom workforce, hiring new, younger employees, and shifting jobs overseas. To keep the number of layoffs as low as possible, IBM has made a practice of encouraging resignations by requiring people who were working from home to report or relocate to an office that was often in an inconvenient, distant location. In some cases, former employees were invited back as contract workers for less pay and fewer benefits.[10]

Age bias can be both institutional (more familiar) and internalized (less so). *Institutional* age bias refers to society's ill-informed stereotypes, for example, older workers seen as too experienced and too expensive in terms of salary and healthcare costs. Negative images of aging "portray older adults as burdens, a drain on society, and incapable of keeping up with the demands of the modern workplace" rather than as active and productive members of society.[11] *Internalized* age bias refers to self-perception, the ways individuals discourage *themselves* from applying for a job or promotion by questioning their competency without cause. Both types of bias are prevalent and harmful, not only to job seekers and their families, but also to businesses that lose out on potential talent. In sum, "the human and social capital of older adults is underutilized due to ageist attitudes, outdated policies, and shortsighted programming."[12] By removing barriers and opening up opportunities for older adults, society will benefit from their productive engagement—whether in caregiving, volunteering, or participating in the paid workforce.

Eden King and colleagues provide another take on internalized age bias called "age meta-stereotyping"—what workers think others believe about them based on the workers' age group, even if there is no actual reason for such thoughts.[13] Yet, say these researchers of industrial and organizational psychology, age stereotyping and meta-stereotyping create artificial generational divides that can interfere with management, training, interpersonal relations, and other work behaviors. (Beliefs about how we differ are nothing new, of course. Social scientists have for years pigeonholed us into cohorts based on age, race, ethnicity, gender, and so on. Charles King's new book on the early cultural anthropologists Franz Boas, Ruth Benedict, Margaret Mead, Zora Neale Hurston, and Ella Cara Deloria portrays their efforts to confront bigotry and widely-accepted attitudes of superiority ("us") versus inferiority ("them") that were "scientifically endorsed" by showing that they were unsupported by science.[14] To this day, however, too many politicians and nativists persist in exploiting "us versus them" thinking.)

With several different generations populating the work place today—the Society for Human Resource Management (SHRM) adds Generation Z (born in the mid-1990s) to the usual four—managers and human resources professionals need to understand that a climate favorable to age diversity and inclusion can improve organizational performance and reduce employee turnover. "By removing the lens of age as a way to view existing or potential employees," SHRM says, "you can shift the focus to their abilities, skills, experience and knowledge, where it belongs." SHRM recommends six practical actions employers can implement to leverage the value of an age-diverse workforce:

- Open apprenticeships to workers of all ages.
- Start a program to assist workers re-entering the workforce after a long absence.
- Facilitate cross-generational mentoring to improve knowledge transfer.
- Raise awareness of intergenerational differences to enhance team functioning.
- Organize employee resource groups that increase workers' engagement and provide mentoring opportunities. These groups may evolve into problem-solving or leadership-development groups.
- Actively recruit talent across all ages to build a diverse, experienced workforce.[15]

Keeping up with the demands of the modern workplace includes keeping up with ever-changing technologies. There's artificial intelligence, for example, and industrial automation, such as robotic process automation. Both are progressing very fast and, once adopted, will likely mean retraining for some workers and displacement for many others. Technological advances do not come without risks. For example, some Amazon order fulfillment center workers are stressed by the rate of work required to keep pace with automated systems in their workplace. Although they are not being replaced by robots, they are under intense pressure to work as productively as robots.[16]

In yet another sphere, new developments in artificial intelligence when used to make the review of job applications more efficient and targeted will potentially help to obscure age discrimination or other bias. An Economist Intelligence Unit study of the evolution of work and the worker foresees the effects of automation on mid-skilled workers who are no longer needed for performance of routine tasks, often in manufacturing. In high demand will be technical workers with specialized skills and senior executives responsible for corporate management, which will exacerbate already increasing social inequality.[17] Noting the risk from automation that will affect professionals doing tasks that can be easily replicated, former secretary of labor and professor of public policy Robert Reich also warns that the mere availability of robots will depress wages in jobs that cannot be done without the human touch.[18]

One persistent stereotype is that young people are "tech-savvy" and older adults are not. Although some older workers do lack essential skills, many others make sure their skills are up to date. Again, *functional* age is the more relevant criterion than chronological age, and hiring managers, trainers, performance evaluators, and organizational leaders should take note. Not only has the nature of work undergone change by becoming digitized, less physical, and more knowledge-based, ideas about where and when work can be performed have also changed. Thanks to proven technological innovations, it is increasingly common for men and women to work from home one or more days a week or work in an office that can be far distant from the central office and get work done on their own schedule. Such flexible arrangements are particularly valued by parents of small children and caregivers of elderly loved ones.

Technology enabled a recruiter of biotech sales representatives to run her business very successfully from home for well over thirty years, starting when her son and daughter were born. "I am self-motivated," she explains. "I enjoy helping clients get ahead in their careers—it keeps my brain active—and like knowing I have something to do when I wake up in the morning. Self-employed and aged sixty-four, I don't have to worry about money and can do everything I want to do, so recently I reduced my hours to allow more time for travel, hiking, biking, and kayaking." A key word in this woman's remarks is "self-motivated."

All too often, managers in the United States and elsewhere in the world hold negative stereotypes about older workers' ability to learn new things and assume they have a declining interest in work. But research into the complexities of motivation and the motivational factors affecting career intentions of a sample of older Spanish workers as they age shows a shift away from competition and status and toward decision-making opportunities, rather than a general decline in motivation.[19] With regard to status as a driving force, other research finds gender differences in a sample of Chinese retirees participating in bridge employment in Beijing. Status-seeking motivates male retirees more than female retirees to choose bridge employment. (However, it is negatively related to volunteer work after retirement.[20])

In addition to questioning their older employees' motivation to work, managers reluctant to encourage extended careers often fail to see older workers' strengths, not only their maturity and years of experience, but also their professionalism and strong work ethic, problem solving skills, self-direction, and abiding interest in learning.[21] Traditionalists and Baby Boomers tend to see themselves as reliable, productive, engaged, and loyal. Unfortunately, managers as well as co-workers belonging to younger generations do not always share that view, particularly when co-workers are vying for training and development opportunities or recognition for their work.[22] Sometimes efforts by human resource managers to target training to the needs of older workers end up backfiring. A Portuguese lecturer on human resources management advises human resources managers to avoid age-segregated practices that can make older workers more vulnerable to negative stereotypes about their competence and that can give the appearance of special treatment. Instead, workplace interventions should include all age groups, open lines of communication, and ensure equal treatment.[23] In sum, too often ageism colors employers' perceptions of older workers. Employers would probably deny having ageist attitudes, yet, according to AARP, two-thirds of workers aged fifty and over are convinced that employers see *age as a disadvantage* when making hiring decisions; nearly four-fifths of workers aged sixty-five and older agree.[24]

An array of organizations alert to issues of aging here and abroad are tackling the problem of ageism. The Pass It On Network,[25] a peer-to-peer learning network for positive aging advocates worldwide, is celebrating its fifth anniversary and its status as one of forty-four newly accredited non-governmental members of the United Nations Open-ended Working Group on Ageing, established by the UN General Assembly by resolution 65/182 in 2010.[26] PION's co-founders, Jan Hively and Moira Allan, attended the ninth session of the OEWGA in July 2018. They report that the working group will consider the existing international framework of the human rights of older persons and identify possible gaps, such as the problem of ageism as a human rights issue in the workplace, and how best to address them, including by considering, as appropriate, the feasibility of further instruments and measures, such as a UN Convention that recognizes the Human Rights of Older People to Autonomy & Independence and to Long Term Care & Palliative Care.

The Pass It On Network also praises a related effort called "Ageing Equal," a seven-week campaign against ageism initiated by AGE Platform Europe to mark the seventieth anniversary of the Universal Declaration of Human Rights. The campaign's launch date in October 2018 also coincided with the United Nations International Day of Older Persons and supports the World Health Organization's (WHO's) coordinated fight against ageism.[27] The WHO defines ageism as "the stereotyping and discrimination against individuals or groups on the basis of their age; ageism can take many forms, including prejudicial attitudes, discriminatory practices, or institutional policies and practices that perpetuate stereotypical beliefs." Put another way, stereotyping is *how we think about* older people, prejudice is *how we feel about* older people, and discrimination is *how we act toward* older people on the basis of age (italics added). Furthermore, says the WHO, "Ageism is everywhere, yet it is the most socially 'normalized' of any prejudice, and is not widely countered—like racism or sexism. These attitudes lead to the marginalization of older people within our communities and have negative impacts on their health and well-being."

One such stereotype, the so-called lump of labor idea, posits a zero-sum game pitting veteran workers against younger aspirants for their jobs. The WHO refutes this myth: "Policies enforcing mandatory retirement ages do not help create jobs for youth, but they reduce older workers' ability to contribute. They also reduce an organization's opportunities to benefit from the capabilities of older workers. Age has not been shown to be a reliable indicator for judging workers' potential productivity or employability."

Tying together the WHO's and United Nations' initiatives on aging and ageism is the International Federation on Ageing (IFA)'s 14th Global Conference, "Towards a Decade of Healthy Ageing—From Evidence to Action."[28] The title responds to the WHO Global Report on Ageing and Health and the subsequent goals of the WHO 2016 Global Strategy and Action Plan which focuses on five strategic objectives:

> commitment to action on healthy ageing in every country; developing age-friendly environments; aligning health systems to the needs of older populations; developing sustainable and equitable systems for providing long-term care (home, communities, institutions); and improving measurement, monitoring, and research on Healthy Ageing. The Global Strategy and Action Plan is a significant and much-needed step forward in establishing a framework for Member States. The IFA, in its formal relations with the WHO, is strongly committed, through the platform of our Global Conference and attending delegates, to contributing to the evidence and partnerships necessary to support a Decade of Healthy Ageing from 2020 to 2030.

Moreover, "the IFA is committed to helping enable older people to do what they value through a deeper evidence-based understanding and has aligned the IFA Global Conference's themes to the WHO's Strategy and Action Plan with links to the UN's Sustainable Development Goals."

Also looking ahead to a global decade of healthy ageing (2020 to 2030), the Global Coalition on Aging repudiates unexamined assumptions about what it means to be old (i.e., decline and deterioration), along with "defining out of economic life our soon-to-be largest age population group, a trend which is both unsustainable and self-defeating." Employers, the coalition warns, need to rethink markets, work, and retirement and invest in lifelong training and education. For, in the "silver economy," aging populations that remain active, engaged, and working can help drive innovation, change, productivity, and wealth creation.[29]

In 2018, European organizations representing employers and labor unions formed a partnership to explore ways to support older workers who want to keep working, to address youth unemployment, and to promote intergenerational knowledge sharing. The partners agree that collaboration leading to innovative solutions to each of these challenges can be mutually beneficial for employers and workers, particularly at a time when European labor markets are undergoing demographic change.[30]

As in Europe, a coalition of organizations and individuals in Australia has formed to confront ageism. After conducting preliminary research to gauge the extent of the problem, EveryAGE Counts launched a national advocacy campaign under the auspices of the Benevolent Society in 2018 "to research the attitudes and beliefs that drive ageism faced by older Australians; raise awareness of ageism; and campaign against the structural barriers caused by ageism, which prevent older people from participating equally in social and economic life."[31] EveryAGE Counts says ageism is pervasive—in the workplace, healthcare, personal lives, and in social and political discussions. An earlier study by Taylor and colleagues of the prevalence and nature of *everyday* discrimination in the Australian workplace—encompassing subtle behaviors, such as exclusion from a work meeting, avoidance, unfriendly communication, and withholding of assistance—found it to be uncommon and pointed out the difficulty of disentangling age discrimination from gender, race, and class.[32] (This research, which was not intended to look for discrimination in the recruitment/hiring process, serves as a reminder to readers to ascertain what was actually being measured before drawing conclusions about discrimination.)

In addition to receiving an income- and asset-tested state-funded age pension, older Australians who need to augment their retirement funds and those motivated by enjoyment or other personal reasons for working in the retirement years often struggle when stereotypes and discrimination pose barriers to employment. And, as in the United States, Australian society is becoming more segregated by age, isolating both old and young people and feeding negative perceptions of older age which in turn raise recruitment barriers when those as young as forty-five are labeled as old. Cognizant of that mindset, Geoff Pearman, managing director and principal age-and-work consultant of Partners in Change, specializes in assisting organizations in Australia and New Zealand to position themselves vis à vis "the age wave" of Boomers in the workforce and for anticipated skills shortages.[33] He helps clients from a variety of sectors, including financial services, health, transport, utilities, government, banking, aged care, and economic development, to develop and put in place practical organizational and workforce development strategies and actions geared to staff retention. "Age-friendly" or (the even newer term) "age-inclusive" initiatives include providing ongoing up-skilling, instituting flexibility policies, and recognition of workers' needs vis à vis health and well-being. For example, Partners in Change offers an "Ageing Workforce Strategy Builder" program in which participating employers develop a practical action plan as well as gain new insights and skills. The four-month program enables organizations to develop a full understanding of their aging workforce and the business risks and opportunities they face regarding the aging population and to design a strategy and action plan specifically for their organization. Each cluster comprises eight organizations that learn and work together. The program is designed for business owners, operations managers, human resources managers, work/health/safety specialists, and local/state/federal government workforce planning and development officers. As a component of the Strategy Builder program organizations are entitled to two hours of in-house consulting. One company, Transport Main Roads Queensland, invited Partners in Change to run a workshop for thirty-four of its managers.

The percentage of employed mature-age New Zealanders (aged sixty-five and up) was nearly 25 percent in 2016 and is projected to exceed 26 percent by 2031. (The projection jumps to 44 percent for people sixty-five to sixty-nine.) "This is not a challenge that is going to go away," Pearman asserts. "This is longevity playing out." Pearman also co-founded Senior Entrepreneurs New Zealand to support people over the age of fifty who want to move into business for the first time. He "passionately" hopes to see senior entrepreneurs gain legitimacy in New Zealand.

AARP invited Geoff Pearman to speak about the work of Partners in Change at its Disrupt Aging: The Future of Work for all Generations Global Summit in Washington, DC. The June 2019 summit launched an international learning collaborative called "Living, Learning & Earning Longer," led by AARP, the World Economic Forum, the Organisation for Economic Co-operation and Development, and fifty employers seeking to identify and share multigenerational, inclusive workforce practices. The partner organizations' project objectives for 2019 and 2020 are to share existing resources and, where knowledge gaps exist, collaborate on new research to help employers build, support, and sustain multi-generational workforces. In addition to conducting extensive desk research, a series of regional workshops will convene a diverse set of international thought leaders to engage in dialogue, share existing resources, highlight meaningful case studies, and consider business rationales and incentives for employers to support a multi-generational, inclusive workforce. The work will culminate in a web-based interactive, to be launched at the 2021 World Economic Forum Annual Meeting in Davos, Switzerland. This interactive will serve as a guide for employers on the policies, practices, and business cases for supporting an age-diverse workforce.

To mark the fiftieth anniversary of the ADEA, AARP interviewed workers about their experience in the workplace, specifically their experiences with age discrimination. To survey "The Value of Experience," AARP's Multicultural Work and Jobs Study tapped a national sample of thirty-five hundred adults ages forty-five and over who were working full-time, part-time, or looking for work in 2017.[34] With the aging of the workforce (projections show 35 percent of the U.S. workforce to be aged fifty or older by 2022), AARP finds age discrimination to be a persistent and common problem (as mentioned previously) not only for older job seekers but also for those already employed who are judged by their age rather than their performance. About three in five older workers (61 percent) have either seen or experienced age discrimination in the workplace. Disaggregated AARP data reveal that unemployed respondents are more likely than employed respondents (74 percent versus 61 percent) to say they have seen or experienced age discrimination. Women are more likely than men (64 percent versus 59 percent) to say they have seen or experienced age discrimination. African Americans/blacks are more likely than Hispanics/Latinx and whites to say they have seen or experienced age discrimination (77 percent versus 61 percent and 59 percent, respectively). In response, AARP is supporting job seekers' networking groups designed to help job seekers in the fifty years and up demographic by providing job search guidance, support materials, and strategies for a new career direction or an encore career. In Massachusetts, the effort is funded by the Executive Office of Elder Affairs and managed by Massachusetts Councils on Aging.

Betty Friedan drew our attention to ageism in her 1993 book *The Fountain of Age* by declaring that aging is not lost youth but a new stage of opportunity and strength. A current leader in the fight against ageism, Ashton Applewhite, agrees. The author of *This Chair Rocks: A Manifesto Against Ageism* and a blogger,[35] Applewhite sees aging as a period of ongoing growth and development especially for those with a sense of purpose and meaningful roles. Absent these, she warns, ageism "damages our sense of self, segregates us, diminishes our prospects, and actually shortens lives." Her 2017 TED Talk reminds us that aging is a natural process, not a problem, a failure, or a disease. Yet ageism remains "the last acceptable prejudice," allowing bias in the media and popular culture conveyed subtly or blatantly. And it is particularly damaging in the workplace where it can be both institutionalized by management and internalized by older workers themselves. Applewhite and colleagues have launched a new website called *Old School* to educate people about ageism and work to dismantle it.[36] *Old School* is a clearinghouse of free, vetted, anti-ageism resources: books and blogs, workshops and PowerPoints, organizations and advocates. Applewhite says the response to *Old School* has been immediate: "If my inbox is any indication, interest in the plight and power of older workers is growing rapidly."

NOTES

1. See http://www.ethelbert-miller.blogspot.com.

2. See http://www.capitalcommunitynews.com.

3. Bowles, Nellie. "In the Digital World, Midlife Crisis Can Hit at 30." *New York Times*, Business, March 10, 2019, 1, 4–5.

4. Coughlin, Joseph. *The Longevity Economy*. New York: PublicAffairs, 2017.

5. Ozimek, Adam, Dante DeAntonio, and Mark Zandi. "Aging and the Productivity Puzzle." Retrieved March 29, 2019, from: https://ma.moodys.com/rs/961-KCJ-308/images/2018-09-04-Aging-and-the-Productivity-Puzzle.pdf.

6. Applebaum, Steven H., et al. "The Effects of Old-Age Stereotypes on Organizational Productivity (Part Three)." *Industrial and Commercial Training*, 48, no. 6, 2016, 303–10.

7. Gonzales, Ernest, et al. "Increasing Opportunities for the Productive Engagement of Older Adults: A Response to Population Aging." *The Gerontologist*, Special Issue: 2015 WHCoA.

8. Lipnic, Victoria A. "The State of Age Discrimination and Older Workers in the U.S. 50 Years After the Age Discrimination in Employment Act (ADEA)." U.S. Equal Employment Opportunity Commission, June 2018.

9. Span, Paula. "The 'Dead Wood' Got Fired Up and Took Back Their Jobs." *New York Times*, The New Old Age, July 10, 2018, D3.

10. See http://features.propublica.org.

11. Brownell, Patricia, and James J. Kelly, eds. *Ageism and Mistreatment of Older Workers—Current Reality, Future Solutions*. New York: Springer, 2013, xii.

12. Morrow-Howell, Nancy, et al. "Approaches, Policies, and Practices to Support the Productive Engagement of Older Workers." *Journal of Gerontological Social Work*, *60*, no. 3, January 2017, 193–200.

13. King, Eden, et al. "Generational Differences at Work Are Small. Thinking They Are Big Affects Our Behavior." *Harvard Business Review, Daily Alert*, August 1, 2019.

14. King, Charles. *Gods of the Upper Air: How a Circle of Renegade Anthropologists Reinvented Race, Sex, and Gender in the Twentieth Century*. New York: Doubleday, 2019.

15. Trawinski, Lori A. "Leveraging the Value of an Age-Diverse Workforce." SHRM Foundation Executive Briefing. Also see www.aarp.org/employerresourcecenter.

16. Condliffe, Jamie. "Amazon's Workers Hate Robots." *New York Times*, Technology, July 22, 2019, B3.

17. The Economist Intelligence Unit. "What's Next: Future Global Trends Affecting Your Organization." SHRM Foundation, February 2014. Retrieved from: http://futurehrtrends.eiu.com/executive-summary.

18. Reich, Robert B. "Barely Afloat in America." *New York Times* Book Review, July 15, 2018.

19. Alcover, Carlos-Maria, and Gabriela Topa. "Work Characteristics, Motivational Orientations, Psychological Work Ability and Job Mobility Intentions of Older Workers." *PLOS ONE*, no. 4, April 27, 2018. Retrieved from: https://doi.org/10.1371/journal.pone.0195973.

20. Zhan, Yujie, Mo Wang, and Jungi Shi. "Retirees' Motivational Orientations and Bridge Employment: Testing the Moderating Role of Gender." *Journal of Applied Psychology*, *100*, no. 5, September 2015, 1319–31. Retrieved from: https://doi.org/10.1037/a0038731.

21. Society for Human Resource Management. "The Aging Workforce—Basic and Applied Skills." Washington, DC: SHRM, January 12, 2015. Retrieved from: http://www.shrm.org/research/surveyfindings/articles/pages/shrm-older-workers-basic-and-applied-skills.aspx.

22. James, Jacquelyn B., et al. *Generational Differences in Perceptions of Older Workers' Capabilities.* Chestnut Hill, MA: Sloan Center on Aging & Work, Boston College, 2007.

23. Oliveira, Eduardo. "Buffers or Boosters? Human Resource Management Practices Shape the Way Older Workers See Themselves in the Workplace." AGEnda Aging & Work Blog. Chestnut Hill, MA: Center on Aging & Work, Boston College, February 8, 2018. Retrieved from: http://agingandwork.bc.edu/blog/buffers-or-boosters-human-resource-practices-shape-the-way-older-workers-see-themselves-in-the-workplace.

24. Kerman, Sarah, and Colette Thayer. *Job Seeking Among Workers Age 50+.* Washington, DC: AARP Research, October 2017.

25. See http://www.passitonnetwork.org.

26. See https://social.un.org/ageing-working-group.

27. See www.who.int.

28. See www.ifa2018.com.

29. *Hodin, Michael. "Ageism, Health, Economics." Blog post, May 17, 2018. Retrieved from:* www.globalcoalitiononaging.com.

30. Flynn, Matt. "Improving How the Older Labor Market is Managed: A New Era of Social Partnership." Boston College, Center on Aging & Work, March 2918. Retrieved from: http://agingandwork.bc.edu/blog.

31. See https://www.everyagecounts.org.au.

32. Taylor, Phillip, et al. "Everyday Discrimination in the Australian Workplace: Assessing Its Prevalence and Age and Gender Differences." *Australasian Journal on Ageing*, 37, no. 4, December 2018, 245–51.

33. See http://partnersinchange.co.nz and *Doing It Differently—Life & Work After 50*, Pearman's guide to journeying through a new stage of life.

34. See https://www.aarp.org/research. Perron, Rebecca. *The Value of Experience: AARP Multicultural Work and Jobs Study.* Washington, DC: AARP Research, July 2018. Retrieved from: https://doi.org/10.26419/res.00177.000.

35. See https://thischairrocks.com.

36. See https://www.oldschool.info.

8

Older Workers as Volunteers and in Encore Careers

CHAPTER OBJECTIVES

1. Addresses volunteer work, survey participants' commitment to volunteering, and their use of free time
2. Highlights the benefits of civic engagement and purposefulness and employment policies that foster productive engagement
3. Describes Encore.org and other movements promoting generational connectedness as an antidote to age apartheid
4. Examines cumulative disadvantage of less-educated, low-skilled older adults with respect to volunteer work, caregiving responsibilities, and continued learning

An inquisitive reader might be wondering why a book about working for pay in later life includes a chapter on volunteering. Well, it may be unpaid, but volunteering *is work*. And many older men and women who are in the labor force as part-timers or full-timers are also working as volunteers. Because there is no financial reward for doing so, what they get for their efforts is an extra measure of satisfaction and sense of purpose.

Across the country, reports the Bureau of Labor Statistics, almost sixty-three million people (a quarter of the population aged sixteen and older) volunteer through or for an organization, reaping personal benefits from civic engagement and collectively saving their communities and society at large billions of dollars. Most often they commit unpaid time to a religious organization, an educational or youth services organization, or a social or community service organization (in that order). Women volunteer at a higher rate than men across all age groups and educational levels. Individuals with a bachelor's degree or higher level of education engage in volunteer activities at higher rates than those with less education, and adults with higher educational attainment are more likely to donate their time to multiple organizations. Just over one out of every four *employed* persons (27.5 percent) is a volunteer, with part-time jobholders edging ahead of full-time jobholders. Older adults donate more hours than younger volunteers. Nonetheless, the volunteer rate tapers off as age increases: the rate for those forty-five to fifty-four years of age is 28 percent, for those fifty-five to sixty-four it is 25.1 percent, and for those sixty-five and older it is 23.5 percent.[1]

Consistent with Bureau of Labor Statistics data, the women who responded to my survey are volunteering at a higher rate than the men, actually at a much higher rate—71 percent of the women compared to 59 percent of the men. When the genders are combined, fully two-thirds of all my respondents are volunteering in addition to working full-time or part-time. They are most often engaged in some type of community service, donating time to a religious institution, doing political work, coaching, fundraising, and babysitting. Babysitting by grandparents who are also working, which can be very enjoyable but also very tiring, differs from the even weightier responsibility of caring for or helping to raise grandchildren while in the labor force. Roughly one-third of the 915,000 grandparents ages sixty and older who were caring for grandchildren were also employed as of 2010, according to the Population Reference Bureau.[2]

Quite a few women and men serve on the boards of non-profit organizations or professional associations, such as an Aspergers/Autism Network, the Lighthouse Guild, the Commission on Aging, and a math teachers association. There is a hospice volunteer who makes pet visits, a person serving meals at a homeless shelter, and a secretary for a local theater group. A psychiatrist in his eighties and working part-time performs evaluations of asylum seekers who are victims of torture and abuse. There are lawyers performing pro bono legal work and at least one lawyer (the fellow mentioned in the previous chapter) who finds time for protesting the Trump regime. One woman's cause is a community garden, another is president of a food pantry, another is an Audubon sanctuary volunteer, and several are mentors to high school students and college students. A full-time journalist in New York City volunteers in the "Girls Write Now" program. A full-time director of a non-profit organization finds the time to lead a college mentoring program pairing thirty-six mentors with an equal number of young women who are business majors, many of them immigrants and the first generation in their families to attend college. (This is similar to the type of volunteer work that motivates Jim Barrows, as the profile in chapter 5 explains.)

⌖

PROFILE: DR. DAVID W. ELLIS, INVESTMENT DISPUTE ARBITRATOR AND BOARD MEMBER

Board service suits eighty-two-year-old Dr. David Ellis of New Hampshire, who is unusually good at fixing institutions, such as museums, science centers, libraries, and colleges and universities. (He also likes to rebuild things like old cars and the vintage steam-powered vehicle that once climbed Mt. Washington.) He draws on his extensive experience in organizational management when serving on boards and when he is asked to consult pro bono with the boards of non-profit institutions that are struggling with strategy, governance, and advancement issues. It helps that he has a science background and first-hand knowledge of higher education administration, having served as the president of Lafayette College in Easton, Pennsylvania, and of Boston's Museum of Science (MOS), to name just a few of his top-level appointments. Although most of his time is donated these days, Dr. Ellis is paid to arbitrate investment disputes for the Financial Industry Regulatory Authority, the regulatory body that governs business dealings between securities firms, brokers, and public investors. The profile that follows describes his volunteer work and the high points of his long and very interesting career.

David Ellis likes a lot of balls in the air at once. He continues to work at age eighty-two because he likes work, being with people, solving problems, meeting challenges, and contributing to the common good. He devotes considerable time pro bono as a consultant to museums, science centers, libraries, institutions of higher education, and other non-profits, and as a board member for non-profit organizations of various types. He can offer his expertise to an outgoing president thinking about next career opportunities or can guide an institution that needs an interim president. Consulting pro bono for the Executive Service Corps of Northern New England is one example. Similarly, he helps a number of non-profit boards with strategy, governance, and advancement issues (e.g., the Forsyth Institute, the Bigelow Laboratory for Ocean Sciences, and the Conservation Law Foundation). A rather exotic endeavor was consulting with the Chilean Navy and the Chilean office of the David Rockefeller Center for Latin American Studies on a proposed museum gallery in Valparaiso and a proposed satellite museum in Antarctica. (The project is on hold owing to a precipitous drop in the price of copper, which is a significant part of the Chilean economy, and to a question of the location due to potential sea-level rise.) He also arbitrates disputes for the Financial Industry Regulatory Authority (FINRA), for which he is paid.

David was brought up around colleges and college presidents, having both his grandfather and his father as role models. Charles Calvert Ellis was the sixth president (1930–1943) and Calvert N. Ellis was the seventh president (1943–1968) of Juniata College, a private liberal arts institution in rural Huntington, Pennsylvania. Juniata was founded by the Church of the Brethren, a Christian community that was established more than three hundred years ago in Germany and is known for its pacifist beliefs. Both his father and grandfather served as Moderator of the Church.

Aside from his father's church duties there were often houseguests, sometimes generals and senators, who came to discuss issues of higher education or religion. Having grown up among pacifists, David faced his "hardest decision": whether to register for the draft as a conscientious objector. He had admired the "seagoing cowboys" (Mennonites, Quakers, and Church of the Brethren members) who after alternative service during World War II had escorted shipments of livestock to ravaged European countries. The cowboys' work endured and is known as the Heifer Project today. Years later he was delighted to meet a "cowboy," Owen Gingerich, who went on to a career as professor of astronomy and the history of science at Harvard and who remains a good friend. "I love people who do different things," David says.

David was drawn to science, in contrast to his father and grandfather who were humanists, partly by experiences in 4-H and from working on a family farm, and partly due to science courses, particularly a course in physical geography taken while at Governor Dummer Academy. He earned his bachelor's degree in chemistry with honors from Haverford College in 1958, along the way getting a taste of research during a summer job at Sunoco. A summer job at DuPont, a stint as a teaching assistant, and a doctorate in chemistry (spectroscopy) in 1962 from the Massachusetts Institute of Technology followed. He enjoyed research and teaching, so accepting a faculty position at the University of New Hampshire (UNH) seemed a logical and timely move. However, after several years he gradually shifted into administrative roles, capped by serving as UNH's chief academic officer for seven years. David points out that chemistry provides a "fabulous background" for going into administration because it teaches the skills of analysis and synthesis. In 1978, his final year at UNH, he represented chief academic officers of institutions in the National Association of State Universities and Land Grant Colleges on its executive committee. He was "among the 'big boys,' meeting some amazing people, having a wonderful experience."

As a person who was "always looking ahead, not to the past" David knew he was ready for the presidency offered in 1978 by Lafayette College. He held the top job there for twelve successful years, raising millions of dollars, including two gifts of ten million dollars apiece. Nonetheless, not only was it time for new challenges, but also David had never been completely comfortable with Lafayette's emphasis on the fraternity system and the college's insistence on competing in Division I athletics with too small a student population. (Lafayette alumni, who recalled the college's success as a football powerhouse in the 1930s, stubbornly insisted on playing in Division I.)

While at Lafayette, David had become the voice of independent colleges and universities in Washington, DC, on behalf of student aid through the National Association of Independent Colleges and Universities, where he served on the board and later as chair. He discovered that he enjoyed lobbying and testifying before legislative committees. Reflecting on how much he believed in making the case for student aid, he told this interviewer about the special satisfaction he took in challenging a congressional naysayer who claimed that college tuition was rising because of student aid and the G.I. Bill—arguments David could easily refute, armed as he was with knowledge of the origins of the G.I. Bill. His father had served on the advisory committee to the House Committee on Education and Labor, which had developed the G.I. Bill.

Throughout their New Hampshire years, in addition to caring for their three daughters, David's wife Marion Schmitt Ellis was highly involved in the local schools and New Hampshire issues, and she began to take courses at Andover-Newton Theological Seminary. After the move to Pennsylvania, she continued her studies, ultimately earning her master of divinity degree at Union Theological Seminary in New York City. That pilgrimage took her fourteen years and five seminaries.

In spring 1989, David spent a sabbatical from Lafayette in the Advanced Management Program at Harvard Business School, which allowed him to consider his next move.

> It wasn't that I was "itchy" to leave Lafayette, in fact I had a strong sense of responsibility to the institution, but after twelve years it was time for a change. I went through the Advanced Management Program for two reasons: considering whether to go into private business (I had an offer), and wanting a better understanding of the corporate world. Although I learned a lot from the program, it made me decide against pursuing a corporate position.

Accepting the presidency of Boston's Museum of Science in 1990 seemed a better fit given his background and skills. David and his family looked forward to putting down roots in the Boston area, where Marion had grown up and her father still lived. However, the first three years at the MOS were very difficult. He had taken over an institution that had quadrupled staff while only doubling attendance, was in the red, and was threatening to eat into its endowment. David had to lay off seventy-seven staff members, slash salaries and benefits for senior-level people, and cut travel. Once the museum's fiscal problems were resolved, David insisted on giving all staff the same bonus despite the objections of some MOS trustees. After those early trials, things ran relatively smoothly, including bringing current science and technology into the museum's exhibits and programs and merging the Computer Museum with the MOS. Emeritus status in 2003 concluded his last full-time job.

Major commitments since then have included one year as senior fellow at the Boston Foundation, extensive consulting in Brazil for the Vitae Foundation on the development of science centers, an interim presidency of the Boston Children's Museum for one and a half years, followed by a nearly two-year stint as interim executive director of Harvard's Museum of Natural History. David's paid work today is occasional consulting gigs and arbitrating disputes for FINRA, whose primary purpose is to protect investors by governing all business dealings conducted between securities dealers, brokers, and all public investors. (According to investopedia.com, FINRA is the single largest independent regulatory body for securities firms operating in the United States.) David first became involved in arbitration in the late 1980s when a Lafayette faculty member who had served on a national labor board invited him to sit in on some hearings, quizzed him about the cases, and invited him to state how he would have ruled. "Next thing I knew, I was on a panel for the American Arbitration Association!"

For relaxation, David and Marion go to their cabin on the Maine coast between Cutler and Lubec, the easternmost point in the United States, often sharing it with their daughters and their families. "It's *way* down east, where you cross to Campobello Island, New Brunswick. The cabin has no electricity and no telephone intentionally, which is fine with me." Another passion is old cars, such as his 1956 two-seater Ford Thunderbird. Then there was the "Locomobile," a steam-powered vehicle, which was similar to the self-propelled Stanley, the first vehicle to climb Mt. Washington, the highest peak in the northeastern United States. The vintage steam car was in pieces when David found it in old barns of his grandfather, and over thirteen years he rebuilt it, including building a new wood body. The car now resides in the museum at the foot of Mt. Washington's auto road.

Reminding me that he always tends to look to the future, David described the house he and Marion built in Newmarket, New Hampshire, which has become their principal home. It has geothermal heating, solar panels for standard electricity, wide doorways that can accommodate a wheelchair should one be needed, and is close to the homes of two of their daughters and their families and not far from the university in Durham. The couple recently signed with a company that provides caregiving services in one's home, should that ever become necessary. Marion compares it to an insurance policy—good to have as they look ahead. Their daughters are grateful.

∽⊗∼

PROFILE: JO-ANNE THOMPSON, TRANSPORTATION COMPANY OWNER

Like David Ellis, business owner Jo-Anne Thompson also devotes a considerable amount of time to board service. However, most of her volunteer work is centered on the public library system in Framingham, Massachusetts (her hometown), where she has been a library trustee for more than thirty years. As a director of the library foundation, she is currently spearheading efforts to raise funds for a "MakerSpace" within the main library. It will be a place filled with high-tech and low-tech equipment and tools with which young people and adult patrons can create, explore, invent, and learn. The MakerSpace initiative follows right on the heels of a successful fundraising project, also championed by Jo-Anne and her foundation co-directors, for the purchase of a new bookmobile for the library that brings library resources to homebound patrons, after-school programs, day care centers, and senior centers, among other sites. It was around the same time she was first elected to the library board that Jo-Anne officially joined the transportation company that her father had founded. Thirty-plus years later, owning and managing the company has become quite stressful as well as more time consuming, for intense competition from aggressive ride-sharing enterprises is testing her business acumen. Jo-Anne reflects on the decision to be an active volunteer in her community in addition to owning and operating a complex transportation business.

> Way back when, I responded to the idea that people should get involved in local government, so I served on the board of the Civic League—home base for civic, recreational, educational, and cultural projects—until it closed in 2011. And I was also elected to the library's board of trustees more than thirty years ago. Board service was very different then. Previous library directors always sat at the head of the conference table and ran the board meetings. Refreshingly, the current director chooses to sit at the foot of the table and the board chair conducts the meeting. Our current trustees make things happen!

Jo-Anne is right about that. She was board chair the year I joined the library board. We are both directors of the foundation that fundraises on behalf of the library. She somehow gets it all done despite being "tied to the transportation business since 1986." Now sixty-five years of age she would like to have more time to travel, see friends, and do more volunteer work. "I have a group of very close friends, half of whom have retired, and two are working part-time, and I am working full-time."

Jo-Anne has worked for forty-nine years overall, starting with her "first real job," which was in the Jordan Marsh Basement store at the former Shoppers World mall.

As owner of Tommy's Taxi, Inc., she manages about fifty employees at any one time.[3] The company operates out of a two-story, red brick and yellow cinderblock building; multiple garage service bays are downstairs, and offices are upstairs. Parked outside is a fleet of yellow taxis with red roofs. The right front fender of each vehicle says "Driven By Excellence." The right rear of each vehicle says "Package Delivery" and "24/7 Airport Service."

Jo-Anne's dad, John "Tommy" Thompson, started the taxi service in 1946 after returning from the war. He drove servicemen undergoing rehabilitation at Cushing Hospital to downtown Framingham in his 1939 Oldsmobile. He always hoped Jo-Anne would go into the business, but her mother wanted Jo-Anne to become a teacher. With a bachelor's degree in English from Skidmore College followed by a master's degree in education from Framingham State College, Jo-Anne did teach high school English for six years. In the early 1980s she took a brief detour by becoming a tech writer and copywriter at Data General, one of the mini-computer companies. However, by the mid-1980s personal computers were emerging, putting big companies like Data General out of business. Jo-Anne anticipated a layoff and decided it was time to join the family business officially. When her dad started talking about computerizing his taxi business, Jo-Anne purchased a computer, printer, and software package and taught herself accounting. "I grew up in the business and knew everyone. I was always involved, working nights and weekends with my dad."

Jo-Anne speaks highly of her co-workers and her customers. She has an easy-going, friendly personality and the gift of making people comfortable around her. The door to her office stood open the whole time I was interviewing her. Several people—drivers and friends—stopped by to ask questions, discuss a problem fare or a great fare, or relate a funny story. She knows every one of her drivers.

A major source of stress comes from ride-share companies encroaching on traditional taxi businesses.

This is a very difficult time in the transportation industry. At meetings of the Taxicab, Limousine and Paratransit Association (TLPA), the talk is "all Uber" all the time. Uber spends millions on lobbying. Competition from ride-shares makes our demand unpredictable. It is hard to retain taxi drivers whose earnings keep dropping. Our drivers are employees, not independent contractors.

That means the company provides the vehicle, fuel, insurance, and employee benefits. In contrast, ride-share drivers are independent contractors who have to pay out of pocket for their fuel, vehicle maintenance, insurance, and so on. Furthermore, ride-share companies do not properly vet their drivers: there is little supervision and little accountability regarding the condition of vehicles. A driver just needs a license and proof of insurance, but there is no guarantee that the person who actually operates the vehicle is the legal driver.

Jo-Anne says congestion is increasing in big cities because ride-share vehicles are cruising around waiting for a call. San Francisco is one example: there are many thousands of ride-share vehicles on the narrow streets, compared with 1,530 medallion (licensed) taxicabs.

I asked Jo-Anne whether she had experienced gender discrimination in the industry, which is predominantly controlled by males. She nods,

At first when I accompanied my dad to industry-wide TLPA meetings, association officials assumed I would be going on the "spouse tour" while the men attended the "real" meetings. Things have changed a lot since then. In addition to Tommy's Taxi, there are at least two other Massachusetts companies (in Somerville and Worcester) headed by women. We have had female presidents of the association. There is a committee called "Women in Transportation" that welcomes new members and steers them to people who can be helpful. I chaired the committee for several years. . . . When the committee is no longer needed—that is, when the number of TLPA board seats held by women is proportional to their representation among owners—that will spell success.

Jo-Anne is not ready to retire. She says she loves her work most of the time, although she cannot travel as often as she would like. "We provide excellent service. We keep our loyal customers. Still, I would like to be in a better place industry-wise." She wants to "ride out the Uber challenge," to see where it goes. "I don't really *get* retirement. How can I give up my work? I'm proud of the company. If we make a mistake, we fix it. I get validation from my work. How do you close the door on that? A person should retire *to* something, not just *from* something."

It is often said that civic engagement and purposefulness benefit those who generously give of their time and talents as much as they help those who are the intended beneficiaries of a social service program. David Ellis, Jo-Anne Thompson, and untold others would agree, as do researchers who study productive engagement. In their American Academy of Social Work and Social Welfare working paper on "Increasing Productive Engagement in Later Life," Nancy Morrow-Howell and colleagues cite the many benefits to individuals who choose productive engagement in later life: maintaining economic security, social ties, and health, as well as sense of meaning, purpose, and value. The paper's authors call out ageist attitudes and outdated social structures that limit participation of older adults in important social roles, including employment:

> To meet the grand challenge of increasing the productive engagement of older adults while maximizing outcomes for society and for older adults themselves, we must improve work environments and employment policies to enable people to work longer, such as strengthening policies to combat age discrimination; restructure educational institutions so individuals can develop new knowledge and skills across the life course; enable older adults to more fully engage in volunteer work and help organizations more fully recognize this talent pool; and support caregiving and other forms of care work in later life to facilitate involvement and reduce negative effects from stress associated with these roles.[4]

Whether it takes the form of paid employment, volunteering, or caregiving, productive engagement can meet many of the social and economic needs associated with population aging, provided that older adults are viewed as a *resource* rather than as a problem. Citing Robert N. Butler on living and contributing longer, Morrow-Howell and colleagues conclude that "society cannot afford to dismiss the human capital of the older population; older adults' productive engagement is a *necessity*, not a luxury."[5]

The Encore movement emphasizes both civic engagement and purposefulness. Operating "at the intersection of passion, purpose, and paycheck," Encore.org grew out of Civic Ventures, the project Marc Freedman founded twenty years ago to encourage retirees to redirect their "prime time" to civic engagement and volunteering. Although his original goal was to get seniors to "swap income for impact" when putting their life experience to good use, retirees' obvious need for income led Freedman to expand his definition of an "encore career" to include potential remuneration as well as personal meaning and social impact. With Dr. Linda P. Fried (currently dean of Columbia

University's Mailman School of Public Health), Freedman conceived of and piloted Experience Corps, a tutoring and mentoring program for seniors (aged fifty and up) that helps students in high-need elementary schools improve their reading literacy skills. Since AARP adopted the program in 2011, Experience Corps has flourished: each year nearly two thousand highly trained volunteers help some thirty thousand youngsters in more than twenty cities boost their literacy skills and their confidence. In 2005, Freedman also founded the Purpose Prize, a sixty thousand dollar award for social innovators aged fifty and over who are using their life experience to make a difference. Now under AARP auspices, the Purpose Prize helps five winners each year "celebrate their achievements and broaden the scope of their work." Three of the 2018 Purpose Prize winners are leading these programs:

- The New American Leaders Project, in which first- and second-generation Americans are trained to run for political office
- Today's Students Tomorrow's Teachers, in which participants mentor culturally diverse and economically disadvantaged high school and college students and help prepare them to become teachers, and
- Access Ability Wisconsin, which provides outdoor adaptive equipment, like an all-terrain wheelchair, to people with physical disabilities.

The Encore Fellowship program is an initiative of Encore.org that helps skilled, seasoned professionals who have retired from a career job transition to "what's next" by arranging a one-year paid placement with a non-profit social purpose organization. Robert Roy, a social worker with a long career as chief executive officer of a residential treatment center for troubled children in the Pacific Northwest, tried consulting and creative writing for a few years after he retired at age sixty-nine. He was anxious to "reinvent himself with a renewed sense of purpose." He eventually found it by becoming an Encore Fellow in 2015 at the Virginia Garcia Memorial Health Center in Hillsboro, Oregon. Roy's non-profit work background made adjusting to his new environment easy, and he was able to help build organizational capacity by coaching the health center's other Encore Fellows, who came from the for-profit business sector and were unfamiliar with agency work. Roy aced his primary assignment to assess and make recommendations for management and oversight of the center's behavioral mental health services program, and when his fellowship year ended he was employed as a consultant to give support and mentoring to the first manager hired to oversee that very program. A little over a year later, the health center made him the part-time coordinator of incoming Encore Fellows. (Nationwide, about one-third of Encore Fellows remain associated with their host organization, as Robert Roy has done; another third find work elsewhere in the social sector.) "My Encore Journey continues on!" Roy enthuses. "At age seventy-nine I look forward to the future!"[6]

As mentioned in chapter 3, Marc Freedman's new book, *How to Live Forever—The Enduring Power of Connecting the Generations*, encourages purposeful engagement through *generativity*. In addition to leading Encore .org, Freedman is an advisor to Generations United, a network of member organizations, partners, and stakeholders working "to improve the lives of children, youth, and older people through intergenerational collaboration, public policies, and programs for the enduring benefit of all."[7] As indicated by the unambiguous title of its latest report, "I Need You, You Need Me: The Young, The Old, and What We Can Achieve Together," Generations United seeks to eliminate age segregation and its negative effects. What Freedman calls "age apartheid" is most evident in retirement communities, senior centers, nursing homes, and higher education. Sharing the Generations United philosophy, Encore.org recently initiated the Generation to Generation (Gen-2Gen) program to help America's youth-serving organizations and communities tap experienced volunteers and make the best use of their talents. The ambitious campaign aims to mobilize one million adults aged fifty and older "to stand up for and with young people today" and "to realize the potential of longer lives, the potential of every child, and the power of older and younger generations working side by side for change."

PROFILE: DOUG DICKSON, ENCORE.ORG REGIONAL NETWORK DIRECTOR

Marc Freedman in California and Doug Dickson in Massachusetts are kindred spirits. After a long career in a corporate setting, Doug became acquainted with Freedman and his ideas about retirees' "second acts for the greater good" when he was working in a firm that assisted older men and women making work and life transitions. Doug became active in the national encore movement and soon co-founded a regional network to support older adults eager to offer their time and expertise for pay or as a donation to non-profit organizations in the Greater Boston area. Doug talks the talk *and* walks the walk. Now seventy-one, Doug has always been attracted to ideas on the frontier, particularly those involving change. He began studying biology at Eastern Nazarene College in Quincy, Massachusetts, but was drawn to cultural anthropology because it revealed the enormous variations in societal norms adopted by people in different places and times. This reinforced the notion that change is both normal and possible.

Upon graduation in 1968, Doug landed "more or less by default" in the business world during a time of political and social upheaval. Having been deferred by his local draft board, he went to work for the health insurance giant Blue Cross Blue Shield. Medicare had been signed into law in 1965 by President Lyndon B. Johnson, and as the local administrator, Blue Cross Blue Shield was adjusting to its expanded role. "I came along at an opportune time," he explains. "The company offered me a role that took advantage of my interest, honed by my study of anthropology, in looking at the organization as a system. My job was to piece together performance across the entire organization, then to identify how to make improvements. It turned out to be total quality management before we knew enough to call it that."

The work focused on business processes, but when Doug became consumer ombudsman, he applied this approach to issues and policies affecting the experience and best interests of customers. One outcome of this work was a number of changes in consumer communications and Doug's becoming head of corporate communications to focus on how the business connected to all of its principal audiences. After twenty-five years of making changes in the company, Doug learned that an organizational shift would change the job he was doing and that he could take another job or leave with severance pay. At age forty-eight, he decided to leave.

Doug became a client of New Directions, an executive outplacement firm in Boston. David Corbett, New Direction's founder, was wrestling with the challenge of helping older clients, mainly business leaders and professionals, plan ahead for their retirement years. Doug's interest was piqued by the possibilities. Clients were not interested in traditional retirements and those that did try that approach often returned looking for alternatives. When Doug was given an opportunity to join the firm to assist clients with their work and life transitions, he collaborated with David Corbett on a concept called Life Portfolio. This idea helped clients view their current and future lives as a series of options that needed to be considered and brought into balance, much as one would manage a financial portfolio. It became the basis for a New Directions curriculum and a book titled *Portfolio Life: The New Path to Work, Purpose, and Passion After 50*, written by David Corbett.

In helping to develop Life Portfolio, Doug became aware of Marc Freedman, co-founder of Experience Corps, then founder of Civic Ventures, now doing business as Encore.org. Marc had just released a book titled *Prime Time: How Baby Boomers Will Revolutionize Retirement and Transform America.* The premise of the book was that longevity and demographic shifts were setting the stage for a new kind of retirement characterized by social purpose—second acts for the greater good. Freedman quotes John F. Kennedy to make his point: "America's wasting resources of incalculable value," and invokes a Robert F. Kennedy expression to hammer it home: "Older Americans don't want to go to the seashore." Programs such as SCORE, Executive Service Corps, Foster Grandparents, and Big Brothers Big Sisters demonstrated how to keep retirees from feeling useless and bored. Now Encore.org was hoping to release their potential for social innovation by operating "at the intersection of passion, purpose, and a paycheck."

While this seemed a rather ambitious goal, it was validated by Doug's experience working with New Directions clients, who were taking their skills, relationships, and experience into entrepreneurial ventures, non-profit leadership, and government service. In 2001, Freedman organized a day-long conference of community leaders in Boston to explore ways to spread the encore idea across the region. Three initiatives emerged from this convening. A group of life coaches, career counselors, and other practitioners, led by Meg Newhouse, formed what became known as the Life Planning Network, a "community of professionals dedicated to helping people redesign and navigate the second half of life." Another group, led by Carol Greenfield, created Discovering What's Next to engage older adults around the idea of "revitalizing retirement." A third group (which failed to gain traction at the time) focused on introducing the non-profit community to the potential for older adults to make significant contributions as both paid and unpaid workers. Sensing another frontier and an opportunity to use his own experience at New Directions to push the encore idea forward, Doug joined all three initiatives.

When Doug retired from New Directions in 2008, he devoted more time to the Life Planning Network and Discovering What's Next, taking leadership roles in each. "The need presented itself and I was available to help out," he says. In 2010, he co-founded the national Encore Network with Nancy Peterson of Encore.org, bringing together the leaders of organizations similar to those in Boston that were emerging in other parts of the country. "We could see there was little connection among the disparate efforts and that we could all benefit enormously by pulling together." Another leading-edge idea was born and, under the guidance of Betsy Werley, the initial group of fourteen has now grown to more than one hundred.

In 2012, another realization led to formation of the Encore Boston Network: if a national network could create collective benefit, why not a regional one? With a group of local encore leaders, Doug co-founded a cross-sector, multi-stakeholder network consisting of organizations (non-profits, government agencies, and mission-driven businesses) and professionals of various sorts (academics, coaches, and advocates who work with and for adults who are fifty and older). According to Doug, what attracts them is the idea of learning from one another, speaking with a single voice on key issues, and doing things collectively that one organization cannot do on its own. "We have taken Marc Freedman's basic concept—engaging older adults to contribute their experience in meaningful ways—and applied it in local communities at the level where people actually live and work."

Some older adults do social purpose work for pay; others donate their time and expertise. Mature Caregivers, for example, trains older adults to provide in-home care to dementia patients for pay in communities across the country. SeniorsHelpingSeniors offers a similar service. ReServe matches people over fifty years of age with non-profits and government agencies to perform a variety of roles for below-market wages. But many organizations offer volunteer opportunities ranging from direct service to clients to office tasks and projects. Big Brothers Big Sisters, for example, matches adults with young people in long-term mentoring relationships. School-based programs, like Generations Incorporated and Jumpstart, offer semester-long or school-year opportunities. And some programs have options for short commitments, like judges for Generation Citizen's two Civics Days each year.

Doug is encouraged by the receptivity to these ideas by non-profit leaders today compared to ten or fifteen years ago. "In a full-employment economy," Doug points out, "the need for older adults performing this valuable work becomes even more urgent. Organizations are more open to embracing a human capital model that favors stable, mature recruits who will stay five years or longer." The key, Doug says, "is to prepare organizations to manage a multi-generational workforce. You can't just drop people into organizations that lack experience in engaging and supporting people over the age of fifty. Those people may get disillusioned and drop out. We help organizations structure appropriate roles, develop pertinent policies and practices, and create a culture that is attractive to older adults." Through the Gen2Gen campaign, Encore Boston Network and Encore.org are developing tools, best practices, workshops, and other opportunities to assist organizations in making this transition. The goal of Gen2Gen is to mobilize people over age fifty to mentor young people, help them thrive, and unite all ages to create a better future.

Doug recognizes that encore opportunities are not for everyone. "Adults fifty-plus have a broad range of needs—financial, emotional, intellectual—and preferences for meeting those needs vary widely. Leisure has its place, and we have to be careful about generalizing in a way that makes people feel they're being judged or excluded," he cautions. He has also heard Encore described as targeting elites who have time on their hands. In fact, people with time and financial security often have the ability to be early adopters. But the need for older adults to contribute exists in every community, and this is especially true when language, cultural sensitivity, and local knowledge are important considerations. "The bottom line is making participation a meaningful experience for everyone who chooses to be engaged in this work."

In addition to his work as part of the encore movement, Doug has led a number of environmental initiatives in his hometown of Newton, Massachusetts, and has served on a variety of boards. He also writes on a regular basis, editing the Encore Boston Network newsletter and contributing to books, guides, and other publications. "It's nice to know that other people can benefit from my experience and, perhaps, connect to new ideas through these channels," he says.

Doug and his wife, Sharon, enjoy gardening and music, among other pursuits. "Both are relaxing and therapeutic," he says. He also delights in spending time with his granddaughter and his two daughters and their husbands.

The Pathways to Encore Purpose Study recently set out to discover the extent to which older adults are actually being "purposeful beyond the self." A collaboration between the Stanford Graduate School of Education and Encore.org, the Pathways study comprised a nationally representative survey of nearly twelve hundred U.S. adults ranging in age from fifty to ninety and more than one hundred in-depth interviews. Researchers found "a big appetite among older adults for purposeful engagement." Nearly one-third were engaged in some form of volunteer work, even when they themselves were dealing with serious problems, and people of color were more apt to be living with purpose than whites.[8] Volunteering in itself only leads to well-being if the activity is purposeful, engaging, and accomplishes something, Stanford researcher Anne Colby notes. She and her colleagues found greater well-being among older adults whose efforts were *pro-social*, such as improving the lives of others or building a better community or teaching what they had learned to others, rather than doing something useful for themselves like augmenting their fiscal situation or pursuing sports and hobbies or continuing their education. ("Well-being" here means joy and satisfaction, not physical health, which was not measured in the Stanford-Encore.org study.[9])

In response to the growing demand for purposeful engagement in encore adulthood, the University of Minnesota has designed a "gap year" for experienced professionals seeking to transition from a career job into a new endeavor that will "leverage their talents for the common good." Senior fellows in the University of Minnesota Advanced Careers Initiative (UMAC) pay fifteen thousand dollars to participate in interdisciplinary courses along with undergraduate and graduate students exploring major societal problems. In the second semester UMAC adds a practicum in which each fellow works on a social impact project at a non-profit organization. By means of formal and informal programming, seminars and discussions, and intergenerational learning experiences, UMAC aims to deepen fellows' understanding of societal issues, both local and global, and enable them to "retool" for new careers and act on that understanding. The university's initiative is at the leading edge of a higher education movement offering seniors who are unwilling to be sidelined (and who can afford the tuition) a learning experience and a meaningful "second act."

Further commentary on the productive engagement of older adults identifies "cumulative disadvantage" stemming from health and economic disparities earlier in life as a barrier for some groups.[10] The idea of having an encore career with a social purpose has wide appeal, but participation in formal encore-type programs by low-skilled, less-educated older adults who need income, depend on benefits, and may also be in poor health is miniscule compared to the participation of their better educated and more affluent peers. (This issue is touched on in Doug Dickson's profile, described previously.) Black and Hispanic older adult volunteers, primarily women, are more likely to have family caregiving responsibilities in addition to or instead of paid work. The National Alliance for Caregiving and AARP estimate that 65.7 million Americans, mostly women, provide unpaid care. Of that total, approximately 13 percent are caregivers aged sixty-five and older. And longer lifespans will only increase the demand.[11]

Offering a different spin on the importance of engagement, continued learning and social connection in the senior years, the Pass It On Network (PION; introduced in chapter 7) is a global peer learning network encouraging aging advocates to learn from one another and spread innovations that support positive and productive aging, including working in the later years. Co-founder Jan Hively, an Encore Entrepreneur and Purpose Prize Fellow, is PION's U.S. liaison. In the years since earning her doctorate at age sixty-nine with a dissertation on "Productive Aging in Rural Communities," Jan has championed older men and women benefiting themselves and their communities by doing meaningful work for pay or on a volunteer basis. Her mantra is "Being is meaningful work." PION co-founder Moira Allan is the Paris liaison and leader of 2Young2Retire Europe and Le Cercle des Seniors Actifs. PION has liaisons in more than fifty countries across five continents. Through shared learning, they "expand the power of older adults to build on their strengths and interests to help themselves, their families, and their communities." Liaisons from Canadian provinces, for example, are developing cross-Canada teamwork to facilitate learning from one another. And South Africa's liaison, Lynda Smith, lets PION colleagues in other countries know how membership is building in 50Plus-Skills, an online skills portal connecting individuals who are over the age of fifty and who have expertise and experience with employers who need their skills, time, and services. Smith, who believes in "refiring" rather than retiring, created 50Plus-Skills to promote "serving, learning, and earning." Workshops and coaching will enable employees within five years of retirement to be better prepared for what comes next. Whether working longer for money, personal meaning, or both, they will lend age diversity to the workplace and benefit economic growth in South Africa.

PION is constantly growing its roster of liaisons and developing links to myriad active aging-focused organizations dedicated to "helping people stay in charge of their own lives for as long as possible as they age and, where possible, to contribute to the economy and society." For example, the European Commission is trumpeting the return of older workers to the labor market following the economic downturn of 2008 that led to job losses and unemployment. The rapid rise in participation of mature workers is offsetting a decrease in the pool of younger workers and the stagnant labor force activity rate of the prime age working population. Another multi-nation group, the Active Aging Consortium Asia Pacific, promotes learning from positive aging approaches. Under the motto "We engage, We create, We share," a January 2018 Active Aging Consortium Asia Pacific conference featured five symposia: active aging, aging in place, intergenerational issues, innovative technology, and health. In August of the same year, the International Federation on Ageing convened its fourteenth global conference in Toronto to plan action steps toward healthy aging (as discussed in chapter 7). Much of this activity has its origins in a proliferation of movements advocating life planning, sageing, healthy aging, re-firing, re-wiring, conscious elderhood, positive aging (and the like) when approaching and reaching one's second act, prime time, bonus years, next stage, and third age (or fourth, for the oldest old).

Roger Hull explains how he is using his bonus years:

Since I was lucky enough to have a career that covered law, appointive politics, diplomatic work, and education (including the presidencies of Beloit College in Wisconsin and Union College in New York for a total of twenty-four years), it may seem hyperbolic to say that what I am doing now in my mid-seventies is more meaningful. But it is.

I created and now run three nonprofits. One, Avon Associates, consists of a group of former college presidents and vice presidents who consult with distressed colleges at no cost. A second, the Help Yourself Foundation, now in its thirteenth syear, provides after-school STEM education on college campuses to at-risk grade-school children. And the third, the Schenectady-WIN Foundation (which just merged with Help Yourself to form the Help Yourself Win Foundation) is a program for under-employed adults that provides them, over the course of twelve to eighteen months, with a high school degree, life skills, construction training, and, at the end of the process, a job.

While I very much enjoyed my paid positions, I find my volunteer work now is truly more meaningful. As both the Talmud and Koran state: If one saves a life, one saves the world. Through these tiny efforts, I think we may save lives.

Carolyn Bruse explains how she is using her bonus years:

Like many women of my generation, my working life took many twists and turns. I worked as the record librarian for the Duke Music Department before my son was born, ran a daycare center for a while, and taught music in a Montessori pre-school when he was a toddler, then returned to graduate school at Brandeis University when he went to kindergarten. About four years into grad school, my marriage broke up, and I worked as an administrative assistant to a sociologist while I lingered over my Ph.D. in music theory and composition. When I finished it, I realized I didn't really like teaching and I was on the brink of running out of money—a very scary time in my life! I did some soul-searching and analysis of my strengths as well as an assessment of the kinds of things I like to do, and put together a résumé hoping to find a job in the growing high tech world. In what seemed like a fluke, I did get a job as a "product designer" (which meant I wrote all the guides and did all the testing of the product). After four years in that job, I moved to a larger (and friendlier) company as a tech writer. Several years later, I became a manager and continued in that role after our company was acquired by Oracle. I enjoyed the work, I enjoyed knowing about technical stuff, and I enjoyed managing. However, Oracle eventually made adverse changes to the way documentation was delivered and to the organizational structure of documentation groups. When I was reassigned to a manager whom I found problematic, I retired as soon as I could. That was eighteen months before I was eligible for Medicare (COBRA provides health insurance, albeit expensive, for eighteen months after you leave a job). During my last few years at Oracle, I was also caring for my mother, which was very difficult, but also very rewarding.

I didn't really agonize at all about what to do in my retirement, having never been so absorbed in my work that I was concerned about losing it. In fact, I was delighted to escape! A friend warned me not to commit to anything in the first year, but unfortunately, she didn't mention that until *after* I'd agreed to be the chair of the music committee at my church. It turned out to be far too much like my old job, so I resigned toward the end of the year, explaining that I was apparently still burned out from my job. Since then, I've tried to avoid agreeing to do managerial work, with limited success.

Instead, I decided to follow up on a much earlier wish (from back in high school, in fact) to play an orchestral instrument. I play the piano, the guitar, and the recorder, and I did a lot of singing of various kinds over the years, but I'd never played an orchestral instrument. After thinking about it quite a bit, I settled on the oboe. I wanted to be able to play in any orchestra, including ones from the Baroque era. That meant choosing an instrument in the string family, which I thought would be too difficult, or the oboe. Little did I know how difficult the oboe is! Serendipitously, I mentioned my interest in playing the oboe to a friend at church, who said she knew a great oboe teacher. I called her the next day and have been taking lessons ever since. We've become good friends too, which is a nice bonus.

After about a year, I managed to join a concert band, although I was still pretty bad as a player! That was ten years ago, and I'm continuing to improve. I recently indulged myself by buying an English Horn (basically an alto oboe). I've gotten involved in a number of music organizations: the Lexington Music Club (I'm on the board), the Concord Band (I help with mundane tasks but steadfastly refuse to be on the board), the Lincoln-Sudbury Civic Orchestra, the Harvard Music Association (a reading orchestra), and the Appalachian Mountain Club's Mountains and Music Committee (I'm co-chair and really wish I wasn't!). I'm also part of a woodwind quintet and have participated in the Buffalo Philharmonic Fantasy Camp, the John Mack Oboe Camp, and several double-reed days at the New England Conservatory, University of Massachusetts, Amherst, and University of New Hampshire. I try (and mostly fail) to practice an hour a day. Having music at the center of my life in my mid-seventies feels right and picks up the thread of who I was as a child and teenager.

Of course, music isn't the only thing in my life. I've also developed an interest in birding, and I've always loved outdoor activities like hiking, snowshoeing, biking, and kayaking, activities I indulge in mostly when I'm on vacation. I also read a lot, both for my book group (novels) and just because (mostly history, sociology, and science). I have four grandchildren, who live in New Hampshire and are all extremely busy. I'd love to see more of them, as I did when they were little, but it's a huge pleasure to spend what time with them is available. I just returned from a trip to New Zealand with my oldest granddaughter who is twenty-one. We hiked, biked, kayaked, and swam with dolphins and both of us had a fabulous time!

And here is Martin Zelnik's brief description of his "non-retired life" after retirement:

To be clear, my motivation for remaining active at age seventy-nine is unrelated to the need to generate income. I have a decent pension from the one job that I actually did retire from after thirty-plus years: professor of interior design at the Fashion Institute of Technology, State University of New York. I enjoy remaining in contact with my design students and colleagues, and, as I am considered one of the "founders" and authors of the interior design department's bachelor of fine arts program, I am still sought out for advice and consultation. (I miss the teaching and student contact but not the bureaucracy.) I also had an architectural and interior design practice for forty years with my late partner, Julius Panero, a colleague on the FIT interior design faculty. Together, we wrote three best-selling design books (reference books still in demand by architects, interior designers, space planners, builders, and construction managers), carried on an active practice, and ventured off into the world of real estate. We did well in all arenas.

I have been motivated, in part, by wanting to show my three sons that one can be productive and active post "retirement." One son is a third-generation architect, and we share an office and a practice. Perhaps the architectural umbilical cord should have been cut a long time ago, but two pairs of eyes and years of experience in architecture are better than one. (I had similar experiences with my dad.) A few years ago, I bought an 18-hole golf course in Florida for my youngest son. (I don't play golf!) He was a pro golfer and a pro caddie on the PGA tour, a tough and demanding career. Rather than wait to settle my estate, hopefully years from now, my son has the opportunity to manage, operate, and eventually own this course, which reassures me about his future.

With respect to my volunteer activities, I find myself motivated by the Hebrew expression "Tikkun Olam," a term referring to repairing the world, doing good for others, and the pursuit of social justice. I gain great satisfaction in volunteering constructively any way I can, particularly with causes related to low-income housing and helping the poor. While a grad student at Columbia University's School of Architecture, I spent three months studying low-income housing in Peru and working with members of the Peace Corps during my research. My late brother, Reggie, also influenced my need to volunteer and remain active. He was a political activist and professor of Russian history at the University of California, Berkeley, who risked his faculty position when he joined with Mario Savio and the Free Speech Movement in the 1960s. Volunteer work is also a form of "psychic income," if you will. Like the gratification that comes from helping and guiding my sons, I get satisfaction from serving as a director of the Bronx chapter of the American Institute of Architecture, the Brandeis University-based National Center for Jewish Film, and the Riverdale (NY) Community Coalition, a community-based organization that advocates for compatible land use and opposes inappropriate zoning changes often sought for by developers.

In addition to volunteering, older men and women engage in a wide variety of leisure-time pursuits as time permits. Table 8.1 presents the preferred leisure-time activities of my current survey respondents. Reading is clearly number one for both men and women. Two-thirds have fitness and exercise routines; however, as discussed in the section on health, more women are into fitness than men. Two-thirds also enjoy opportunities for traveling; again, women mention it more than men. Both genders say they spend time using the computer and doing internet searches, gardening, making and listening to music, and doing crossword puzzles. Sports, however, are a much bigger draw for the men than the women (nothing new to report there). Women appear to spend more time using social media and attending adult education classes (non-credit) than men do. Less than a quarter of the respondents checked other creative and cultural pursuits, such as writing and art projects. Dance is popular with fourteen respondents, all but two of whom are women. Only eight people are involved in a religious program, which is somewhat surprising for this older population—typically, people become more religious as they age—but it is consistent with national trends showing an exodus from organized religion. Three hardy souls are in advanced degree programs (for credit).

The different kinds of "other" leisure time activities reported by respondents generally conform to traditional feminine and masculine stereotypes. Many of the older women are socializing with friends and spending time

Table 8.1. Survey Respondents' Use of Leisure Time

Leisure Time Activities	Men	Women	Combo
Reading	81%	82%	82%
Fitness, exercise	58%	72%	65%
Travel	56%	73%	65%
Computer, internet	29%	34%	32%
Gardening	32%	32%	32%
Music	35%	23%	29%
Crossword puzzles	25%	33%	29%
Sports	41%	17%	27%
Adult learning class (non-credit)	11%	35%	24%
Writing	25%	21%	23%
Social media	8%	29%	20%
Art	11%	22%	17%

Note: n = 168. Activities are in rank order based on combining men's and women's responses. Respondents could check multiple leisure time activities and add others.

with family members. (No doubt lots of the older men also socialize and visit with family members, but they seem unwilling to say so on a survey!) Both the women and the men are well aware that working in the retirement years can put them out of sync with retired friends or a spouse or partner who has already stopped working. Seldom, however, do they say they will join the ranks of retirees just to be more available for lunch dates. Instead, they trot out the old saw: Together for richer or poorer, in sickness or in health, but not for lunch!

Some of the older women in my study are playing tennis, swimming, biking, hiking, kayaking, and pursuing other outdoor activities, whereas others are knitting, sewing, making handicrafts, doing interior decorating, scrapbooking, and quilting. One woman is creating and stylizing graphics and ad copy with Photoshop. (Right now, it is strictly for fun, she says; perhaps after gaining enough expertise, she will offer her services for a fee.) Cultural pursuits include going to the theater, museums, art galleries, symphony, ballet, and opera. They often watch films and television. A few enjoy cooking and entertaining or playing mahjong, canasta, bridge, or other card games. Two women practice meditation, and one relaxes by watching birds and the river flowing by in her back yard. An assortment of other activities includes playing the piano, participating in book groups, sorting and purging (part of downsizing?), genealogical research, and unspecified personal projects.

"I work twelve to fourteen hours a day and have almost no free time," grumbles a sixty-two-year-old research scientist. "I don't have a lot of leisure time!" cries a seventy-seven-year-old clinical social worker and marriage and family therapist. "I am a bit of a misfit in some ways, being an older woman who is actively employed. Most people are well retired by my age; however, I would not give up what I do for anything! I am being paid for my experience and my expertise, and I have kept up both electronically and with current advances in the field."

"I am fortunate that attending press briefings at several museums and opening night at several theaters is part of my work," says the seventy-six-year-old executive director of the Penn Quarter Neighborhood Association in Washington, DC, whose profile appears in chapter 2. She regularly goes to see plays, films, and the ballet, and does her best to find time to be with friends and family.

The "other" leisure time activities reported by older men in my study include woodworking (Steve Holmes' profile in chapter 5 mentions making reproductions of Shaker furniture), boatbuilding, playing in a poker game, reading newspapers, repairing computers for friends and neighbors, automobile maintenance, and following favorite sports teams. Outdoor pursuits popular with the older men are fishing and duck hunting (Dean Moore's profile in chapter 4 cites them as favorite pastimes), camping, skiing, sailing, playing golf, and boating, as well as vacationing at a camp on the Maine coast and going to the beach. As we saw in his profile in chapter 4, David Feldman has taken up triathlons in his senior years. Creative outlets mentioned by some include making videos, playing the violin, yoga, singing, attending concerts, and going to the movies. In addition to traveling, two men tell of spending time with their wives, another notes that he spends time with friends, and another is planning a wedding with his daughter who lives abroad. Doug Dickson, whose profile is earlier in this chapter, especially enjoys spending time with his granddaughter. Assorted other activities include walking the dog, unspecified community activities, and "B. S.-ing" about today's media and political issues.

NOTES

1. U.S. Bureau of Labor Statistics, "Volunteering in the United States," News Release. USDL-16-0363. Washington, DC: U.S. Department of Labor, February 25, 2016. Retrieved from: www.bls.gov/ops.

2. Scommegna, Paola, and Nadwa Mossaad. "The Health and Well-Being of Grandparents Caring for Grandchildren." *Today's Research on Aging*, no. 23. Population Reference Bureau. Washington, DC: December 2011.

3. See www.tommystaxicab.com.

4. Morrow-Howell, Nancy, et al. "Increasing Productive Engagement in Later Life." Grand Challenges for Social Work Initiative Working Paper No. 8. Cleveland, OH: American Academy of Social Work and Social Welfare, 2015, 4.

5. Ibid., 5.

6. See https://encore.org/efn-profile/robert-roy.

7. See www.gu.org.

8. Colby, Anne, and Jim Emerman. "Is a Purposeful Retirement Overrated?" *MarketWatch*, June 21, 2018. Retrieved from: https://www.marketwatch.com/story/is-a-purposeful-retirement-overrated-2018-06-21/print.

9. Suttie, Jill. "How to Find Your Purpose in Midlife." *Greater Good Magazine*. Greater Good Science Center, University of California, Berkeley, March 8, 2018. Retrieved from: https://greatergood.berkeley.edu/.../how_to_find_your_purpose_in_midlife.

10. Gonzales, Ernest, et al. "Increasing Opportunities for the Productive Engagement of Older Adults: A Response to Population Aging." *The Gerontologist*, Special Issue: 2015, WHCoA, 1–10. Retrieved from http://gerontologist.oxfordjournals.org.

11. Ibid., 3.

Men and Women Working Longer— Concluding Thoughts

CHAPTER OBJECTIVES

1. Recaps the major themes of *Aging, Work, and Retirement*
2. Sums up research findings about individual, organizational, and socio-economic perspectives on later-life participation in the labor force
3. Reviews extrinsic and intrinsic rewards, particularly job satisfaction and life satisfaction, associated with working longer

When my primary career ended ten years ago, I was not ready to retire and dreaded landing on the shelf, even temporarily. In fact, "Not (Yet) on the Shelf" was the working title of my first book about older workers choosing to stay on the job past conventional retirement age. The expression means counted out, canned or laid off, eliminated, discarded, bypassed, out of use, and (just as depressing) out of circulation. Equally bad are "over the hill" and being "put out to pasture," a saying that one online dictionary erroneously classifies as "humorous." No way is it humorous to make demonstrably capable individuals leave their jobs because they are considered to be too old. It is like being consigned to the scrapheap or given the heave-ho when thought to be no longer of use. Then there is "dinosaur," which is both self-explanatory and insulting.

As stated previously, functional age is the more relevant criterion than chronological age for the purpose of making employment decisions or with respect to the wisdom and practicality of decisions about health, housing, transportation, and any number of different contexts. The World Health Organization, for one, is making functional ability the metric for determining public health success. Healthy aging, says the World Health Organization, is "the process of developing and maintaining the functional ability that enables well-being in older age . . . the degree to which people can be or do what they value . . . determined by the intrinsic capacity of the individual, the physical and social environments he or she inhabits, and the interaction between the individual and these environmental characteristics." Better health plus greater longevity are helping to drive demographic and labor market shifts that operate in conjunction with broader socio-economic changes. Simply put, with aging increasing at an unprecedented rate in our country and globally, government policymakers realize that the labor force participation rate of older workers should rise significantly. (This will, in turn, provide much-needed contributions to our ailing Social Security System.) As a consequence, the employment picture for older workers has changed dramatically here and abroad since the 2008 recession.

The argument in favor of functional age as the more relevant criterion applies not only to macro-level social policymaking but also to micro-level workplace *hiring, training, performance, and retention decisions.* At the organizational level, *there is growing awareness that business leaders,* faced with looming labor shortages in many categories (particularly shortages of skilled knowledge workers), *can ill afford to ignore older workers and what they contribute on the job.* As stated in chapter 1, this thinking represents a noticeable turnaround for employers who have freely shed their older, experienced workers and now are beginning to realize how much they need them and their valuable store of institutional knowledge. The so-called Boomer brain drain is a big waste. Thus, whether in the for-profit or non-profit sector, there is much to be learned from *Aging, Work, and Retirement* and kindred studies. Hiring managers, trainers, performance evaluators, and organizational leaders (plus those studying how to manage people and organizations) would be wise to take note *and* take action.

On the individual level, there is growing awareness of the many intrinsic and extrinsic rewards that come with working in the retirement years. And, as we have seen, reaching retirement age no longer has to mean an abrupt and permanent end to one's primary career. Retirement can be a process, a transition, or even more than one transition. The terms phased retirement, bridge employment, and *un*retiring describe viable alternatives to the "cold turkey" exit experience. Paid work, volunteer jobs, and so-called encore careers all allow older men and women to remain engaged, productive, and purposeful whether they are working full-time or part-time, for themselves or for an employer, in a brand new field or on a well-trodden career path. By recounting compelling stories of individuals who are choosing to work past conventional retirement age and focusing on what that decision means to them, this volume highlights their accomplishments and gives voice to the feelings of immense satisfaction they derive from their jobs. Under favorable working conditions with opportunities to learn, older professionals can experience a sense of personal efficacy and fulfillment. Yes, they appreciate the income and in many cases depend on it, but that is not what really motivates them to keep working. In sum, it does not seem to be too much of a stretch to assume a connection between their job satisfaction and their life satisfaction.

The following quote from George Bernard Shaw's 1905 play *Man and Superman* reinforces the point beautifully. (Allan Shedlin, whose profile appears in *Men Still at Work*, shared the quote with me.)

> This is the true joy in life, being used for a purpose recognized by yourself as a mighty one. Being a force of nature instead of a feverish, selfish little clod of ailments and grievances complaining that the world will not devote itself to making you happy. I am of the opinion that my life belongs to the whole community and as I live it is my privilege—my privilege—to do for it whatever I can. I want to be thoroughly used up when I die, for the harder I work the more I love. I rejoice in life for its own sake. Life is no brief candle to me; it is a sort of splendid torch which I've got a hold of for the moment and I want to make it burn as brightly as possible before handing it on to future generations.

Like the Shaw quote, each of the profiles in this volume illustrates one or more important aspect of working in the retirement years. Whereas each profile tells a special story of persistence and professional achievement, the one that follows is truly unique because its subject hits so many buttons. Early shaper of the field of gerontology—check. One of Next Avenue's "Top 50 Influencers in Aging" today—check. Nationally recognized speaker, author, syndicated columnist, and consultant to employers and employees on aging and retirement issues, including *work* as part of retirement—check. Co-founder of Project

Renewment discussion groups for career women exploring next steps—check. Staying informed, helping to create change, and learning all the while—check. Meet Helen Dennis.

c∞o

PROFILE: HELEN DENNIS, "INFLUENCER IN AGING," CONSULTANT, SPEAKER, AUTHOR, SYNDICATED COLUMNIST

How did Helen Dennis get to be one of Next Avenue's Top 50 Influencers in Aging?[1] The seventy-seven-year-old has always had exceptionally good timing, yet becoming a nationally recognized speaker, author, syndicated columnist, and consultant was hardly a simple or straightforward process. When Helen was a graduate student in clinical psychology at California State University, Long Beach, she needed to come up with a master's thesis topic. In the library she found a book on cognition and aging that piqued her interest. She wrote and defended her thesis on "Remotivation Therapy for Older Adults" in 1976, and, though she did not know it at the time, launched her career in the field of aging and retirement. Since the faculty at Long Beach lacked expertise in the field of aging at that time, she went to the newly established Davis School of Gerontology at the University of Southern California (USC)[2] to find a sympathetic ear. That was when James Birren, early researcher on aging, founding dean, and the "father" of modern gerontology, was dean of the school.

USC invited Helen to teach part of a course based on her thesis as a guest lecturer in the summer institute. The Andrus Gerontology Center subsequently hired her to direct two mental health grants, which led to her next major assignment: directing a USC centennial celebration on the theme of Work, Aging, and Retirement, a three-day event for a thousand participants. Helen was hooked on the subject. Her director then asked Helen to head up the area of retirement and retirement planning. She hesitated, telling him she had completed a lot of research and gone to retirement programs where everyone was saying the same thing and it seemed rather boring. Her director replied, "Then it's your job to make it less boring." That turned a switch for Helen. "As a girl raised in the 1950s I believed I had two choices if I didn't like something: be quiet or walk away quietly. This 'make it less boring' comment made me realize I could help create change if something was wrong or lacking."

Helen stayed at USC for about fifteen years, developing new courses in collaboration with business school faculty, such as Aging and Business and Aging and Marketing, and earning teaching excellence awards. "I began my career when the field was young and we were learning from one another. I am eternally grateful for the opportunity," she muses. When David Peterson, another leader in early gerontology at USC, invited Helen to teach a course with him on retirement planning, it was "a seminal experience to be learning from the best."

During this phase of her career, she was a corporate wife with two young children. Pursuing a doctoral degree, a tenure track position, or an administrative role was not what she wanted to do. She was very comfortable as a lecturer and project director. The next step was self-employment, which made the most sense; she became a consultant on retirement education in 1990. USC became a client as she continued teaching and took on clients from Fortune 500 companies, universities, and non-profit organizations.

Today, employers seek Helen's help with age issues in management, age discrimination, and strategies for engaging older workers in productive ways. Too often, however, she finds a wide gap between what corporate leaders say is important and what they actually do. Sessions for employees have also been in demand: she has assisted more than twenty thousand employees—corporate executives, factory workers, physicians, engineers, accountants, faculty, staff, and rabbis in all parts of the country—to prepare for the *non*-economic aspects of retirement. Her seminars on preparing for the next chapter of life address, for example, attitudes toward aging, slowing the aging process, preparing for an encore career, use of time, maintaining relationships, and end-of-life issues.

Writing became an obvious extension of her work. After editing two books, *Retirement Preparation* in 1984 and *Fourteen Steps in Managing an Aging Workforce* in 1988, she began a weekly syndicated column on "Successful Aging" that is published in ten southern California newspapers with a readership of 1.6 million, as well as online. To date she has written over eight hundred columns on an array of subjects. When venturing into less familiar territory she does her homework and checks with experts; she leaves medical and financial advice to other columnists.

Helen has been in demand as an expert witness in class action age discrimination cases, as well. "That work was another great learning experience," she declares. "I learned not to be intimidated under pressure while supporting a point of view—defending an opinion while saying as *little* as possible. Quite a challenge!"

Timing also played a role in the development of Project Renewment (a cross between retirement and renewal). In 1999, Bernice Bratter called Helen to inquire whether she knew of any research or program for a career woman like herself who was nearing retirement and wondering "what's next?" Helen and Bernice met for a four-hour lunch and shortly thereafter for a four-hour dinner with a group of like-minded women to identify issues and discuss ideas for forming what they decided to call "renewment" groups. According to Helen, "renewment is positive, suggesting rebirth, choices, vitality, opportunity, and personal growth. It implies that decisions about this new life stage can be intentional rather than defined by the needs and expectations of others. Since career women retiring today are the first and largest generation to define themselves by their work, there are few role models." Once Project Renewment was born at that initial dinner meeting, thirty-five to forty more groups have formed and grown virally, not only in this country but also abroad.[3] Helen defines Project Renewment as a mini-movement rather than a formal organization or a business; some groups come and go, discussion topics do the same. "Inadvertently we have developed many enduring communities of women across the country, some meeting for twenty years." A colleague has referred to renewment groups as "self-styled learning communities."

Wanting to share their experience and perspectives more widely, in 2008 Helen and Bernice co-authored *Project Renewment: The First Retirement Model for Career Women*, with the paperback edition published in 2013. It was an *L.A. Times* bestseller. In addition to essays, the book contains a guide and informal curriculum with tips on forming a group and examples of questions and answers that lead to rich discussions. Helen describes her modus operandi as Create and Release. Thus, with respect to Project Renewment: "We put it out there and just watch where it goes."

Public speaking engagements provide another avenue for disseminating information about the "new" retirement. Helen has given numerous keynote addresses for businesses, non-profit organizations, and retirement communities about the new life stage and trends in employment and retirement. She has always done a considerable amount of pro bono work, having served as president of five non-profits over the years. She currently is on the leadership team of three: the Village Movement, advocating aging in place and staying connected to community; Encore.org, offering new ways of giving back during post-retirement years; and the American Society on Aging (ASA), creating a Corps of Accomplished Professionals (CAPs), people who have had long-term involvement with the ASA. "My principal contribution to the CAPs (along with others) is suggesting ways to capture the talents of active *emeriti* who made their mark in the field and to create meaningful roles for them and ways to give back to the Association. CAPs keeps them connected to the ASA and to one another, thereby meeting both professional and personal needs. We've barely scratched the surface, yet I think the CAPs model could become a prototype for other organizations."

When Helen gets the inevitable question, "Are you *still* working?" she is apt to reply that she challenges conventional expectations and has no intention of retiring in the traditional manner because work is fundamental.

I love the challenge of writing my column every week. In order to help create change, one needs to be informed about what's happening in society. I'm learning all the time. Since I began thinking about and talking about aging forty-some years ago, it has invaded every aspect of American life—work, leisure, health, housing, and so on. The field of aging has become multidimensional. There are more players—one positive sign is the increasing number of students enrolling in USC's gerontology programs. And with expanded research has come increased awareness of older adults' capabilities and how to tap their knowledge and experience, not just focusing on the downsides of aging.

Helen knows there is a long way to go before ageism is eradicated.

Age as a topic often gets lost in the shuffle altogether or gets subsumed under "inclusion." There is lots of talk about the longevity revolution, which is encouraging and frustrating at the same time. Encouraging because a long life can be rewarding and meaningful, frustrating when it is not. On the plus side, one of the biggest changes in gerontology since its early years is growing acceptance of *work as part of retirement and seeing older adults as a resource rather than a liability.* Dynamic change is truly exciting; it defines aging and its potential.

⁙

Men and women who are already working in the retirement years and members of the pre-retirement generation following right behind them can take heart and more than a few lessons from the stories in this volume. With increasing numbers of older workers deciding to stay in the workforce by choice or out of necessity, they will have lots of company. I heard my own daughter saying the other day that she (like my Millennial grandson) is one of those who expects to be working *forever*. My daughter and I bracket the Baby Boomers—she qualifying at the youngest end and I at the oldest. (Well, okay, to be more accurate, I am a few years past the oldest end of the Boomers.) Her reasoning at this stage is largely colored by college tuitions for the kids, a mortgage, growing her business, dealing with health insurance costs, and other financial pressures. Yet I would like to think that many of the intangible, non-pecuniary rewards that can be enjoyed by older working professionals will supersede the utilitarian concerns that preoccupy her and the women and men of her generation today, should she and they choose to keep working in the retirement years.

NOTES

1. Next Avenue is PBS's source of news and information for people over fifty.

2. The USC Davis School of Gerontology was established in 1975 with a gift from Leonard Davis, whose generosity enabled USC to offer the country's first doctoral, master's, and bachelor's degree programs in gerontology. Having co-founded AARP with educator Dr. Ethel Percy Andrus in 1958, Davis went on to pioneer in the development of insurance for older Americans. He along with AARP was instrumental in creating the Ethel Percy Andrus Center at USC, which houses the Davis School of Gerontology, as a memorial to his friend.

3. See www.projectrenewment.com.

Bibliography

AARP Research. "Staying Ahead of the Curve 2013—The AARP Work and Career Study." January 2014. Retrieved from: http://www.aarp.org/research.

Alcover, Carlos-Maria, and Gabriela Topa. "Work Characteristics, Motivational Orientations, Psychological Work Ability and Job Mobility Intentions of Older Workers." *PLOS ONE*, no. 4, April 27, 2018. Retrieved from: https://doi.org/10.1371/journal.pone.0195973.

Alderman, Liz. "The Middle Class Shrinks in Europe." *New York Times*, Business, February 16, 2019, B1, B4.

Applebaum, Steven H., et al. "The Effects of Old-Age Stereotypes on Organizational Productivity (Part Three)." *Industrial and Commercial Training*, *48*, no. 6, 2017, 303–10.

Azoulay, Pierre, et al. "Age and High-Growth Entrepreneurship." March 23, 2018. Retrieved from: http://mitsloan.mit.edu.

Barnes-Farrell, Janet L., and Russell A. Matthews. "Age and Work Attitudes." In *Aging and Work in the 21st Century*, edited by Kenneth S. Shultz and Gary A. Adams. Mahwah, NJ: Erlbaum, 2007, pp. 139–62.

Beehr, Terry A., and Misty Bennett. "Working After Retirement: Features of Bridge Employment and Research Directions." *Work, Aging, and Retirement*, *1*, no. 1, 2015, 112–28. Retrieved from: https://doi.org/10.1093/worker/wau007.

Beier, Margaret E., and Ruth Kanfer. "Work Performance and the Older Worker." In *The SAGE Handbook of Aging, Work and Society*, edited by John Field, et al. Los Angeles: SAGE, 2013, 97–117.

Bennett, Jessica. "Older and in Power, Unwilling to Remain Unseen." *New York Times*, January 9, 2019, A1, A17.

Bosworth, Barry, Gary Burtless, and Kan Zhang. "Later Retirement, Inequality in Old Age, and the Growing Gap in Longevity Between Rich and Poor." Washington, DC: Brookings Institution, January 2016, 12–13.

Bowles, Nellie. "In the Digital World, Midlife Crisis Can Hit at 30." *New York Times*, Business, March 10, 2019, 1, 4–5.

Bronshtein, Gila, et al. "The Power of Working Longer." Stanford Institute for Economic Policy Research, Working Paper 17-047, January 2018.

Brown, Alyssa. "In U.S., Average Retirement Age Up to 61." Gallup Poll. Washington, DC, May 15, 2013. Retrieved from: www.gallup.com/poll/162560/average-retirement-age.aspx?utm.

Brown, Melissa, et al. "Working in Retirement: A 21st Century Phenomenon." 2008 National Study of the Changing Workforce. Families and Work Institute, July 2010.

Brown, S. Kathi. "What Are Older Workers Seeking?" An AARP/SHRM Survey of 50+ Workers. Washington, DC: AARP, June 2012.

Brownell, Patricia, and James J. Kelly, eds. *Ageism and Mistreatment of Older Workers—Current Reality, Future Solutions*. New York: Springer, 2013, xii.

Brundage, Vernon Jr. "Profile of the Labor Force by Educational Attainment." *Spotlight on Statistics*. Washington, DC: U.S. Bureau of Labor Statistics, August 2017.

Burke, Ronald, et al. "The Aging Workforce: Individual, Organizational and Societal Opportunities and Challenges." In *The SAGE Handbook of Aging, Work and Society*, edited by John Field et al. Los Angeles: SAGE, 2013, 1–20.

Calvo, Esteban. "Does Working Longer Make People Healthier and Happier?" Center for Retirement Research at Boston College, Issue Brief, Series 2, February 2006.

Carlstedt, Anita B., et al. "A Scoping Review of the Incentives for a Prolonged Work Life After Pensionable Age and the Importance of 'Bridge Employment.'" *Work*, 60, no. 2, 2018, 175–89. Retrieved from: https://doi.org/10.3233/WOR-182728.

Carstensen, Laura L. "In Search of a Word That Won't Offend 'Old' People." *The Washington Post*, December 29, 2017. Retrieved from: https://www.washington post.com/opinions/in-search-of-a-word-that/2017/12/29/76640346-b808 -11e7-a908.

Casey, Rebecca, and Ellie Berger. "Enriching or Discouraging? Competing Pictures of Aging and Paid Work in Later Life." Population Change and Life Course Strategic Knowledge Cluster Discussion Paper Series, *3*, no. 3, article 3, March 2015. Retrieved from: http://ir.lib.uwo.ca/pclc/vol3/iss3/3.

Casselman, Ben, and Jim Tankersley. "A Booming Economy? Women Don't Share Men's Rosy Viewpoint." *New York Times*, October 28, 2018, 25.

Chang, Michelle, and Dan Kopf. "The Number of Americans Working in Their 70s Is Skyrocketing." *Quartz at Work*, June 3, 2019. Retrieved from: https://qz.com/ work/1632602/the-number-of-Americans-/.

Colby, Anne, and Jim Emerman. "Is a Purposeful Retirement Overrated?" *MarketWatch*, June 21, 2018. Retrieved from: https://www.marketwatch.com/ story/is-a-purposeful-retirement-overrated-2018-06-21/print.

Coleman, Joseph. *Unfinished Work: The Struggle to Build an Aging American Workforce*. New York: Oxford University Press, 2015.

Condliffe, Jamie. "Amazon's Workers Hate Robots." *New York Times*, Technology, July 22, 2019, B3.

"Coping With the 100-Year-Life Society." *The Economist*, *429*, no. 9118. November 17, 2018.

Coughlin, Joseph. *The Longevity Economy*. New York: PublicAffairs, 2017.

DeSilver, Drew. "More Older Americans Are Working, And Working More Than They Used To." Washington, DC: Pew Research Center, June 20, 2016.

Duhigg, Charles. "Wealthy, Successful and Miserable." *New York Times Magazine*, February 24, 2019, 26–27, 60.

The Economist Intelligence Unit. "What's Next: Future Global Trends Affecting Your Organization." SHRM Foundation, February 2014. Retrieved from: http:// futurehrtrends.eiu.com/executive-summary.

Eichar, Douglas M., et al. 'The Job Satisfaction of Older Workers." *Journal of Organizational Behavior*. December 1991. Retrieved from: https://doi.org/ 10.1002/job.4030120705.

Eisenberg, Richard. "Working in Retirement: Wishful Thinking?" *Next Avenue*, December 13, 2017. Retrieved from: www.nextavenue.org/working-retirement -wishful-thinking.

Erdheim, Jesse, and Michael A. Lodato. "Generational Differences in Older Workers and Retirement." In *The Oxford Handbook of Retirement*, edited by Mo Wang. New York: Oxford University Press, 2013, 573–87.

Fairlie, Robert W., et al. "2017 Kauffman Index of Start-up Activity, National Trends." Ewing Marion Kauffman Foundation, May 2017.

Farrell, Chris. *Purpose and a Paycheck—Finding Meaning, Money, and Happiness in the Second Half of Life*. New York: HarperCollins, 2019.

Fideler, Elizabeth F. *Women Still at Work: Professionals Over Sixty and On the Job*. Lanham, MD: Rowman & Littlefield, 2012, 2017.

Fideler, Elizabeth F. *Men Still at Work: Professionals Over Sixty and On the Job*. Lanham, MD: Rowman & Littlefield, 2014.

Fideler, Paul A. *Social Welfare in Pre-Industrial England—The Old Poor Law Tradition*. New York: Palgrave Macmillan, 2006, 150.

Flynn, Diane Johnson. "7 Insights on Ageism That May Surprise You." PBS Next Avenue, Work and Purpose, July 16, 2019.

Flynn, Matt. "Improving How the Older Labor Market Is Managed: A New Era of Social Partnership." Boston College, Center on Aging & Work, March 2018. Retrieved from: http://agingandwork.bc.edu/blog.

Fry, Richard. "Baby Boomers Are Staying in the Labor Force at Rates Not Seen in Generations for People Their Age." Pew Research Center, July 24, 2019.

Gallup-ShareCare Well-Being Index, 2017. "State of American Well-Being 2017." Retrieved from: http://wellbeingindex.sharecare.com.

Goldin, Claudia, and Lawrence F. Katz. "Women Working Longer: Facts and Some Explanations." National Bureau of Economic Research, 2016. Retrieved from: http://www.nber.org/papers/w22607.

Goldin, Claudia, and Lawrence F. Katz. "Women Working Longer: Increased Employment at Older Ages." National Bureau of Economic Research and University of Chicago Press, 2018.

Gonzales, Ernest, et al. "Increasing Opportunities for the Productive Engagement of Older Adults: A Response to Population Aging." *The Gerontologist*, Special Issue: 2015, WHCoA, 1–10.

Greller, Martin M. "Hours Invested in Professional Development During Late Career as a Function of Career Motivation and Satisfaction." *Career Development International*, *11*, no 6, October 2006, 544–59. Retrieved July 21, 2019. from: https://doi.org/10.1108/13620430610692944.

Haddadin, Jim. "Economy, Housing Crunch Grow." *Framingham TAB*, May 25, 2018, A3.

Haider, Steven J., and David Loughran. "Elderly Labor Supply: Work or Play?" Working Paper no. 2001-04. Chestnut Hill, MA: Center for Retirement Research, Boston College, September 2001. Retrieved from: https://ssrn.com/abstract-285981.

Hannon, Kerry. "The Courage to Change the World." *New York Times*, Visionaries, May 27, 2018, F2.

Hannon, Kerry. "Reaping the Benefits of an Aging Work Force." *New York Times*, Special Section on Retirement, March 4, 2018, 7.

Harkness, Helen. *Don't Stop the Career Clock—Rejecting the Myths of Aging for a New Way to Work in the 21st Century*. Palo Alto, CA: Davies-Black Publishing, 1999.

Harpaz, Itzhak, and Xuanning Fu. "The Structure of the Meaning of Work: A Relative Stability Amidst Change." *Human Relations*, *55*, no. 6, 2002, 639–67.

Hedge, Jerry W., and Walter C. Borman, eds. "Advancing Research and Application in Work and Aging." In *The Oxford Handbook of Work and Aging*. New York: Oxford University Press, 2012, 697–98.

Hodin, Michael. "Ageism, Health, Economics." Blog post, May 17, 2018. Retrieved from: www.globalcoalitiononaging.com.

Hyman, Louis. *Temp: How American Work, American Business, and the American Dream Became Temporary*. New York: Viking, 2018.

Irving, Paul. "When No One Retires." *Harvard Business Review*. The Big Idea—The Aging Workforce, November 2018.

Irving, Paul H., and Rita Beamish, eds. *The Upside of Aging: How Long Life is Changing the World of Health, Work, Innovation, Policy, and Purpose.* Hoboken, NJ: John Wiley & Sons, 2014, 4, 93.

Irving, Paul, Rita Beamish, and Arielle Burstein. "Silver to Gold—The Business of Aging." Report from the Summit on Business and the Future of Aging. Santa Monica, CA: Milken Institute Center for the Future of Aging, 2018.

James, Jacquelyn B., et al. "Generational Differences in Perceptions of Older Workers' Capabilities." Sloan Center on Aging & Work, Boston College. Chestnut Hill, MA: 2007.

James, Jacquelyn B., et al. "Insights on Activity in Later Life from the Life & Times in an Aging Society Study—Engaged as We Age." Sloan Center on Aging & Work, Boston College. Chestnut Hill, MA: January 2012. Retrieved from: http://www.bc.edu/content/bc/research/agingandwork/archive_pubs/EAWA_JustDoIt.html.

James, Jacquelyn B., et al. "Optimizing the Long Future of Aging: Beyond Involvement to Engagement." In *The SAGE Handbook of Aging, Work and Society*, edited by John Field, et al. Los Angeles: SAGE, 2013, 477–92.

Kerman, Sarah, and Colette Thayer. *Job Seeking Among Workers Age 50+.* Washington, DC: AARP Research, October 2017.

King, Charles. *Gods of the Upper Air: How a Circle of Renegade Anthropologists Reinvented Race, Sex, and Gender in the Twentieth Century.* New York: Doubleday, 2019.

King, Eden, et al. "Generational Differences at Work Are Small. Thinking They Are Big Affects Our Behavior." *Harvard Business Review, Daily Alert*, August 1, 2019.

Klampe, Michelle. "Working Longer May Lead to a Longer Life, New OSU Research Shows." Corvallis, OR: Oregon State University, April 27, 2016. Retrieved from: https://today.oregonstate.edu/archives/2016/apr/working-longer-may-lead-longer-life-new-osu-research-shows.

Knapton, Sarah. "Retirement Causes Brain Function to Rapidly Decline, Warn Scientists." *The Telegraph*, News/Science, January 22, 2018.

Kolko, Jed, and Claire Cain Miller. "As Labor Market Tightens, Gender Lines Blur." *New York Times*, Business, December 16, 2018, 7.

Kooij, Dorien, et al. "Older Workers' Motivation to Continue to Work: Five Meanings of Age." *Journal of Managerial Psychology*, *23*, no. 4, May 2008, 364–94. Retrieved July 21, 2019, from: https://doi.org/10.1108/02683940810869015.

Krivkovich, Alexis, et al. "Women in the Workplace 2018." McKinsey & Co. and LeanIn.com. October 2018.

Leppel, Karen, et al. "The Importance of Job Training to Job Satisfaction of Older Workers." *Journal of Aging Social Policy*, *24*, no. 1, 2012. Retrieved from: https://www.ncbi.nim.nih.gov/pubmed/22239282.

Lewis, Gregory. "The Most In-Demand Hard and Soft Skills of 2018." LinkedIn Survey, January 22, 2018. Retrieved from: https://business.LinkedIn.com/talent-solutions/blog/trends-and-research/2018/the-most-in-demand-hard.

Lipnic, Victoria A. "The State of Age Discrimination and Older Workers in the U.S. 50 Years After the Age Discrimination in Employment Act (ADEA)." U.S. Equal Employment Opportunity Commission, June 2018.

Lund, Susan, et al. "The Future of Work in America: People and Places, Today and Tomorrow." McKinsey Global Institute, July 2019.

Maestas, Nicole, et al. "Working Conditions in the United States: Results of the 2015 American Working Conditions Survey." Santa Monica, CA: RAND Corp, August 2017. Retrieved from: https://www.rand.org/pubs/research_reports/RR2014.html.

Mahler, Elizabeth, and John Thompson. "Is It Time to Put Retirement Out to Pasture?" June 2018. Retrieved from: http://rslive.bslcore.com/myArticle.php?aid=44243.

McNeely, R. L. "Age and Job Satisfaction in Human Service Employment." *The Gerontologist*, *28*, no. 2, April 1988.

Merrill Lynch/Bank of America. "Work in Retirement: Myths and Motivations." June 2014. Retrieved from: www.ml.com/retirementstudy.

Miller, Claire Cain. "The Gender Pay Gap Is Largely Because of Motherhood." *New York Times*, The Upshot, May 13, 2017.

Morrow-Howell, Nancy, et al. "Approaches, Policies, and Practices to Support the Productive Engagement of Older Workers." *Journal of Gerontological Social Work*, *60*, no 3, January 2017, 193–200.

Morrow-Howell, Nancy, et al. "Increasing Productive Engagement in Later Life." Grand Challenges for Social Work Initiative Working Paper No. 8. Cleveland, OH: American Academy of Social Work and Social Welfare, 2015, 4.

Munnell, Alicia H., and Steven A. Sass. *Working Longer—The Solution to the Retirement Income Challenge*. Washington, DC: Brookings Institution Press, 2008, 14.

Munnell, Alicia H., et al. "Does Socioe-conomic Status Lead People to Retire Too Soon?" Issue Brief no. 16-14. Chestnut Hill, MA: Center for Retirement Research at Boston College, August 2016.

Murphy, Edward D. "Workplace Churn Prods More Companies to Consider Hiring Seniors." *Maine Sunday Telegram*. Retrieved March 17, 2019, from: www.press herald.com/2019/03/17/workplace-churn-prods-more-companies-to-consider -hiring-seniors.

National Center for Health Statistics. "Health, United States, 2017: With Special Feature on Mortality." U.S. Department of Health and Human Services. Hyattsville, MD, 2018.

Oliveira, Eduardo. "Buffers or Boosters? Human Resource Management Practices Shape the Way Older Workers See Themselves in the Workplace." AGEnda Aging & Work Blog. Chestnut Hill, MA: Center on Aging & Work, Boston College, February 8, 2018. Retrieved from: http://agingandwork.bc.edu/blog/ buffers-or-boosters-human-resource-practices-shape-the-way-older-workers -see-themselves-in-the-workplace.

Ozimek, Adam, Dante DeAntonio, and Mark Zandi. "Aging and the Productivity Puzzle." Retrieved March 29, 2019, from: https://ma.moodys.com/rs/961- KCJ-308/images/2018-09-04-Aging-and-the-Productivity-Puzzle.pdf.

Paul, Kari. "The Wage Gap Starts at Home: Boys Are Paid More Than Girls for Household Chores." July 15, 2018. Retrieved from www.MarketWatch.com.

Perron, Rebecca. *The Value of Experience: AARP Multicultural Work and Jobs Study*. Washington, DC: AARP Research, July 2018. Retrieved from: https:// doi.org/10.26419/res.00177.000.

Porter, Eduardo. "Abandoned America." *New York Times*, Sunday Review, December 16, 2018, 1, 6.

Quinn, Joseph, Kevin Cahill, and Michael Giandrea. *Early Retirement: The Dawn of a New Era?* New York, NY: TIAA-Cref Institute, 2011.

Rathke, Lisa. "Pole Vaulter, 84, Sets Her Sights on More Records." March 22, 2019. Retrieved from: https://apnews.com/d30e7bb0b8ad42a09e9782a8cbe98ef1.

Reich, Robert B. "Barely Afloat in America." *New York Times* Book Review, July 15, 2018.

Robin, William. "Becoming a Force While Trying to Avoid Disaster." *New York Times*, Arts, November 10, 2018, C2.

Rushton, Charlotte. "Inaugural McKinsey & Co. Women in the Workplace 2017 Legal Study." October 31, 2017.

Rutledge, Matthew, et al. "How Much Does Motherhood Cost Women in Social Security Benefits?" Working Paper 2017-14. Boston College, Center for Retirement Research, 2017.

Sanzenbacher, Geoffrey T., Steven A. Sass, and Christopher M. Gillis. "How Job Changes Affect Retirement Timing by Socio-economic Status." Brief no. 17.3. Chestnut Hill, MA: Center for Retirement Research at Boston College, February 2017.

Sass, Steven. "How Do Non-Financial Factors Affect Retirement Decisions?" Issue Brief no. 16-3. Chestnut Hill, MA: Center for Retirement Research at Boston College, February 2016.

Scommegna, Paola, and Nadwa Mossaad. "The Health and Well-Being of Grandparents Caring for Grandchildren." Today's Research on Aging, no. 23. Population Reference Bureau. Washington, DC: December 2011.

Shultz, Kenneth S., and Gary A. Adams, eds. "In Search of a Unifying Paradigm for Understanding Aging and Work in the 21st Century." In *Aging and Work in the 21st Century*. Mahwah, NJ: Erlbaum Associates, 2007.

Simon, Ruth. "Booming Job Market Can't Fill Retirement Shortfall." *Wall Street Journal*, December 21, 2018, A1, A9.

Slaughter, Anne-Marie. *Unfinished Business*. New York: Random House, 2015, 14.

Smyer, Michael, and Marcie Pitt-Catsouphes. "The Meanings of Work for Older Workers." *Generations*, *31*, no.1, Spring 2007, 26. Retrieved from: http://hdl.handle.net/2345/763.

Society for Human Resource Management. "The Aging Workforce." Alexandria, VA, June 2014. Retrieved from: https://www.shrm.org/resourcesandtools/

hr-topics/behavioral-competencies/global-and-cultural-effectiveness/
documents/7-14%20roundtable%20summary.pdf.

Society for Human Resource Management. "The Aging Workforce—Basic and
Applied Skills." Washington, DC: SHRM, January 12, 2015. Retrieved from:
http:www.shrm.org/research/surveyfindings/articles/pages/shrm-older-workers
-basic-and-applied-skills.aspx.

Soergel, Andrew. "Poll: 1 in 4 Don't Plan to Retire Despite Realities of Aging."
Associated Press/NORC Center for Public Affairs Research, July 7, 2019.

Soergel, Andrew. "Seniors More Likely to Work Longer in Big Metropolitan Areas."
The Denver Post, June 10, 2019. Retrieved July 9, 2019, from: https://www.
denverpost.com/2019/06/10/metro-area-seniors-working-jobs-retirement/.

Span, Paula. "The 'Dead Wood' Got Fired Up and Took Back Their Jobs." *New York
Times*, The New Old Age, July 10, 2018, D3.

Stanford Center on Longevity. "The Cognition and Retirement Study: Is Working
Longer Good For You?" September 2014. Retrieved from: http://longevity
.stanford.edu/the-cognition-and-retirement-study-is-working-longer-good-for
-you/.

Stanford Center on Longevity. "Seeing Our Way to Financial Security in the Age of
Increased Longevity." Sightlines Special Report, October 2018. Retrieved from:
http://longevity.stanford.edu/wp-content/uploads/2018/10/sightlines-financial
-security-special-report-2018.pdf.

Sterns, Harvey L., and Dennis Doverspike. "Aging and the Training and Learning
Process in Organizations." In *Training and Development in Work Organizations*,
edited by I. Goldstein and R. Katzel. San Francisco: Jossey-Bass, 1989, 299–332.

Stewart, Janet Kidd. "Older Workers Are Staying on the Job; Here's Why." *Star
Tribune*, July 3, 2019. Retrieved from: .

Suttie, Jill. "How to Find Your Purpose in Midlife." *Greater Good Magazine*.
Greater Good Science Center, University of California, Berkeley, March 8, 2018.
Retrieved from: https://greatergood.berkeley.edu/.../how_to_find_your_purpose
_in_midlife.

Taylor, Phillip, et al. "Everyday Discrimination in the Australian Workplace:
Assessing Its Prevalence and Age and Gender Differences." *Australasian Journal
on Ageing*, *37*, no. 4. December 2018, 245–51.

Toossi, Mitra. "Labor Force Projections to 2024: The Labor Force is Growing, But Slowly." *Monthly Labor Review*. Washington, DC: U.S. Bureau of Labor Statistics, December 2015. Retrieved from: https://doi.org/10.21916/mlr.2015.48.

Toossi, Mitra, and Elka Torpey. "Older Workers: Labor Force Trends and Career Options." *Career Outlook*. Washington, DC: Bureau of Labor Statistics, U.S. Department of Labor, May 2017. Retrieved from: https://www.bls.gov/careeroutlook/2017/article/pdf/older-workers.pdf.

Toossi, Mitra, and Leslie Joyner. "Blacks in the Labor Force." *Spotlight on Statistics*. Washington, DC: U.S. Bureau of Labor Statistics, February 2018.

Toossi, Mitra, and Teresa L. Morisi. "Women in the Work Force Before, During, and After the Great Recession." *Spotlight on Statistics*. Washington, DC: Bureau of Labor Statistics, U.S. Department of Labor, July 2017. Retrieved from: https://www.bls.gov/spotlight/2017/women-in-the-workforce-before-during-and-after-the-great-recession/home.htm.

Transamerica Center for Retirement Studies. "18th Annual Transamerica Retirement Survey." TCRS 1364-0618, June 2018. Retrieved from: https://www.transamericacenter.org/docs/default-retirement-survey-of-workers/tcrs2018_sr_18th_annual_worker_compendium.pdf.

Trawinski, Lori A. "Leveraging the Value of an Age-Diverse Workforce." SHRM Foundation Executive Briefing. Also see: www.aarp.org/employerresourcecenter.

U.S. Bureau of Labor Statistics. "Labor Force Characteristics by Race and Ethnicity, 2017." BLS Report no. 1076. Washington, DC: U.S. Department of Labor, August 2018.

U.S. Bureau of Labor Statistics. "Usual Weekly Earnings of Wage and Salary Workers, Second Quarter 2019." Washington, DC: U.S. Department of Labor, July 17, 2019.

U.S. Bureau of Labor Statistics, "Volunteering in the United States," News Release. USDL-16-0363. Washington, DC: U.S. Department of Labor, February 25, 2016. Retrieved from: www.bls.gov/ops.

U.S. Bureau of Labor Statistics. "Women in the Labor Force: A Databook." BLS Report no. 1071. Washington, DC: U.S. Department of Labor, November 2017. Retrieved from: https://www.bls.gov/opub/reports/womens-databook/2017/home.htm.

Van Dam, Andrew. "A Record Number of Folks Age 85 and Older Are Working, Here's What They're Doing." *The Washington Post*, July 5, 2018. Retrieved from:

Vinney, Cynthia. "Fluid Versus Crystallized Intelligence: What's the Difference?" ThoughtCo. September 17, 2018.

Weiss, Bari. "Australia's Fastest 92-Year-Old Woman." *New York Times*, Sunday Review, January 6, 2019, 9.

Zhan, Yujie, Mo Wang, and Jungi Shi. "Retirees' Motivational Orientations and Bridge Employment: Testing the Moderating Role of Gender." *Journal of Applied Psychology*, *100*, no. 5, September 2015, 1319–31. Retrieved from: https://doi .org/10.1037/a0038731.

Resources

AARP (Jennifer Schramm): www.aarp.org

Acting Our Age: Women's Lives at 85+ (Susan D. Goodman): https://actingourageblog.com

Age Lab, Massachusetts Institute of Technology (Joseph F. Coughlin): www.agelab.mit.edu

American Society on Aging: www.asaging.org

Boston College, Center on Aging & Work (Jacquelyn James): https://www.bc.edu/research/agingandwork

Boston College, Center on Retirement Research (Alicia Munnell): https://crr.bc.edu

Boston College, Sloan Research Network on Aging & Work (Jacquelyn James): http://sloanresearchnetwork.bc.edu

Changing the Face of Aging, "Work and Aging": www.changingthefaceofaging.com and www.daughtersintheworkplace.com

Encore.org (Marci Alboher and Marc Freedman): www.encore.org

Encore Boston Network (Doug Dickson): www.encorebostonnetwork.org

Gerontological Society of America: www.geron.org

Heldrich Center for Workforce Development (Carl E. Van Horn):
www.heldrich.rutgers.edu

Innovate + Educate (Jamai Blivin): www.innovate-educate.org

Life Planning Network (Bruce Frankel): www.lifeplanningnetwork.org

Milken Institute, Center for the Future of Aging (Paul Irving):
www.milkeninstitute.org

National Bureau of Economic Research: www.nber.org

Partners in Change (Geoff Pearman): http://partnersinchange.co.nz

Pass It On Network (Jan Hively and Moira Allan): www.passitonnetwork.org

PBS Next Avenue (Richard Eisenberg): www.nextavenue.org

Revolutionize Your Retirement (Dorian Mintzer): www.revolutionizeretirement
.com

Society for Human Resource Management: www.shrm.org

Stanford University, Center on Longevity (Laura Carstensen and Martha Deevy):
www.longevity.stanford.edu

This Chair Rocks (and *Old School* ageism resources) (Ashton Applewhite):
https://thischairrocks.com/blog

Transamerica Center for Retirement Studies (Catherine Collinson): www
.transamericacenter.org

Urban Institute (Richard Johnson): www.urban.org

U.S. Department of Labor, Bureau of Labor Statistics: www.bls.gov

Work and Family Researchers Network: www.wfrn.org

Index

AARP, 7, 13, 95, 157, 161–62, 215; SHRM Survey, 100; Work and Career Study, 62

AAUW, 114–15

Active Aging Consortium, 186

ADEA, 18, 139, 152–53, 154, 162

age: awareness, 39; bias/discrimination, 6, 18, 65, 72, 153, 156–57,162; chronological, 18, 19–20, 38, 156, 195; definitions, 17, 19; dependency challenge in Japan, 130; functional, 18, 19, 38, 156, 195, 196; and economic life, 153, 160; and hiring decisions, 153, 157; life span concept of, 18, 38; median, 18, 69; organizational, 18; psychosocial, 18; wave, 160. *See also* retirement

age-diverse, 1, 13, 15, 155, 162

age-friendly, 1, 12, 13, 61, 62, 83, 84, 118, 160

age-inclusive, 160

Ageing Equal, 158

ageism, vi,14, 66, 83, 139, 143, 146, 151, 152, 157, 158–59, 160, 162–63, 201; as human rights issue, 158

Age-Smart, 6

aging, vi, 5, 7, 162; disrupt, 161; healthy, 117

Alboher, Marci, 215

Allan, Moira, 158, 216

American Society on Aging (ASA), 7, 201, 215

Applewhite, Ashton, 162, 216

apprenticeships, 155

arts, 90

Asset and Health Dynamics Among the Oldest Old (AHEAD), 37–38

Attenborough, Sir David, 3

Australia, 160

automation, 23, 91, 155–56

Babkirk, Barbara, 84

Baby Boomers, 7–8, 9, 18, 21, 83, 157, 160, 202; brain drain, 196

About the Author

Elizabeth F. Fideler, Ed.D., is a founding member of the Sloan Research Network on Aging & Work at Boston College. Her primary research and writing interests focus on the latest trends in labor force participation and uncover the reasons women and men bypass conventional retirement age and stay on the job. *Aging, Work, and Retirement* updates Dr. Fideler's previous studies: *Women Still at Work—Professionals Over Sixty and On the Job* and *Men Still at Work—Professionals Over Sixty and On the Job*, both available from Rowman & Littlefield Publishing. Fideler is also the editor of Rowman & Littlefield's new, comprehensive handbook on aging and work, forthcoming spring 2021. She can be reached at lizpaulfideler@gmail.com and on Facebook and LinkedIn. She is an experienced presenter and the author of numerous articles and reports in addition to her books.

www.ingramcontent.com/pod-product-compliance
Lightning Source LLC
Chambersburg PA
CBHW050428280326
41932CB00013BA/2035

* 9 7 8 1 5 3 8 1 3 9 6 1 5 *